Human Diversity
and the Culture Wars

HUMAN DIVERSITY AND THE CULTURE WARS

A Philosophical Perspective
on Contemporary Cultural Conflict

Philip E. Devine

PRAEGER

Westport, Connecticut
London

Library of Congress Cataloging-in-Publication Data

Devine, Philip E.
    Human diversity and the culture wars : a philosophical perspective
on contemporary cultural conflict / Philip E. Devine.
        p.   cm.
    Includes bibliographical references and index.
    ISBN 0–275–95205–3 (alk. paper)
    1. Multiculturalism. 2. Political correctness.
3. Multiculturalism—Controversial literature. 4. Political
correctness—Controversial literature. 5. United States—
Civilization—20th century. I. Title.
BD175.5.M84D48   1996
306′.0973—dc20   96–15319

British Library Cataloguing in Publication Data is available.

Library of Congress Catalog Card Number: 96–15319
ISBN: 0–275–95205–3

First published in 1996

Praeger Publishers, 88 Post Road West, Westport, CT 06881
An imprint of Greenwood Publishing Group, Inc.

Printed in the United States of America

The paper used in this book complies with the
Permanent Paper Standard issued by the National
Information Standards Organization (Z39.48–1984).

10 9 8 7 6 5 4 3 2 1

Copyright Acknowledgment

The author and publisher gratefully acknowledge permission to reprint the following:

Selections from John Kekes, *The Morality of Pluralism*. Copyright © 1993 by Princeton University Press. Reprinted by permission of Princeton University Press.

To Patrick

Contents

Preface

I have always been fascinated by the diversity of ways of life and by the differing belief-systems that arise from and justify these ways of life. But I have also been disturbed by the exploitation of *diversity* to justify a militantly intolerant relativism, which gained strength in American politics after 1972 or 1973 and whose future as I write this is uncertain. My own experience has sustained both my belief in the importance of human diversity and my conviction that the way such diversity is commonly invoked in politics and the academy is more than questionable. The focus of my discussion is the United States, a highly diverse country and the one I know best. But radical diversitarianism is if anything more troubling if one's perspective includes Nova Scotia, Rwanda, and Bangladesh. Even if we imagine replacing the United States with larger or smaller political units (or even with both), the problem of human diversity will not go away and may even be intensified.

During my graduate school years, I was asked to fill out one of many forms by which I identified my "cultural heritage." Having received a decent education in the Western tradition, I included both "Jewish" and "Greek" among my answers, though to my knowledge I have neither Jewish nor Greek ancestors—not, I suspect, what the framers of the questionnaire had in mind. From 1972, when I received my Ph.D. from the University of California at Berkeley, to 1990, when I was appointed to my present position at Providence College, I was a gypsy scholar teaching at a wide variety of colleges and universities. I visited the Harvard Law School during the academic year 1980–1981, and there observed the battle between the "crits" and the liberals, before the standards of academic civilization broke down. I taught at Saint Cloud State University in Minnesota when it was taken over by the politically correct faction, who among other things procured a consent decree mandating reeducation sessions for faculty on affirmative action.

Since I am something of a convert to the importance of cultural issues in politics, I need to reaffirm my awareness of the importance of political issues of the conventional ("who gets what?") sort. Yet cultural issues still have a certain priority in my mind. First, if the whole social enterprise collapses, in one of the many ways contemporary men and women imagine, the question of distribution of its burdens and benefits will cease to be of any importance. Second, our ability to think together about issues such as justice in health care—which involve, among other things, our attitude toward death—is now in serious question. For our politics has degenerated into squabbles of the most degraded sort.

On a more intellectual level, I have endeavored to avoid the suggestion that cultures—whether our own or that of the Balinese—are homogeneous, coherent, and isolated entities independent of the men and women who live in them. We are both social and idiosyncratic beings, assimilating in our own distinctive ways the complex and messy heritage within which we are required to live. It will, indeed, be a core thesis of this book that the Western humanistic tradition, with its emphasis on the dignity and uniqueness of each individual, provides the only acceptable resolution of cultural conflict.

One implication of the culture wars is the large number of verbal issues that require attention. I intensely dislike the use of linguistic nuances as badges of partisan affiliation, a dislike increased by a study of the Yugoslav experience, in which one's choice of alphabet became a test of national loyalty. And it is impossible to appease determined ideologues. I have attempted to use language in a way in which I am personally comfortable, while at the same time avoiding writing anything that will grate on the ears of readers of goodwill.

Writers on political correctness (PC) tend to content themselves with the vaguest possible definition of their topic. In their book *Political Correctness, For and Against* (New York: Rowman and Littlefield, 1995), Jan Narveson and Marilyn Friedman speak of "a diverse array of the most controversial cultural and academic issues of our day" (p. vii). Friedman writes of "calls for diversity and multiculturalism" (p. 2)—a formulation that raises more questions than it answers. Narveson suggests that "political correctness takes the view that the ones who do less well, and are correspondingly less well treated by academic institutions, are somehow being mistreated" (p. 51), leaving it an entire mystery why anyone should think such a thing. The expression *PC* was seriously meant by its Leninist originators, though its reference was rather different from that now in vogue. It is now, however, generally used by its opponents, and generally though not invariably resisted by those to whom it is applied. In fact, the emergence of the word *PC* signaled a significant decline in the power of PC itself.

In this book, *political correctness* will be used in the narrow sense of a militant and intolerant relativism, not (for example) as a general word for orthodoxies and party lines of all sorts. To be sure, not all people called "PC" are relativists: some Afrocentrists believe that it is just plain true that Plato learned his philosophy from Egyptian priests. But even these Afrocentrists are influenced by a relativistic historical methodology that encourages each group to write its own history, and in so doing create a myth that serves its needs. Nor is the designation of PC as a form of relativism intended as a quick dismissal: relativism of their sort, though heterodox among professional philosophers, has been for some time close to orthodoxy in the social sciences, and has been accepted as well by many historians, even when they have not drawn the conclusion that antirelativism is a threat to peace. In any event, I believe I have picked out a real phenomenon, and one of some importance in contemporary cultural conflicts.

I will speak of the *cultural Left* and the *cultural Right*, while trying hard not to confuse them with the political variety, despite considerable sympathy with Irving Howe's objections to this usage. I will speak of *Roman Catholics*, but shorten the expression to Catholics after its first appearance in each chapter. (Occasionally I will shorten the *Roman Catholic Church* to *the Church*, since, as Lenny Bruce observed, the Roman Catholic Church is, as a matter of cultural-historical fact, "the only the Church.")

Americans partly of African descent will be called *black people* (not *blacks*), *African Americans*, and, when I desire especially to emphasize their racially and culturally mixed character, *Negroes*. Members of the majority race will be called *white people* (not *whites*), and sometimes *European Americans*. Neither *American Indians* nor *Native Americans* is completely satisfactory; the two terms will be used as synonyms, as will *nonwhites* and *persons of color*. The other two major "racial" groups in the United States will be called *Hispanic Americans* and *Asian Americans*, even though the former is almost entirely a bureaucratic artifact. I have decided not to use *gay* to refer to male homosexuals, partly because I regret the loss of a translation for the German *frölich*, but more importantly because of its false—and in view of the AIDS epidemic, absurd—suggestion that male homosexuals lead carefree lives. Similarly, *straight* questionably suggests that heterosexuals are free of sexual or other kinks.

The word *progressive* refers to those who think of themselves, rightly or wrongly, as contributing to the improvement of the world. I prefer not to use the word *reactionary*, though something of its sense is conveyed by words such as *restorationist* and *traditionalist*. *Men* (though not *mankind*) will be used of males only, but to avoid the etherealizing tendencies of much contemporary language I will frequently prefer *men and women* (or *human beings*) to *persons*. *Human beings* is used of members of the human species, while *person* marks a moral and metaphysical claim. I speak of *fetuses* when the moral standing of nascent human life is taken as open to question, and *unborn children* when it is not. (I see no excuse for the expression *pre-born*.) For the most part, I use *he* generically, except where the context requires a male individual. I refer to God with capitalized masculine pronouns, also to be understood generically.

This project is continuous with my earlier work on relativism and the ethics of killing. Many of its ideas were worked out in essays and reviews published in the *New Oxford Review* and in my contributions to Providence College's course in the Development of Western Civilization. Early drafts of portions of this book were read to the Modern Language Association in 1993 (by proxy), to the Popular Culture Association in 1994, and to the Providence College Colloquium series in Western Civilization in 1995. Chapter 9 is forthcoming in *Religious Studies*. Chapter 10 draws on my chapter on "'Conservative' Views of Abortion" published in the abortion volume of *Advances in Bioethics*, edited by Rem Edwards, and Chapter 8 is adapted from my Commentary in the Winter 1995 issue of *Responsive Community*. Discussions with friends, students, and colleagues, most of all with Mark Henrie, Joseph Ryshpan, Patrick Walker, Celia Wolf-Devine, and Michael Wreen, have been invaluable in the development of this book. I am indebted to Robert J. Rafalko and Joel Wilcox for reading the work in draft, and to several anonymous readers for their comments on Chapter 9. Thanks also are due to Patrick Walker for proofreading the text, and for his help with the index, and to Betty Pessagno for her careful copyediting.

A word of apology will conclude this Preface. One theme of this book is the diversity of diversity: that when we think of difference we should not only think of black people and homosexuals, but also of Jehovah's Witnesses and Hasidic Jews. Moreover, every difference is different: race is not culture is not sexual psychology is not religion. Nonetheless, I cannot mention every possible sort of diversity: if the reader finds himself different from others in a way not mentioned here (say, inability to drive a car), I tender him my regrets in advance.

Introduction: Taking Diversity Seriously Enough

Cultural conflicts can be found at all times and all places. The context of my discussion of these conflicts will be the contemporary United States, since it is the country I know best, though I hope that my arguments will be relevant to the problems of other nations as well. The very diversity of America requires Americans to pay constant attention to human nature, as a source of standards for the life of men and women.[1] But the question of human diversity has concerned the Western tradition from its beginnings, as a quick examination of the "dead white males" of the European "canon" will confirm.[2]

The present phase of our culture wars can be dated from 1967–1973, a period that began with Susan Sontag's proclamation that the white race was the cancer of human history and concluded with the attempt, by a Republican Supreme Court Justice, Harry Blackmun, to resolve the abortion dispute by imposing a relativistic consensus on the rest of us.[3] By now even those people who have not experienced cultural conflict in intimate ways have at least received mailings from some group inciting them against others.[4]

On the one side, the crude and egomaniacal Rush Limbaugh has gained immense popularity. As Thomas Bryne Edsall reports, "In dozens of American cities and towns one can find 'Rush Rooms' where lunch is eaten in reverent silence as Limbaugh speaks for 180 minutes, except for commercial breaks and the news."[5]

On the other side, many secularists and "mainstream" Christians—ironically, those who speak most unctuously about homophobia—are phobic about fundamentalists. An agnostic psychohistorian is impressed with the dedication of some fundamentalist leaders, and portrays both leaders and rank and file as beset by the same anxieties that the rest of us are, and, like all human beings, interpreting their experience with the help of their tradition. Nonetheless, he responded to their prayers for his pregnant wife and unborn child by "praying against . . . the group and all their dangerous ideas, vowing to myself that if something happened to my unborn baby I would hold them accountable."[6] In 1980, a Southern Baptist leader incurred public censure by proclaiming that God does not hear the prayers of Jews;[7] only the devil, it appears, hears those of fundamentalists.

There are not one but at least two culture wars going on in contemporary America: ordinary folk argue about abortion, pornography, and school prayer, while academics fight about the curriculum. In these conflicts, the "cultural Left" as it is usually called, takes *diversity* as its watchword. But it will be the thesis of this book that the votaries of diversity do not take it seriously enough. If their vision included Mormons, believers in creation science, and "rednecks" as well as black people, women, and homosexuals, they would reach conclusions they themselves would describe as "conservative."

WHAT IS A CULTURAL CONFLICT?

Cultural issues include bioethical issues from reproductive technology through abortion and euthanasia to the definition of death, educational issues at every level, issues in sexual morality, and issues concerning the nature and purposes of families. They have to do with our existence as biological and historical entities, arising from the union of our parents, sooner or later leaving the stage of human existence, and hoping to transmit something of ourselves to literal or metaphorical progeny. Hence they divide us not as rational "persons," but as men and women caught up with one another, both biologically and culturally, whether we will it or not.

Many culture warriors are engaged primarily in venting their hostility toward men and women whose attitudes and ways of life offend them. And it is always useful to believe in the depravity of one's market or political rivals. Thus even the tiniest differences form an explosive combination with rivalry for scarce resources. A shared customary morality, like shared customs and traditions of all sorts, makes it easier for an embattled group to unite shared interest with mutual affection, and thus enables it to struggle more effectively against its foes.[8] On the other hand, radical positions on cultural issues provide an excellent way of covering retreat on issues concerning the distribution of power and privilege. Nor can issues of power and privilege be ignored when we address cultural conflicts: a serious cultural conservative, for example, needs to look at the cultural effects of the flight of capital.

Nonetheless, regret about the importance of cultural politics is misplaced. For many social policies will bear fruit, if at all, only in generations none of whose members now exist. Nor is it possible to treat these generations as already existing, only "downstream" from us in time: their existence and character depend on the reproductive and other decisions we make now.

THEORETICAL PERSPECTIVES

In a remark that foreshadows the Enlightenment, Descartes complains that

given the fact that we were all children before being adults and that for a long time it is our lot to be governed by our appetites and our teachers . . . , it is almost impossible for our judgments to be as pure or solid as they would have been had we had the full use of reason from the moment of our birth and never been led by anything but our reason.[9]

I cannot prove that some philosopher, prophet, or poet will not come along and refound culture, but I see no prospect of any such refounding. The indiscriminate rejection of tradition does not mean liberation, but rather a sullen nihilism completely consistent with brutal attitudes toward women, toward real and supposed homosexuals, and toward members of other races. Regret at having been born an infant is, in any event, misplaced.

Yet the illusion that we are able to refound civilization is deeply ingrained in our culture. And many of us regret, not having been born an infant, but our particular infancy and the cultural and biological ancestry it carried with it. David Bromwitch aptly describes the resulting conflict as between "a culture of assent" and a "culture of suspicion."[10] These cultures converge on a cynical acceptance of the status quo, however unjust, absurd, or even brutal it may appear. But Bromwitch is insufficiently attentive to human beings' need for traditions in which to raise their children, especially if they are going to protect them against cynicism.[11]

We may conclude that some form of cultural conservatism is now mandatory, including some attention to the religious dimension of our tradition.[12] But cultural conservatism need not entail political conservatism, since it is always possible to criticize existing practice in terms of our civilization's deepest commitments.

All cultural traditions, including our own, marginalize some ways of life. Liberal social agendas marginalize traditional people, and feminist social and intellectual agendas put sympathetic males in Kafkaesque double binds. Thus Susan Moller Okin, in her widely admired discussion of justice and the family, criticizes John Rawls for using *man, mankind, he,* and *his* generically, and then finds fault with Alasdair MacIntyre for using fraudulently gender-neutral language in presenting the philosophy of Aristotle.[13]

THE CULTURAL SPECTRUM

We are the beneficiaries or victims of not one but many traditions, each of them with its own set of external and internal problems. MacIntyre lists the Enlightenment, Nietszcheanism, and what he calls Thomism. But there are many others: the Jewish community has been divided over the question "Who is a Jew?" and more narrowly over the status of a person with a Jewish father and a Gentile mother—issues of little interest to non-Jews.[14]

Once we admit our dependence on tradition for our ability to make judgments of all sorts, the issue that arises is how restrictively the tradition within which we work is to be interpreted. I here propose a sort of phenomenology of the spirit, though one not linked to Hegel's metaphysical doctrines. Thus, I survey the cultural spectrum, directing my attention not to particular issues but to divergent ideological and methodological perspectives.

What divides such perspectives is, in the first instance, the range of interpretations of authoritative texts (and likewise of unspoken traditions) they authorize. At the one extreme, even the most difficult texts have a plain meaning, departure from which is a sign of folly or criminality; at the other, such texts mean whatever an individual or group wants them to mean at a given time, and for that reason are incapable of guiding either theory or practice.

Within this spectrum we can understand the contemporary phenomenon called political correctness (PC), neither denying its reality nor exaggerating its power. We are familiar with the many manifestations of PC, both sinister and silly; my favorite is the professor of American history who was reprimanded by the dean for quoting Theodore Roosevelt as calling Woodrow Wilson "pusillanimous."[15] But politically incorrect men and women have no difficulty holding down prestigious professorships (or comfortable think-tank positions), winning public notice for their work, or getting elected to public office.

In my view, PC represents not some sort of menacing conspiracy, but Left-liberalism adrift and in retreat, which has had recourse to a sanctimonious and intolerant relativism in order to protect its beliefs and programs from criticism. Those who dislike its manifestations, in education and elsewhere, need above all to propose and defend alternatives, and in doing so to show the vitality of the tradition in which they are working.

The cultural Left clamors against the idea of a common human nature, from which can be derived universally binding moral and other standards, and invoke "respect for diversity" as a rationale for tolerance. But tolerance is possible as long as there are agreed-upon, though not necessarily well-defined, limits on how far any party will press its advantages. These may be found in a code that defines certain acts as "not done" (for example, one that holds that cheating at cards is the ultimate offense). But in a heterogeneous society, and even more so in a heterogeneous world, something more articulate and philosophically defensible is required. The Western tradition includes the merger of disparate and themselves internally diverse cultures—chief among them the Greek and the Hebrew—and a radical critique of customary practice, cast in the form of story rather than of a philosophical theory.[16] Hence it would seem to provide just what a diverse world requires.

But fundamental to our cultural conflicts is a suspicion that the Western ·experiment has proved a failure, and the best we can hope for is pleasure, comfort, and security as we await the inevitable end. Many writers have used the metaphor of male impotence to express social and cultural sterility; in a recent novel, P. D. James uses infertility of both men and women to the same effect.[17]

This suspicion goes back at least to the First World War, but was reinforced by the Second and the threat of a Third. In America it was further reinforced by a prolonged, bloody, and unpopular war in Southeast Asia, one of whose principal architects now concedes that it was, to put the matter at its lowest, a strategic error. The role of the civil rights movement in these developments is more complicated. At its outset it was as far as possible from an attack on the core Western tradition: Martin Luther King's "Letter from a Birmingham Jail" is entirely traditionalist in its arguments, and even Malcolm X embraced Islam rather than Buddhism or deconstruction. Even the Marxism embraced by some activists hardly amounts to a total rejection of the West. But encounter with the realities of power politics, and the massive inertia of human society, led some adherents of the civil rights movement to nihilism (and in particular to the sloganistic rejection of the Western tradition as racist, sexist, and homophobic). There is no way of protecting idealistic political movements from the messiness of social reality, but the outcome in this case does seem to reflect a wider cultural malaise.

For the despairing cultural Right, the Bible (or St. Thomas Aquinas, or the Great Books) is a tribal totem, with whose help we may be able to keep the barbarians away, at least for a while. Such works in fact form part of a conversation into which some of the "barbarians" at least can be invited. The despair of the cultural Left has been eloquently expressed in a notorious essay by Sontag:

The truth is that Mozart, Pascal, Boolean algebra, Shakespeare, parliamentary government, baroque churches, Newton, the emancipation of women, Kant, Marx, Balanchine ballet *et al.* don't redeem what this particular civilization has wrought upon the world. The white race is the cancer of human history, it is the white race, and it alone—its ideologies and inventions—which eradicates autonomous civilizations wherever it spreads, which has upset the ecological balance of the planet, which now threatens the very existence of life itself.[18]

In my view, the fact of human diversity requires a strong and coherent cultural tradition, embodying a shared conception of human nature—however difficult it may be to find or create such a thing. But we must accept the ambiguous performance of this tradition, judged by its own ideals, as part of the inevitably mixed character of human life. We should neither chauvinistically defend everything each representative of our tradition has done, nor reject the tradition as a whole because all of its representatives (except Jesus and, for Roman Catholics, the Virgin Mary) have been sinners. (Nor should we limit our critique to trite examples such as slavery.)

We remain dependent on our tradition for our capacity to make the critical judgments, even upon its most august representatives. Richard Rodriguez has summed up the educational implications well:

Did anyone attempt to protect the white middle class student of yore from the ironies of history? Thomas Jefferson—that great democrat—was also a slaveowner. Need we protect black students from complexity? Thomas Jefferson, the slave-owner, was also a democrat.[19]

NOTES

1. An informative discussion is Merle Curti, *Human Nature in American Thought* (Madison: University of Wisconsin, 1980).

2. See Arlene W. Saxonhouse, *Fear of Diversity* (Chicago: University of Chicago Press, 1992).

3. Most contemporary references to the 1960s are historically inadequate. The early sixties—the period of Martin Luther King, the Second Vatican Council, and the Peace Corps—had a very different character from that of the late sixties. And the notion that the Fall of Humanity took place in 1968 will not withstand the gentlest scrutiny.

4. As experts in direct mail solicitation observe, "You've got to have a devil. If you don't have a devil you're in trouble." Robert Smith of Carver, Mathews, and Smith, quoted in James Davison Hunter, *Culture Wars* (New York: Basic, 1993), p. 167.

5. Thomas Byrne Edsall, "America's Sweetheart," *New York Review of Books* 41, 16 (October 16, 1994): 10.

6. Charles Strozier, *Apocalypse* (Boston: Beacon Press, 1994), p. 166. The child was fine.

7. Dr. Bailey Smith, then head of the Southern Baptist Convention. His statement was apparently endorsed by Jerry Falwell, who subsequently recanted under pressure. See *Facts on File*, October 24, 1980, p. 811.

8. On the mechanisms at work here, see Andrew Bard Schmooker. *The Parable of the Tribes* (Berkeley: University of California Press, 1984).

9. René Descartes, *Discourse on Method*, Donald A. Cress, trans. (Indianapolis, Ind.: Hackett, 1980), p. 7.

10. David Bromwitch, *Politics by Other Means* (New Haven, Conn.: Yale University Press, 1994), p. 126.

11. Ibid., see especially Bromwitch's polemical remark against George Will at p. 66.

12. The erstwhile Marxist Eugene Genovese now appeals to the Christian tradition, and more specifically to Galatians 6:7 ("God is not mocked"), as the measure of moral responsibility. (See "The Question," *Dissent* [summer 1994]: 372.) But he continues to identify himself as an atheist ("The Riposte," *Dissent* [summer 1994]: 387). The result is altogether perplexing.

13. Susan M. Okin, *Justice, Gender, and the Family* (New York: Basic Books, 1989), pp. 44–45, 90–91.

14. On cultural conflict among Jews, see Jack Wertheimer, *A People Divided* (New York: Basic Books, 1993).

15. For journalistic accounts, see Richard Bernstein, *Dictatorship of Virtue* (New York: Knopf, 1994) and John Leo, *Two Steps Ahead of the Thought Police* (New York: Simon and Schuster, 1994). The best satirical treatment is James Finn Garner, *Politically Correct Bedtime Stories* (New York: Macmillan, 1994).

16. I am here indebted to Charles Taylor, especially "Justice After Virtue," *After MacIntyre*, John Horton and Susan Mendus, eds. (Notre Dame, Ind.: University of Notre Dame Press, 1994), ch. 2.

17. P. D. James, *The Children of Men* (New York: Knopf, 1993).

18. Susan Sontag, "What's Happening to America?" *Partisan Review* 34 (winter 1967): 57–58.

19. Richard Rodriguez, *Days of Obligation* (New York: Viking, 1992), p. 169.

PART I
THE CULTURAL SPECTRUM

For since language is the impress of the mind, how does it come to pass, that men, who are born for the social life, do not communicate with each other in the same language? This defect, seeing that it is repugnant to nature, Moses declares to be adventitious; and pronounces the division of tongues to be a punishment, divinely inflicted upon men, because they impiously conspired against God.

Calvin, *Commentaries on Genesis*, on 11:1

There is no such person in existence as the general Indian.

E. M. Forster, *A Passage to India*

1

From Fundamentalism to Pluralism

Inquiry is possible only because we work within traditions that were founded before we arrived on the scene and will continue, or at least so we hope, after we leave it. People sometimes aspire to unify their cultural standards under the aegis of a philosophy or a religion, but in fact these standards form an inherited conglomerate, which can be sorted out into a number of conflicting traditions. In contemporary America the most influential traditions are Judaism, Roman Catholic and Protestant Christianity, the Enlightenment (and the scientism and technocracy that have developed out of it), Romanticism, Liberalism, Feminism, and (under the guise of the "New Age" movement) Gnosticism. All of us participate in more than one of these traditions, for example, liberalism and Roman Catholicism.[1]

All of the traditions on which we rely for guidance are now assaulted, not only by external challenges, but also by ambiguities and conflicts arising within them, which are possible sources of both growth and decay. Theory and practice are often at odds. The exponents of every tradition must deal with quarrels among its adherents, attempts to show that it is fundamentally irrational, attacks on its continued vitality, and unabashed violations of its most central tenets. Cultural conflict occurs not so much among as within existing communities—so much so that distinctions such as that between Protestant, Catholic, and Jew (and even more so such as Methodist and Baptist) are of sharply limited utility in understanding it.[2]

The resulting issues are of two sorts. There are particular questions of belief, practice, and ritual—some of them hard for outsiders to understand. But traditions as a whole also keep, lose, or regain their capacity to shape thought and action. At the most abstract level we are dealing with a party of stability and a party of change. But human society is always changing, and even the most ardent devotees of change need standards by which to decide which changes are progress and which retrogression. It is not sufficient, for example, to say that a "progressive" change responds to the deficiencies of the existing order: the Nazis responded to Weimar Germany's lack of economic stability, cultural cohesion, and political leadership.

Some conceptual apparatus will now prove useful. *Relativism* holds that claims of truth are made only within certain "frameworks," and that those whose frameworks differ should not regard one another as wrong, but only as different. In earlier work I carelessly interpreted relativists as holding that "people have employed incompatible standards in making assertions about the same subject matter."[3] I now prefer to say that men and women have employed standards that have led them into mutual incomprehension and practical conflict, without suggesting that there must be a "subject matter" about which they disagree.[4]

Some relativists believe that men and women cannot be held responsible for adhering to standards that they have no reason to accept. Others, however, attempt to impose, as universal laws, principles whose grounding is in the desires and practice of particular groups. And even the softer form of relativism is not necessarily tolerant, since it is not always possible for those whose "values" differ radically to avoid one another, or to avoid discussing "sensitive" issues. And, when collective decisions have to be made, relativism cuts away the common ground that otherwise might make reasoned deliberation possible.[5]

Frameworks (like beliefs) are not only abstract entities, but also psychosocial constructions existing in time. Hence, however well entrenched a framework may be, it is vulnerable not only to intellectual refutation but also to erosion through cultural and political change. A *nihilist* generalizes the experience of transiency and concludes from them that *no judgment of value can survive reflection*—a judgment that can easily be extended from morals to the judgments of value (of coherence and simplicity, say) made in theoretical contexts.[6] While we are in the grip of an appetite or emotion, it may be impossible for us to be indifferent to what it leads us to value, or to doubt what it prompts us to believe. But, in a cool hour, these pursuits may prove empty. Similarly, the beliefs that we accept as a matter of animal faith may turn out, as in Hume, to be rationally indefensible.

In this Part, I attempt a "phenomenology of the spirit," setting out a range of responses to our cultural situation, ranging from fundamentalism on the "Right" to postmodernism/deconstruction on the "Left." I shall set out the various interpretative styles in a broadly Hegelian fashion, arguing that the deficiencies of fundamentalism lead naturally to traditionalism, and so forth. Whether political correctness, for example, is now in vogue or *passé* at some time or place is irrelevant to my concern: I attempt to portray a person or group's movement from position to position. And I take the risk of constructing a representative version of each of the positions considered, which may not do justice to the nuances of some particular writer's approach.

My purpose in this Part is not to defend my own allegiances or to do justice to the nuances of individual positions, but to provide the reader with a workable map of the relevant territory, with enough historical detail to support the contention that I am dealing with the way people in fact think rather than a mere construction of my own mind. My discussion will be limited, for the most part, to alternatives within the core Western tradition, since I lack the competence to discuss Zen, Hinduism, or Islam.

I assume that, although human beings often reason badly, the rules of good reasoning nonetheless regulate an activity in which human beings in fact engage, so that the practice of reasoners is for that reason relevant to our understanding of these rules.[7] I do not, however, believe in Hegel's principle of determinate negation: there is not one, but many, ways in which we can remedy the deficiencies of a position. Moreover, the stages in my dialectic do not represent a progress to Absolute Knowledge, but a cycle in which the dissolution of the binding force of tradition leads to its authoritative reassertion or replacement by some other tradition. Whether we are dealing with an upward or a downward spiral, or a cycle on level ground, I do not know.

FUNDAMENTALISM

Lurking behind fundamentalism is the ideal of an interpretative Eden in which no one ever doubted what the rules of life were. People broke these rules, but no one proposed a fresh understanding of them to warrant his conduct. Such was the situation of Adam and Eve before the Fall; even the Serpent did not suggest that God would approve the eating of the fruit of the Tree of Knowledge. But it is not the situation of anyone today.

For its adherents, fundamentalism is not an interpretative strategy but simple fidelity to authoritative sources. Thus a church historian endorsed by Bob Jones defines (Protestant) fundamentalism as "unqualified acceptance and obedience to the Scriptures."[8] But a definition that supposes that the fundamentalists are right in their central contentions is question-begging. Nor should *fundmentalism* be used as an all-purpose term of abuse for those whose religion is stricter than one's own; as Leon Wieseltier observes, "It is not fundamentalist to wish to apply your religion to your private and public life."[9]

Fundamentalism is best understood as the hardening of a tradition in response to threat.[10] Fundamentalists are best understood as responding to the perceived weakness, in the face of challenge, of even the most conservative mainstream representatives of tradition. They therefore separate themselves, more and more, from their weaker brethren, when they cannot secure their expulsion from the community. As a fundamentalist church historian puts it:

While [Protestant] Fundamentalists prior to 1930 had separated primarily from worldliness, and the Fundamentalism of the 1930s and 1940s had separated primarily from modernism, mid-twentieth century Fundamentalism had come to the conviction that, in the face of a new enemy within the camp, they must also separate from disobedient evangelicals.[11]

In short, fundamentalism is an impulse, a rhetorical strategy, and an interpretative method before it is a distinctive body of doctrines and practices.

Fundamentalists characteristically hold that the interpretation and application of authoritative texts is self-evident to any "right-thinking" man or woman,[12] and that anyone who would adapt them to the felt necessities of the time is "both a traitor and a fool."[13] But literal interpretation is not quite the issue, since many of the texts invoked by fundamentalists are explicitly figurative in character. Fundamentalists innovate, though usually without consciousness of innovation; the millenarianism characteristic of Protestant fundamentalism[14] can be understood as a stiffening of resistance to the modern world—both by emphasizing those elements of the Christian tradition most offensive to self-consciously modern men and women, and by asserting that the modern world itself is destined for imminent destruction. Similarly, contemporary "creation science" is a hardening of positions taken by theologically conservative writers in the nineteenth century, who were quite willing to accept an ancient Earth.[15]

While the word *fundamentalism* is customarily used only of Protestants and Muslims, the Hasidic-secular continuum among Jews exhibits the interpretive issues with great clarity. In Orthodox Judaism, for example, the banning of women's prayer groups (mixed prayer groups being out of the question) displays a fundamentalist approach to questions of practice.[16] To venture briefly outside the West, Swami Dayanada Sarasvati, founder of the Hindu revival movement Arya Samaj, makes one of the most remarkable fundamentalist theoretical moves when he draws a line *within* the Hindu canon, dismissing its later portions as corrupt.[17]

TRADITIONALISM

Fundamentalists attempt to avoid interpretation altogether, and in that way to prevent the erosion of their tradition. But no text or tradition is self-applying, and so fundamentalism always involves a sort of pretense. Traditionalism is an attempt, more sophisticated than fundamentalism, to prevent the erosion of a cultural tradition, by finding within it an authoritative core and interpreting the rest accordingly. In order to evaluate this strategy, we need first to distinguish four senses of *tradition*: (1) tradition in the naive conservative sense of what everybody until just recently believed, (2) the inherited conglomerate of which we are all beneficiaries or victims, (3) particular traditions such as Christianity and Marxism, and (4) tradition in the normative sense (Tradition, or what John Finnis calls "high tradition").[18]

Those traditionalists closest to fundamentalism treasure the very unreflective character of inherited attitudes—and their consequent immunity to skepticism and to planned revision. One reason for this attitude is a fear that individuals who critically evaluate their tradition will revise it to favor their particular passions, and that the tradition will for that reason dissolve. A traditionalist of this sort will reject the thought that he represents one school of thought among others: the schismatic Archbishop Lefebvre, for example, has written, "I am not the head of a movement, even less the head of a particular church. I am not, as they never stop writing, 'the leader of the traditionalists.' "[19] For once the traditionalist has identified himself as a traditionalist, at least one game is up: he can no longer present himself as a representative of what "everyone knows" (or believes)—or what everyone knew or believed until outside agitators came on the scene.

Militant traditionalists are prepared to oppose their understanding of tradition to that of their community's leaders. But their attempts to formulate reasons to support their understanding lead them into paradox. Lefebvre calls on the faithful to invoke "the catechism of their childhood" to warrant disobedience to contemporary church authority.[20] But there is no reason to suppose that the catechism of one's childhood should always take precedence over present doctrine, or even that everyone's childhood catechism will say the same thing. The same paradox arises when Burke praises unreflective thought and defends his position by arguments. For one cannot reflectively adopt a principle of unreflectiveness: the most one can do is defend prejudice for literal or figurative children, while reserving the privilege and burden of reflective thought for a few. (It is unfortunate that the word *prejudice* came to be used only of racial animosities and the like: no one, however sophisticated, can get along without some unreflective attitudes.)

Nietzsche's proclamation that God is dead cannot mean that there once was a God but now there is no longer one. Though only an atheist would have put it in quite this way, his statement is most charitably interpreted as referring to the death of orthodoxy in the distinctively traditionalist sense. By this I mean not the disappearance of religious belief, the end of truth, or even the end of officially sanctioned opinion, let alone the end of intolerance (though we might define a Nietzschean world as one in which it is possible to entertain the illusion that no one, or no one intelligent, believes in God).

I mean the end of unquestioned and unquestionable beliefs, practices, and prohibitions, usually though not invariably thought of as ordained by

God, in terms of which all other matters can be judged. For anything the *Zeitgeist* may have to say about it, we can believe that there is a God, or that heterosexual monogamy is the only legitimate (or at least the best) form of sexual life. But we must now deal not only with religious indifference but also with open atheism, and not only with the ever popular violations of heterosexual monogamy, but also with the fact that many people repudiate it even as an ideal.

There are some ideas not in question in most circles—such as that there is a morally significant difference between adults and small children. But even this agreement continues only as long as no group arises to challenge it openly. Some of the hysteria about child sexual abuse—to the neglect of a careful examination of the question of guilt or innocence—arises not from the horror of the act, real though it is, but from the need to hold on, at any cost, to a departing consensus.

But accepting Nietzsche's account of our cultural situation does not imply that we have escaped the power of tradition. For, in the broadest sense, *tradition* refers to any inherited belief or practice, or even to the objects, such as buildings, which figure in such beliefs or practices.[21] My tradition thus consists in everything that I bring to the consideration of a problem, before I sort out the relevant considerations and move toward a resolution.

Our language is both an important element in our heritage and a useful symbol for the other elements. We do not choose our first language, and while learning it we are at the same time being inducted into an entire way of life. Language can adapt to meet new needs, but it can also degenerate. Traditionalists invoke the older language of the Book of Common Prayer, the Authorized Version of the Bible (and now even the Revised Standard Version), and the Tridentine mass, to defend a sense of transcendence they believe recent developments in their religious communities have compromised or destroyed. And Nietzsche's remark—"I fear that we are not getting rid of God because we still have faith in grammar"[22]—is the motto of those in the humanities who reject all tradition as repressive.

In most uses of *tradition*, however, the word carries a claim of antiquity ("so far as the memory of man runneth not to the contrary"). But it is not clear how old our data must be to count as traditional. The policies of the present administration or the present Congress do not represent tradition in this sense, but the New Deal, it is easy to argue, does. The best criterion is that *tradition* refers to those cultural data that arose before I myself entered the fray (roughly in adolescence).

Different men and women have widely different early experiences, and thus different conceptions of the traditional. In order to retrieve lost traditions, one must identify oneself with one element in one's inherited conglomerate, and interpret the world and one's tasks within it in terms of that element, even as one interprets that element in terms of one's world. Before doing so, one must make judgments on the relative vitality of the traditions and subtraditions that contend for one's allegiance. To accept a tradition is also to identify oneself with the community whose tradition it is.

For the members of a community defined by a tradition, its elements have a given quality—one independent of the personal responses or beliefs of its particular members. Such traditions involve a self-conscious attempt at continuity: men and women do things in part because their biological or spiritual ancestors did them. Such traditions claim, rightly or wrongly, a coherence that a mere inherited conglomerate lacks. For that reason, they include a claim to evaluate new forms of theory and practice as compatible or incompatible with the standards of the tradition—for example condemning some forms of investigation as "unscientific." Finally, traditions define what is important and what is trivial. (As Charles Taylor has pointed out, one cannot define one's identity by devoting one's life to wriggling one's toes in warm mud.)

In order to serve their purposes, cultural standards need to meet five tests. First, they need to be shared with others, so that we can use them to help coordinate our activities with them in the pursuit of shared goals. Second, they must be coherent, so that a reflective man or woman can affirm them without undue internal strain. Third, they should coordinate human behavior, in that the tasks assigned to one group of men or women should mesh with those assigned to others. Fourth, it is necessary that men and women be trained in a morality from childhood on it, so that they will adhere to it in situations of emergency and temptation. (Burke makes much of this last point.) Fifth, their dictates need to be clear and stable enough to prevent opportunists from adopting whatever interpretation suits their present purposes. In all these respects, contemporary cultural standards fall woefully short.

Traditionalists identify a core tradition and see departures from it as mutually reinforcing; even those that may seem to be supported by good reasons are adopted at the cost of destroying the coherence of morality and thus rending the fabric of social life. Many of them hold that we made a wrong turning at some point in our near or distant past—say, in the fourteenth century—though identifying this point presents serious difficulties. It is the task of political theory to discover the divine original behind the confusion of present-day *mores*, and the task of political practice is to reproduce at least a simulacrum of it in society. But traditionalists need to face the charge of nostalgia in Christopher Lasch's sense: "Strictly speaking, nostalgia does not entail the exercise of memory at all, since the past it idealizes stands outside time, frozen in its perfection."[23]

There is, moreover, an enormous variety of idealized, fictional, and semifictional pasts to which one can appeal in politics, and adherents of different pasts are sometimes allies and sometimes enemies. Any idealized past can serve as a metaphor of any other. Archbishop Lefebvre has said that "Vatican II is 1789 in the Church."[24] And all the lesser falls identified by traditionalists are diminished similitudes of the expulsion from Eden.

"Paleoconservatives" are distinguished by the belief that our tradition cannot assimilate new elements without destroying itself; and, in America, that the process of disintegration began with the New Deal, if not earlier—say, with the Northern victory in the Civil War or even with the Declaration of Independence or the emigration of British settlers who found their inherited social and political order oppressive. The most consistent paleoconservatives are those who deny the legitimacy of all American institutions on the basis that they are founded on the displacement of the Native American population—or those feminists who reject the whole of the Western tradition as "androcentric," and look back to a primeval matriarchy.

We thus arrive at the central paradox of conservative thought: the fact that the social order conservatives are attempting to protect results from many revolutions contains within itself the seeds of instability, and thus can be stabilized only by changing it in (perhaps radical) ways. Many movements with radical implications—the Reformation, for example—got their start with attempts to retrieve an authentic tradition covered up by the practice of the groups in which they arose. And accepting things-as-they-are means, among other things, accepting ongoing change of a disturbing sort. De Maistre attacked the French Revolution by invoking force and Providence as the source of political authority, and ended up defending the French Revolution as a punishment for the sins of France.

PROGRESSIVE CONSERVATISM

Traditionalists may win every interpretive battle and still lose the war. They deprive the traditions they are trying to defend of the capacity to respond to new challenges, and for that reason they are reduced to awaiting the end of the world. Of course, the world *may* end: no one has ever proved that our inductive arguments will continue to hold, though we are well advised to continue to use them. But we cannot count on its ending either, and in the meantime we are obliged to do the best we can with what we have. This argument forms the foundation of the progressive conservative attitude.

Progressive conservatives, while differing on much else, concur in arguing as follows. Neither the cultural Right nor the cultural Left can possibly win, though both can lose, if our society transforms itself into a bloody mess on the Yugoslav model. For the Right proposes, like William F. Buckley, to stand in front of cultural history and cry "Stop!" And the Left attempts entirely to break its continuity. Hence none of us has any alternative but to make the best sense we can of the tradition or traditions that have formed us.

By "progressive conservatism" (or less euphoniously, "conservative pro-gressivism") I thus mean a set of attitudes toward cultural innovation that was standard during the nineteenth century. Old-fashioned reformers and revolutionaries believed, in the biblical phrase, that truth was great and would prevail if given a fair chance to do so—or at least that the errors which survive a fair contest are tolerable, given the generally unsatisfactory character of human life (though for some of them, it would take a bloody upheaval for the desired result to come to pass).

Nineteenth-century reformers assumed that there was an objective order that grounded normative principles which in part supported, and in part condemned, the existing state of things, and enabled us to work toward changing this state of things in a coherent way. Such changes were then called "progressive," and proposals designed to block them were stigma-tized as "reactionary." In this scheme, conservatives are in implicit or explicit dialogue with those who propose to change inherited ideas and practices. Moreover, a conservative need not acquiesce in every change that takes place, and at some point will become a reformer, even of a radical sort. For the "progressive conservative" framework has a role for the retrieval of truths lost to view. But the upshot of the process is the retention of what is good in our traditions, and the setting aside of what is bad or no longer relevant.

I will be adopting progressive conservatism as a working hypothesis in the arguments of this book. But it is no longer possible to believe in the scientifically discoverable laws of history on which some progressive con-servatives have relied.[25] (These include the "law" of inevitable seculariza-tion, whether asserted by hopeful unbelievers or by despairing believers.) It is thus easy to dismiss the beliefs underlying progressive conservatism as projections of our hopes onto an unknown and unknowable future; they are defensible, if at all, as a matter of faith and hope rather than knowledge.

PLURALISM

In a recent book, John Kekes[26] confronts the widespread belief that our morality is disintegrating by reason of its inability to resolve conflicts (pp. 3–9). His response is a restatement of the ideas of Isaiah Berlin and Michael Oakeshott (p. xi). Their "pluralism," he argues, does not imply relativism. For the abandonment of the "monistic" claim that there is a general method for resolving moral conflicts does not imply that we cannot settle such conflicts reasonably, nor does it prevent us from setting limits on the range of acceptable modes of life, nor from speaking meaningfully of moral progress.

But Kekes's grounds for rejecting monism are not persuasive. Against the Platonic and Christian claim that there is a *summum bonum* that trumps all other goods, and thus enables us to resolve conflicts among them, he asks:

Why should we reject the thoughtful testimony of millions of reasonable people, including ourselves, that they, and we, often want to realize two values but that the nature of these values is such that they cannot be realized together? Why should we doubt this evidence that comes from the contexts of radically different societies, separated by vast historical, cultural, environmental, and psychological differences? There does not appear to be a convincing answer. (pp. 65–66)

But Christian theology at least has an explanation of our failure to accept the Christian *summum bonum*: the doctrine of original sin.

The doctrine of original sin yields results, both practical and theoretical, at least within hailing distance of Oakeshott and Berlin. A Christian who takes the doctrine seriously can, for example, agree with the following passage from Berlin's "Two Concepts of Liberty," as long as we understand *final solution* as one brought about by human efforts within history.

One belief, more than any other, is responsible for the slaughter of individuals on the altars of the great historical ideals. . . . This is the belief that somewhere, in the past, or in the future, in divine revelation, or in the mind of an individual thinker, in the pronouncements of history or science, or in the simple heart of an uncorrupted good man, there is a final solution. (pp. 85–86 n. 5)

Kekes's own approach to moral conflict is also unsatisfactory. He repeatedly informs us that "pluralism . . . denies the overridingness of any value" (p. 92 and elsewhere), or again "one of the most important implications of pluralism is that no value should be unqualifiedly endorsed" (p. 109). Even the continuation of a treasured way of life cannot always override all other claims. Yet, in his view, both individuals and groups can settle moral conflicts reasonably. For, *"except in the most extreme situations*, the value of our conceptions of the good life, or the value of the traditional system of values to which we adhere will be greater than either of the two values whose conflict we are facing" (p. 25, emphasis supplied).

It might seem that Kekes is offering a traditional solution of the problem of moral conflict—namely, that if first-order goods such as friendship, knowledge, and pleasure are incommensurable, the conflict can be resolved by appeal to higher-order goods such as marriage. But while, in his view, first-order goods are grounded in a common human nature, the criteria of reasonable conflict resolution are based in individual or collective choice, though he insists that neither individuals nor societies enjoy unlimited discretion. In his own words, "the causes of conflicts are facts in the world; the norms for resolving conflicts is our response to those facts" (p. 94).

But Kekes's position implies that solutions to conflicts have a metaphysical and epistemological status inferior to the moral conflicts themselves. Thus he is, in practice, more skeptical about morals than are stock subjectivists or relativists, for whom the goodness or badness of pain, and the rightness or wrongness of euthanasia, are alike matters of individual or collective response. He provides, in fact, the contrast necessary to give ethical noncognitivism the power it needs effectively to undermine morality.

The same is true of Kekes's discussion of the nature of moral limits. He rightly points out that our moral imagination can devise evil as well as good ways of life, and that it is therefore necessary to define limits to its legitimate scope. These limits are provided by what he calls "deep conventions" (pp. 118–121), which protect human beings in their lives, their liberties, and their ability to pursue their chosen goals. At the same time, he carefully qualifies the resulting limit: in his view, acts such as "murder, dismemberment, and enslavement are evil, *unless extraordinary circumstances make them otherwise*" (p. 119, emphasis supplied). The issue is thus whether such extraordinary circumstances can be defined in such a way as not to erode the force of the required limits.

Kekes's appeal to human nature to establish moral limits suffers from serious deficiencies.[27] For the time being, however, I shall consider one good that is taken as fundamental in virtually all moralities, that of life.

Kekes makes it clear that even life is, though a primary, not an overriding value: it can be overridden for the sake of "freedom, justice, autonomy, prosperity, adventure, privacy, free trade [!], civic harmony, and countless other values" (p. 123). If so, no social practice can be criticized as failing adequately to take the value of life into account: even the Nazis did not deny the value of life, though they subordinated it to racial integrity and social solidarity. And he defends the Dinka custom of burying aged spearmasters alive, on the supposition that the relevant Dinka beliefs concerning the transmission of life from the spearmaster to his people are true (pp. 125 ff.). In rejecting the defense of live burial in terms of its symbolic meaning, he relies on the fact that "the Dinka tradition has remained strong even after Sudanese authorities outlawed live burial" (p. 130). If it had not, perhaps even a symbolic interpretation would have sufficed to defend this practice.

Kekes's analogy between live burial and blood or kidney donation (p. 127) ignores the fact that, though blood or kidney donation may sometimes be harmful to the donor, the practices are not in general lethal. He also ignores the fact, that beliefs such as that the ritual death of a spearmaster is necessary to the welfare of his people, and the metaphysical presuppositions that underlie such beliefs, are themselves open to relativistic questions. For differences of world-view generate different factual pictures as well as different moral beliefs.

Kekes's example of moral progress concerns shame. Individuals progress as they move from propriety-shame, which depends on how we appear to others, through honor-shame, in which we accept the opinions of others as our own, to worth-shame, in which "we care about being a certain way and we do not care about appearances" (p. 153). Similarly, a tradition progresses insofar as it enables its adherents to progress from propriety-shame to honor-shame to worth-shame (p. 154). "Part of the reason why this movement constitutes progress is that it gives us greater control of our own lives" (p. 153).

But this movement cannot, on pluralistic premises, constitute unambiguous progress. As Kekes acknowledges, "it may happen that [in adopting worth-shame] we progress toward morally noxious commitments" (p. 153). And the moral individualism that underlies worth-shame itself has significant costs. To the extent that people cease to be ashamed of offending against conventional moral standards, to that extent these conventions lose their power to maintain solidarity among, and coordinate the behavior of, the members of society. It then becomes easier to throw off moral restraints altogether and adopt the opportunistic strategy of supporting whatever moral code best serves one's immediate interests. At least on pluralistic premises, the choice between individual autonomy and social cohesion is tragic.

If pluralists are right, individual autonomy cannot in general override social custom. So much is implicit in the contrast Kekes draws between liberalism and pluralism (ch. 11). A refusal to take individual rights as trumps also follows from his assertion that

an acceptable level of law-abidingness, order, prosperity, and social solidarity are as important as the four values liberals favor [freedom, equality, the protection of human rights, and Rawlsian justice], and they are important for exactly the same reason; their claims must be recognized by all conceptions of the good life. (p. 206)

One might expect that Kekes's position would at least imply some sort of liberal-conservative compromise in politics, especially in view of his invocation of Oakeshott and Berlin as mentors. But he holds that ethical pluralism is consistent not only with a liberal or a conservative social philosophy, depending on the concrete historical situation, but also "with some form of radicalism, like anarchism or libertarianism" (p. 208). If so, pluralism seems to be entirely without normative content.

The case would not be changed if we were to take a hard Kantian line and equate morality with autonomously chosen as opposed to merely conventional principles of conduct, while admitting pluralism in value theory. For we would still have to face the implications of Kekes's contention that "if pluralism is correct, there must be conflicts in which moral values are reasonably overridden by nonmoral values" (p. 162). For among these nonmoral values must be included conformity to conventional "moral" standards, and indeed to nonmoral customs such as eating turkey at Thanksgiving. If "all things considered, agents may [reasonably] put love, beauty, creativity, and so on ahead of the common good in many contexts" (p. 178), they may with equal reason favor adherence to the *mores* of some group with which they identify, even when these *mores* require immoral acts such as private violence against deviants. If aesthetic considerations, and the demands of a career, can override the demands of morality (pp. 163 ff.), the same is true of the maintenance of a treasured custom.

To admit a multitude of principles, without establishing any order among them, is to authorize any result that an individual or group might happen to reach. The order needed to escape this result does not demand a foundationalist meta-principle: the love of God or our devotion to a certain way of life will also do what is required. But the form of pluralism defended by Kekes (and, very likely, that defended by Oakeshott and Berlin as well) precludes such an appeal. It is thus an appropriate prologue to the avowedly relativist views to be considered in the following chapter.

Nonetheless, something like the pluralism considered here is the best that can be done on strictly naturalistic premises. For any form of life adopted (and perhaps even any form of life imagined) by human beings is in some sense a human form of life, however extreme or perverse it may seem to outsiders. And unwillingness or inability to invoke a transcendent normative principle to place limits on such forms of life implies the loss of normativity reflected in the pluralist's inability consistently to override any consideration that, at least persistently, moves human beings to action. It remains for Richard Rorty to draw the implications.

When the secret police come, when the torturers violate the innocent, there is nothing to be said to them of the form "There is something within you that you are betraying. Though you embody the practices of a totalitarian society which will endure forever, there is something beyond those practices which condemns you."[28]

The collapse of pluralism into relativism or nihilism has broad metaphysical and epistemological implications. Interpreting Wittgenstein, Hilary Putnam writes:

On the one hand, to regard an assertion or a belief or a thought as true or false *is* to regard it as being right or wrong; on the other hand, just what sort of rightness or wrongness is in question varies enormously with the *sort* of discourse.[29]

But we await reasons for rejecting the claim that even the most noxious ideologies are a "sort" of discourse, with immanent criteria of rightness or wrongness; and that reality constraints can be evaded by the simple expedient of inventing new forms of discourse. We may accept what Putnam calls the "natural realist" perspective: the world somehow constrains our ability to indulge in metaphysical-epistemological-linguistic fantasy.[30] But we need to be told more about how this happens. It is not sufficient that the Nazis were, as a matter of historical fact, defeated.

NOTES

1. Relations between these traditions are discussed in R. Bruce Douglass and David Hollenbach, eds., *Catholicism and Liberalism* (Cambridge: Cambridge University Press, 1994).

2. How this came about is discussed in Robert Wuthnow, *The Restructuring of American Religion* (Princeton, N.J.: Princeton University Press, 1988).

3. Philip E. Devine, *Relativism, Nihilism, and God* (Notre Dame, Ind.: Notre Dame University Press, 1989), p. 43.

4. John Koller of Rensselaer Polytechnic Institute first pointed out this problem to me.

5. See my essay, "Relativism, Abortion, and Tolerance," *Philosophy and Phenomenological Research* 48 (1987): 131–138.

6. Cf. Friedrich Nietzsche: "What does nihilism mean? *That the highest values devaluate themselves.* The aim is lacking; 'why' finds no answer." *The Will to Power,* Walter Kaufman and R. J. Hollingdale, trans., Walter Kaufman, ed. (New York: Vintage, 1968), sec. 2.

7. I am here responding to concerns expressed in Gordon Graham, "MacInytre's Fusion of History and Philosophy," in John Horton and Susan Mendus, eds., *After MacIntyre* (Notre Dame, Ind.: University of Notre Dame Press, 1994), ch. 9.

8. David O. Beale, *In Pursuit of Purity* (Greenville, S.C.: Unusual Publications, 1986), p. 3. Italics in original.

9. "The Jewish Face of Fundamentalism," in Norman J. Cohen, ed., *The Fundamentalist Phenomenon* (Grand Rapids, Mich.: Eerdmans, 1990), p. 195. Stephen L. Carter elaborates this point in *The Culture of Disbelief* (New York: Basic Books, 1993).

10. For a psychological study of fundamentalism, see Robert Jay Lifton, *The Protean Self* (New York: Basic Books, 1993), ch. 9; and, more fully, Charles B. Strozier, *Apocalypse* (Boston: Beacon Press, 1994). But there should be no question of reducing fundmentalist ideas to emotional responses.

11. Beale, *In Pursuit of Purity*, p. 9. Beale lists the following as representing theologically unreliable "broad evangelicalism": the Moody Bible Institute, Jerry Falwell, Calvin College, the Southern Baptist Convention, the Lutheran Church-Missouri Synod, and Oral Roberts University (pp. 268–269).

12. On the centrality of common-sense epistemology in the hermeneutics and polemics of American fundamentalism, see George M. Marsden, *Fundamentalism and American Culture* (New York: Oxford University Press, 1980), especially ch. 24.

13. The words of a Catholic integralist, Don Felix Sandra y Salavny, *El Liberalismo es Pecado* (1886), as cited in Peter Steinfels, "The Failed Encounter," in Douglass and Hollenbach, eds., *Catholicism and Liberalism*, pp. 40–41.

14. Ernest R. Sandeen, *The Roots of Fundamentalism* (Chicago: University of Chicago Press, 1970). Strozier also emphasizes fundamentalist "endism."

15. Ronald L. Numbers, *The Creationists* (Berkeley: University of California Press, 1992). I discuss the practical and theoretical issues raised by "Creationism" in Chapter 9.

16. For the Jewish situation, see Jack Wertheimer, *A People Divided* (New York: Basic Books, 1993); on the banning of women's prayer groups, see pp. 122–123.

M. Herbert Danzger, *Returning to Tradition* (New Haven, Conn.: Yale University Press, 1989), pp. 260–261, reports: "At the very same time the sexual mores of society have become more permissive, current practice in Orthodoxy has shifted in a traditionalist direction."

17. Daniel Gold, "Organized Hinduisms," in Martin Marty and R. Scott Appleby, eds., *Fundamentalisms Observed* (Chicago: University of Chicago Press, 1991), p. 544.

18. See Finnis's *Moral Absolutes* (Washington, D.C.: Catholic University of America Press, 1991), for example, pp. 32, 34.

19. Archbishop Lefebvre, *An Open Letter to Confused Catholics*, Father M. Crowley, trans. (Leominster, Eng.: Fowler Wright, 1986), p. 14. I am indebted to Mark Henrie for supplying me with a copy of this book.

20. Ibid., pp. 135–136. At p. 150 he appeals from the present Pope to St. Pius V.

21. Edward Shils, *Tradition* (Chicago: University of Chicago Press, 1981). See also George Allan, *The Importances of the Past* (Albany, N.Y.: SUNY Press, 1986), and Garrett Barden, *After Principles* (Notre Dame, Ind.: University of Notre Dame Press, 1990).

22. Friedrich Nietzsche, *Twilight of the Idols*, R. J. Hollingdale, trans. (Harmondsworth, Eng.: Penguin, 1988), p. 38.

23. Christopher Lasch, *The True and Only Heaven* (New York: Norton, 1991), ch. 3; quotation on p. 83.

24. Quoted by Peter Steinfels, *New York Times*, July 1, 1988.

25. For a witty account of the reasons for this result, as well as its implications, see Alasdair MacIntyre, *After Virtue*, 2nd ed. (Notre Dame, Ind.: University of Notre Dame Press, 1984), ch. 8.

26. John Kekes, *The Morality of Pluralism* (Princeton, N.J.: Princeton University Press, 1993). Parenthetical references in this section are to this book.

27. See ch. 6 under "The Project Continued."

28. Richard Rorty, *Consequences of Pragmatism* (Minneapolis: University of Minnesota Press, 1982), p. xlii.

29. Hilary Putnam, "Sense, Nonsense, and the Senses," *Journal of Philosophy* 91, 9 (September 1994): 515.

30. In Putnam's words, "The notion that our words and life are constrained by a reality not of our own invention plays a deep role in our lives, and is to be respected . . . [To understand it, we should look] at the ways in which we endlessly renegotiate—and are *forced* to renegotiate—our notion of reality as our language and our life develops." Ibid., p. 462.

2

From Neoconservatism to Deconstruction

We now continue our survey of the cultural spectrum, in its more skeptical side. Neoconservatism has been described as the political philosophy of a liberal who has been mugged—if not literally, then by the realization that social change may turn out to mean social disintegration. At a deeper level, however, it is to be understood as a conservative form of relativism, for which these results are inevitable (or at least cannot be avoided by planning), since there is nothing outside society to guide us in our efforts at reform.

NEOCONSERVATISM

Let us suppose that our moral and other standards are contingent human constructions. Any attempt to get outside these constructions, in order to improve them, leads only to nihilism. The simplest form of the resulting relativism counsels us, in the absence of answers to ultimate questions, to accept the standards of our society. As long as we retain an intuitive sense of what these standards require, and as long as such standards have even a *prima facie* claim on our acceptance, we can use relativistic arguments to undercut all possible ways of criticizing them.

Conservative relativism is best represented in our world by the neoconservative movement. For the core of neoconservatism is the reaffirmation of the Western way of life, central to which neoconservatives take to be a capitalist understanding of liberty, against radical attack.[1] The central neoconservative strategy is to refuse to ask the question of social justice, where older forms of conservatism would have affirmed the justice of existing institutions.[2] The effect is relativism, mitigated by ascribing to the nation-state (or, in older versions, to the "Free World") a set of norms—or at least a common interest—and attempting to hold all individuals and groups within the community to their observance. Hence orderly discourse within the national community (and possibly among allies) is possible on neoconservative premises, though dialogue with the alien enemy is not.

Allan Bloom and Roger Scruton represent neoconservatism among philosophers. Bloom is known for his polemics against "soft" relativism, but his own antirelativism is at best ambiguous. He writes:

Nonphilosophic men love the truth only so long as it does not conflict with what they cherish—self, family, country, fame, love. When it does conflict, they hate the truth and regard as a monster the man who does not care for these noble things, who proves they are ephemeral and treats them as such. The gods are the guarantors of the unity of nature and convention dear to most men, which philosophy can only dissolve. The enmity between science [i.e., philosophy] and mankind at large is, therefore, not an accident.[3]

In practice, this means endorsing the relativism Bloom officially deplores, at least for those men and women unable to follow Bloom's philosophers on their voyage into the abyss.

Scruton affirms that "the culture of Europe, and the civilization that has sprung from it, are not yet dead"—a judgment that he commends as "unfashionable."[4] But Scruton's defense of traditional culture is compromised by his advocacy of the Platonic doctrine of the noble lie.[5]

One example of neoconservative cultural criticism is Michael Medved's polemic against the movie industry.[6] He documents the nihilism of one strand of popular culture: its debunking of every ideal or moral standard, leaving the gratification of sexual and aggressive instincts as the only spring of action. He contends that moviemakers' aspirations toward artistic integrity lead them to nihilism; the market, he believes, is culturally healthy. He writes of an unattractive (and unsuccessful) movie entitled *Life Stinks* (or, in an earlier version, *Life Sucks*):

It is not within purview of this book to debate this fundamental proposition: I will make no attempt to determine whether, in point of fact, life either "stinks" or "sucks." I will submit, however, that few Americans outside of Hollywood would agree with such sentiments.

So popular opinion as reflected in the market (except when it favors the violent rap lyrics "our children consume with such notable gusto") is the arbiter of the most important human issues. In a similar vein Saul Bellow is said to have remarked that when the Zulus produce a Tolstoy, we will read him.

Hilary Putnam criticizes neoconservatism, under the name of "cultural imperialism," which he treats as a form of realism.[7] The ground of his criticism is that "our culture, unlike totalitarian or theocratic cultures, does not have 'norms' which decide philosophical questions." We may grant that the standards of belief and action that prevail in contemporary Western societies (and indeed in all contemporary societies) are in flux, and for that reason also in confusion. But those who engage in adult-child sex are aware that they are deviants. And Jehovah's Witnesses are aware that they belong to a *cognitive* minority. Moreover, Putnam himself argues in ways that suppose that at least the academic subculture has philosophical norms; he concedes, against his own interest, that the radical fact-value distinction he endeavors to refute is now "institutionalized," that is to say embodied in our social practice.[8] It appears that all-pervasive norms are invisible, at least until they are somehow challenged.

Despite the Leftist rhetoric of many of its sponsors, radical human diversity is a conservative doctrine—whether neoconservative or quietistic or fascistic depends on the further assumptions of those who hold it. For if there is no common human nature, or if what nature exists is too scanty to be available for political use,[9] our mutual relations, if we somehow avoid collapse into a war of each against all, will be governed by customary standards which, though they do not satisfy the inquiring mind, can become "second nature" through use and custom. I assume that most—not all—human beings are social creatures who accept the customs with which they were brought up unless some powerful motive intervenes.

These standards will vary from class to class, from family to family, from region to region, and from gender to gender. Diversities of this sort, and the conflicts they generate—as opposed to the radically unified political community proposed by Plato—are to be expected given the diversity of human beings. But a rough compromise among the various sorts of people that inhabit our world may nonetheless be possible. No more than the customary moralities that prevail in the various segments of society, however, can this compromise be expected to satisfy the inquiring mind.

Those—call them "fanatics" or "insane" or "psychopaths"—who for whatever reason are unable or unwilling to accept the social covenant must be killed or expelled to guarantee its stability. How much coercion one thinks necessary to preserve law and order will determine whether the resulting conservatism is, relatively speaking, humane or brutal (for some repression will be necessary in any view). But the intellectual who attempts to reform society according to a prewritten script for social justice, or who points to the incoherence of social practice as evidence of its instability, is in any case a menace. Against this line of reasoning, reformers need to argue—and the more radical they are the more they need to argue it—that social institutions may fall short of principles of justice grounded in our common humanity.

On one issue at least the conservative is right. To the extent that our society has norms, both of belief and of action, we are well advised to follow them in the absence of anything better. But the social order that conservatives defend already contains within itself powerful elements producing change. For that reason, conventional opinion leaves ample room for critical reflection, even apart from our limited capacity to transcend our cultural background. Reflectively to praise unreflective "prejudice," as Burke does, is to demand self-deception. There is in fact more than a little doubt, whether our norms are rich and coherent enough to amount to an implied philosophy (or even a pictured social ideal), rather than a grab bag of beliefs and practices ranging from the celebration of Halloween through the repudiation of insider trading to the belief that those who work hard will be rewarded with worldly success. Defense of the status quo, just because it is the status quo, is in any event never sufficient.

RELATIVISTIC LIBERALISM

In contrast to the neoconservative endorsement of existing social norms, relativistic liberals attempt to maintain as many traditional liberal positions as possible, even when they tend to undermine the mores. Relativistic liberals are prepared to support reforms in the interests of greater respect for diversity and of greater equality of power and wealth, largely ignoring the possibility that these two ends may be in deep conflict. (As noticed above, much human diversity is linked to differences of social position.)

Relativistic liberals take their positions without the belief either in progress or in transhistorical moral standards that advocacy of radical reform most naturally supposes. For the simplest form of relativistic liberalism, relativism is explicitly a foundation for tolerance.[10] More complex forms of relativistic liberalism include those philosophies that screen out background pictures of human nature and flourish from their discussions of political justice, even if they claim transconventional status for their statements about justice.

Such theories sometimes accomplish the screening-out of background pictures by fashioning, and attempting to impose, a conception of "public reason" that excludes all such background pictures, even if both true and rationally held, from public discussion.[11] Sometimes they invoke a "thick" veil of ignorance, excluding conceptions of the good life from deliberation about political justice.[12] I also include among relativistic liberals Richard Rorty, who excludes any criticism of present practice on moral grounds, while rejecting the conservative label this position normally is thought to involve.[13]

Merely proceduralist liberals, who accept whatever results may emerge from a liberal democratic political process, are also relativistic, except insofar as they believe that liberal democratic procedures are in some sense morally privileged. There are also intellectual proceduralists, who concede everything to relativists but the norms of "procedural rationality."[14] Lastly, those critics of liberalism called "communitarian" are relativistic, unless they are prepared to affirm the existence of a supracommunal standard for resolving such questions as what forms of community are legitimate and which take precedence in cases of conflict.

The purpose of these strategies is to preserve, within a general acceptance of the cultural and political status quo, a role for minority cultures and for standards of procedural justice independent of any party. But their effect is to sanction a permanent plurality of outlooks, each of them effectively insulated from rational criticism, and for that reason likely to become more and more chaotic until the possibility of coherent discussion among the various groups composing society disappears. They require relatively stable power relationships among communities holding differing views of human nature and the good life in order to assure their stability. Without such favorable circumstances, men and women ranging from radical feminists to Evangelical Christians will reject relativistic liberalism in favor of the maxim, "If you're losing the game, change the rules."

HISTORICISM

The deficiencies of relativistic liberalism have led to calls for a philosophy that recognizes the historical contingency of the balance of cultural forces and the possibility of new ways of life, and thus also makes possible social criticism and political engagement outside the "knowledge sector." Older forms of historicism—Marxist, Hegelian, and others—carried with them the dubious implication that future might is right. The new historicism in literary studies, while rightly insisting on the placing of literary texts within their sociohistorical context, combines a murky oppositional politics with a muddled attempt to evade the unpleasant implications of older forms of historicism.[15]

On the political ramifications of the movement, the following passage is, I am afraid, typical:

To ask what is the intrinsic political meaning or content of the new historicism . . . is to pose the question in terms which wipe out the assumptions on which many critics who are routinely called new historicists might base a reply. Consequently, the following remarks proceed from a different question: what are the historical situations of the new historicism and how have they defined the nature of its exchanges with explicitly political discourses?[16]

From the *Iliad* to T. S. Eliot and the *Partisan Review*, the connections between literature and politics have been real and important. One might disagree with the politics that informs contemporary literary theory, but few of my readers (I hope) will endorse Eliot's anti-Semitism either. What is wrong with contemporary literary theory is that it does not provide a political perspective on literature; rather, it replaces interest in literature with political advocacy. Moreover, the politics of contemporary literary theorists does not go beyond rejecting the status quo just because it is the status quo, and in consequence identifying with (almost) all discontented people, whatever their reason or lack of reason for discontent—a feckless form of politics in my judgment. (In fact, their concern is limited to an official list of oppressed minorities, but the list could be changed without altering the essential point.)

The leading new-historicist critic, Stephen Greenblatt, indulges in a rhetorical trick of importance for the present inquiry. Writing of the spiritual crises of the Renaissance, he observes:

To the reader who believes, as I do, that all religious practices and beliefs are products of the human imagination, these charges [made by Protestants and Catholics against one another] have a melancholy and desperate sound. It is as if the great crisis in the Church had forced into the consciousness of Catholics and Protestants alike the wrenching possibility that their theological system was a fictional construction; that the whole, vast edifice of church and state rested on certain imaginary postulates; that social hierarchy, the distribution of property, sexual and political order bore no guaranteed correspondence to the actual structure of the cosmos.[17]

The existence of rival outlooks, and the resulting suspicion that the whole business is a mere imaginative construction, afflicts Marxists, left-Liberals, and evolutionary biologists[18] quite as much as Protestant and Catholics. Greenblatt acknowledges this when he writes, at the end of his book, of his "overwhelming need to sustain the illusion that [he is] the principal maker of [his] own identity." If we seriously consider the assumption that the social world is an illusion, then politics, whether conservative, reformist, or radical, becomes impossible (as Greenblatt is, of course, aware).

In philosophy, the thought of Alasdair MacIntyre gives some promise of producing a sounder historicist approach, though so far his meta-narrative remains both sketchy and arbitrary. The political payoff of contemporary historicism, both in literature and philosophy, remains meager. The moral, spiritual, and political problems faced by St. Thomas More are like those of twentieth-century people in some respects, but some features of his situation are of historical interest only: the validity of the marriages of the great is not now a political issue. Whether historicist political thought can do better remains to be seen.

Cornel West proposes radical historicism as an alternative to standard forms of relativism and objectivism, and attributes the result to Marx (see especially chs. 1–3)[19]—with what accuracy I need not consider here. Radical historicism also attempts to supply what is lacking in both relativistic liberalism and the new historicism—a political perspective of real use outside the knowledge sector.

According to West, radical historicism consists in the following seven propositions:

1. "There can be moral truths or facts." (p. 10)

2. "[Moral truths or facts] are always subject to revision." (p. 10)

3. "Such moral truths or facts are always relative to specific aims, goals, or objectives of particular groups, communities, cultures, or societies." (p. 10)

4. Yet radical historicism "affirms the universalizability of such truths or facts is established relative to the specific groups, communities, cultures, or societies." (p. 10)

5. "Universalizing particular ethical judgments has nothing to do with an Archimedean point" of the sort traditionally sought by philosophers. (p. 11)

6. "The radical historicist approach [to a 'hard objectivist' view such as Kant's] would not to be to reject its philosophic status, but rather to explain its historical emergence and social function and cultural role during its dominance, and to describe and explain its decline." (p. 12)

7. In other words such views are to be treated as data for historical inquiry rather than as philosophical positions to be refuted.

Hence the radical historicist need not attempt to engage cultural expressions that fail to accord with his program. He need only expose them as ideological expressions of a way of life, or more bluntly a system of power relations, which, he hopes, is destined to pass from the scene. But the question remains, what reasons might be given for this expectation or for regarding it as morally worthy. One possible answer is that radical historicism is a form of relativism: there are no grounds for choosing among ways of life, only an endless power struggle.

The answer to the question of whether radical historicism is a form of relativism depends on our understanding of propositions 6 and 7. If historicists do not reject, but simply ignore, the truth claims proposed by Kant or Plato, they have withdrawn from the debate over relativism to pursue political activism. There is nothing necessarily wrong with this withdrawal, but it does not make traditional philosophical problems go away. For, as long as human beings differ deeply in outlook, the question of relativism will continue to be posed.

Historicists might, on the other hand, treat Plato and Kant's views as an object of historical inquiry in a way intended to give reasons why everyone should ignore their arguments. Then we are dealing with frank relativism of the sort defended by Joseph Margolis. Margolis advocates "a philosophy of the free spirit, of all those unwilling to let *any* premise count as privileged or fixed."[20] Yet at least one premise is privileged in Margolis's account—relativism itself. He frankly describes his relativism as "a prejudice in the old sense, in the sense of (discerning) the deep preformative themes of our operative judgment horizontally formed by the very practice of historical life"[21]—in other words, a dogma. This dogma's claim to our assent lies in the alleged fact that we all assent to it, even if some of us claim not to do so.

Another issue concerns the interpretation of West's proposition 2. Does the revision of moral truths or facts mean only that we can have good reasons to change our opinion of moral issues? Or does it mean that moral truths themselves can change, so that slavery, for example, might have been morally acceptable in the ancient world but not in the nineteenth century? If change of opinion is meant, but if the changes take place without reason (or if the reasons consist only in the changing goals, purposes, and responses of individuals and groups), once again radical historicism is a form of relativism. Similarly, West is a relativist if moral change is brute historical fact. West can only escape relativism by arguing that moral change is a result of the existence of new knowledge, alternatives not previously in existence, or changes in the consequences of our decisions. West could also avoid relativism by explaining moral change in terms of changes in the conventional meanings of our acts, provided the implications of these changes are governed by a constant principle such as not treating humanity as a mere means.

At least if West intends the relativistic implications of his formulations, his philosophy implies a virulent form of intolerance. For moral claims will be relative in their justification to the purposes and conventions of particular groups, which in our world frequently come into conflict. Yet they will be absolute and universal in their claims. For answers to the question of relativism other than West's, if there is no reason to expect people to acknowledge a moral claim, even after they have had an opportunity to examine its grounds, it is not reasonable to hold them to it. But historicists of West's sort will be led to regard their opponents as "pigs," who neither can accept nor be excused for rejecting "progressive" moral and political positions.

Hence historicists will regard their moral and political adversaries as wrong rather than just different, while at the same time believing themselves incapable of persuading them of the rightness of their position. There is no distinction, on this sort of ground, between elements of their customary morality that they may reasonably believe to have universal binding force and elements that reflect the idiosyncrasies of a particular cultural mix. It is hard to imagine a better intellectual basis for the extirpation of deviants.

West, however, is a Christian, and his Christian beliefs might provide him with a way of pointing beyond endless war. But these beliefs remain extrinsic to radical historicism as he understands it. And the lessons he draws from them are not adequate to the requirements of his argument. For he acknowledges some tension between historicism and Christian faith

(p. xxvii). His view of Christianity is insufficiently developed to handle this tension. However laudable it may be "to look at the world through the eyes of its victims,"[22] victimology is not an adequate response to the problem of relativistic intolerance (or to any other social problem). Too many groups these days claim victim status: there have been, for example, support groups for the HIV-negative (this is not a misprint). And victims or their representatives regularly victimize others once they gain power.

Moreover, West makes it clear that his radical historicism might at some point require him to reject Christianity.[23] He might conclude that "another tradition provides a more acceptable and enabling moral vision."[24] One way he might be led to do so is by searching for principles by which to govern, once he and his friends have won the political struggle and the appeal to victimology is no longer persuasive. Then West or his followers could shed their Christian principles and rule ruthlessly.

A simpler form of historicism—we may call it social Darwinism writ large—makes success in the struggle for existence itself the criterion for the acceptance or rejection of ideas. Richard Rorty concedes the intellectual high ground to fascism and maintains that, when it comes to the choice between two ways of life,

I cannot appeal to such a "fact of the matter," any more than a species of animal that is in danger of losing its ecological niche to another species, and thus faces extinction, can find a "fact of the matter" to settle the question of which species has the right to the niche in question.[25]

Views are more likely to prevail in the struggle for existence if their advocates believe them to be true in a full-blooded sense, rather than adopting them as hypotheses to be tested by their capacity for ensuring group survival. Hence historicism of Rorty's sort invites each politically active group *both* to regard itself as a company of *Übermenschen*, entitled to rewrite the rules of society to suit itself; *and* to claim objective truth for its principles. Questions of consistency are not likely to bother people in such a frame of mind, and "victors' morality" is its natural result.

But in fact world-views are not organisms and rarely if ever become extinct. (There are still, for example, Russian Old Believers.) Nor is success in the marketplace of ideas—or, what is not the same thing, success among the educated classes—the same thing as transmitting one's genes to future generations.

POLITICAL CORRECTNESS (PC)

James Davison Hunter describes the politically correct (PC) outlook as follows:

a position is so "obviously superior," so "obviously correct," and its opposite is so "obviously out of bounds" that they are beyond discussion and debate. Indeed to hold the "wrong" opinion, one must be either mentally imbalanced (phobic—as in *homophobic*, irrational, codependent, or similarly afflicted) or, more likely, evil.[26]

My present interest is more specific—in those people who think of themselves as liberal and progressive but are nonetheless intolerant in this way.

PC advocates characteristically hold that there is no such thing as political correctness, but only women and men united against entrenched social evils. A party that (half-) denies its own existence is something of a novelty.[27] In response, we should neither deny the existence of PC nor overestimate its power. Politics has always had an impact on high culture. The attempts made in the contemporary academy to silence conservatives (by whatever definition) have had relatively little practical success in the academy and have met with utter disaster elsewhere.

PC has its roots in more respectable intellectual and political positions. It is the refuge of Marxists who have lost their faith in an order in history, or at least in the ability of human beings to understand that order. But mainstream liberals also must bear considerable responsibility for the growth of the PC phenomenon. For the central strategy of relativistic liberals is to impose silence on positions and arguments that transgress the limitations liberals impose on public discourse.

The crucial ingredient in the formation of the PC outlook is despair of the progressive aspirations entertained by one's forbears (or one's earlier self), and the resulting adoption of a fortress mentality by groups who used to try to change the world. Thus PC is a way of protecting liberalism from the threats posed by its intellectual concessions to relativism, as much as by its concrete policy failures, by surrounding "progressive" programs such as affirmative action with taboos, and by attempts to maintain a monopoly of "intelligent" opinion in their defense, whether or not these causes are progressive by any other standard.

Jung Min Choi and John W. Murphy provide a rare explicit defense of political correctness (especially chs. 2 and 3).[28] They proceed on the assumption that all opposition to the PC program is conservative in inspiration, understanding conservatism to include both a belief in the necessary beneficence of the market and a commitment to metaphysical realism. The connection suggested by this conjunction is hardly self-evident, despite the rhetoric of some conservatives and the hostility to the reality principle evident in some parts of the Left. Thus Choi and Murphy write: "While the critics of PC charge that it is totalitarian, they are the ones that adhere to a central tenet of dogmatism" (p. 155).

Stanley Fish has frankly informed us that "There's No Such Thing as Free Speech and It's a Good Thing, Too."[29] But Choi and Murphy attempt to reassure us that "the adverse reaction of PC'ers is not simply to unpopular speech, but to language that is inflammatory and harmful" (p. 131)—neither attending to the problems involved in drawing a line between what is protected and what is not. And Murphy at least holds a view of language designed to make such lines permeable. As he writes elsewhere, "postmodernists do not aspire to bask in the pure light of reality, but rather to wallow in the mire of opinion. They work with slimy concepts, rather than the rigorous axioms of logic."[30] The result is sophism of the crudest sort: I can call for the suppression of my opponents as "racists," while claiming to be a champion of free speech.

But there is more to PC than the harassment of "conservatives" in our colleges and universities. Choi and Murphy have articulated its epistemological basis in the following way:

According to the thesis adhered to by Leotard and Wittgenstein, the influence of language cannot be overcome. Direct access to reality, in other words, is impossible, because every phenomenon is thoroughly mediated by language use. That is what Jacques Derrida means when he declares that "nothing exists outside of the text." Nothing avoids the influence of interpretation, and thus reality should be viewed as simply a linguistic invention. Fact, truth, and so forth can be approached only through the nuances of speech. In this sense, Roland Barthes writes that "objectivity is only one image-repertoire among others." (p. 57)

Consequently, "truth . . . is a linguistic concept and variable" (p. 63).

Despite such frank avowals, Choi and Murphy deny that PC is relativistic, thereby showing that the word *relativism* is as open to manipulation as any other. They cite Fish as holding that "a host of regions exist [remember, Fish believes that "values are regional"] with each one having its own normative structure" (p. 94). But this is exactly what relativists on any reasonable definition believe. They also affirm the possibility of "*Ideologiekritik*," but in their hands, such criticism is limited to rejecting the claims of (other) ideologies to represent universal human interests (pp. 95–96). PC as they formulate it escapes this critique by frankly avowing its own relativism, while at the same time refusing to accept the word.

Thus, despite the avowals of some of its adherents, I understand PC to be an attempt to put relativism to work for nominally progressive political purposes. Its impact on political discourse outside the academy (and other elite intellectual circles) is both ironic and devastating. For all groups, elite intellectuals, as much as any other, have (often unstated) norms of discourse that exclude some possible positions and favor others. But intellectuals also claim to be independent thinkers, capable of subjecting to critical scrutiny all social norms, whether of thought or of behavior. The effect of PC is to undermine this claim and to expose intellectuals as one group among others, whose norms people outside the intellectual and subintellectual world have no reason to accept. As a result, even liberal norms to which nearly all reflective people will assent, such as the one that forbids us to call Jews the children of Satan, lose their authority.

POSTMODERNISM/DECONSTRUCTION

Samuel Wheeler III's observations on interpreting Jacques Derrida apply to the postmodern project as a whole.

The discussion must explicate analyses which claim that all the explicating terms are inappropriate, since the presuppositions of the applicability of those terms are being challenged by those very analyses. It must describe arguments in a text in which the standards of good argument are among the very items being questioned.[31]

In terms of the history of ideas, the postmodern epoch is usually dated from about 1972 and linked with changes in the structure of the Western economy, from an emphasis on the production of goods to reliance on the mobility of capital.[32] As a school of thought, postmodernism represents the final step in the cultural dialectic traced here: the collapse of PC and other forms of relativism into outright nihilism. As such, it includes not only the abandonment of claims to consistency, but also the dissolution of the very self who makes the mutually contradictory judgments to which the nihilist is committed. In this section I accept the inevitable risk of distortion involved in attempting to impose order on a self-consciously chaotic movement and sum up postmodernism in eleven theses.

1. Postmodernism is not so much a philosophical as (broadly speaking) a theological movement.

We may describe the religion that postmodernists expound as a species of neo-Gnosticism.[33] The postmodern movement proclaims the irrationality of the universe and our entrapment in it. An elite of privileged knowers is aware of our true situation and is therefore able to show us the way out. Thus postmodern thought consists in a commentary on the words of the wise (chiefly Nietzsche and the later Heidegger, but sometimes also Freud), with the intention of drawing from them a liberating lesson. Like the philosophers of late antiquity, the goal of postmodern thinkers is peace of mind, in this case the ability to play with inherited ideas without being troubled by their (incoherent) content.

2. "God is dead." This is the primary postmodern text, on which all else is commentary.

Nietzsche's proclamation of the death of God is not to be confused with the traditional atheistic claim that there is no God and never was one. His claim is rather to be understood as an interpretation of our cultural history, as excluding belief not only in the God of Christianity and Judaism, but also any God-surrogate such as History, Law, Nature, Progress, Reason, Science, Tradition, or Truth—at least when these ideas are thought of as carrying with them any stable meaning. We must, above all, sacrifice the concept of Humanity (and hence also of human nature).[34] (How on such assumptions we can exclude anything, even fundamentalist Christianity, I do not know.)

3. With God's death comes the death (or inexorable decline) of "metaphysics," that is, of any belief in a knowable structure in either self or world.

Postmodernists regard the metaphysical tradition in all its forms as exploded (not as refuted). This premise most of all implies a radical rejection of the belief in a rational God, a rational world, and rational people, which undergirded the Enlightenment attempt to improve society through education and politics. The Aristotelian notion of adapting one's standards to an order immanent in the human material also makes no sense on postmodern premises. For there are no natural kinds, marked out by common nature. This ban specfically excludes appeals to common sense in political discourse, and hence also one common strand of democratic argument, the appeal to the good sense of ordinary men and women. Instead, the radical heterogeneity of human beings implies that all order, whether conceptual or social, can only be founded on deception or force.

4. Reality, both internal and external, is chaotic.

Postmodernists reject the possibility that reality in itself may have a structure that we cannot know. Hence they affirm that reality is chaotic, and not just our attempts to understand it, though as antimetaphysicians they cannot take seriously such statements about reality as it is in itself. Chaos extends also to the self that, on superficial views of the matter, might be liberated by the destruction of traditional systems of order. For a postmodernist, as much as for Hume,

The mind is a kind of theatre, where several perceptions successively make their appearance, pass, re-pass, glide away, and mingle in an infinite variety of situations. . . . Nor have we the most distant notion of the place where these scenes are represented, or of the materials, of which it is compos'd.[35]

Thus Gary Wills describes a postmodern self in politics when he writes,

To see [President] Clinton in two different contexts can be like looking at two entirely different persons. . . . Clinton lives so thoroughly in one situation that he seems to have no memory or anticipation of counter-situations. . . . He adapts so well to the present that he disregards any bearing it might have on the past or the future.[36]

5. The illusion of order, whether entertained by oneself or by others, must be destroyed or at least weakened.

Systems of order are not only mere constructs; they are also to be exposed as such. For, postmodernists believe, it is not possible to sustain an illusion of order once one has squarely faced the fact of chaos. (Why this belief does not suppose a belief in Truth and Human Nature I do not know.) Here the postmodernist differs from the disciples of the Grand Inquisitor, who propose to protect the mass of mankind from a reality they cannot endure. Instead, postmodern thinkers undertake an assault on all the structures by which human beings govern their lives.

6. In the service of a postmodern perspective is every method of dialectical and intellectual trouble-making (usually called deconstruction).

Deconstruction differs from traditional skepticism in that it undermines not only our claims to know, but also our ability to express our beliefs in intelligible language. Thus Derrida makes two moves that go beyond the armory of traditional skepticism: (1) writing "under erasure," so that he can make assertions while severing their implicit claims to truth or adequacy; and (2) insisting that the possibilities surrounding a concept are inescapably linked to it.[37] (Relatedly, he will take the copyright notice, or even a word that does not occur in the text but in his judgment should, as the keys to its understanding.) In this way he can disavow any apparent implication of his claims, however clear the reasoning involved may be, while demanding that his opponents accept even the faintest suggestions of their own.

7. The practical implications of postmodernism vary almost without limit.

One possible outcome of the postmodern argument is Michel Foucault's remark: "I do not appeal to any 'we'—to any of those 'we's' whose consensus, whose values, whose traditions constitute the framework for thought and define the conditions under which it can be validated."[38] But another and more moderate version of deconstruction is also possible—one that preserves the residues of the tradition in order to play in its ruins. Thus Derrida supports, through a group called GREPH (Groupe de Recherches sur l'Enseignement Philosophique), a curriculum in which Plato is studied in the *lycées*.[39] No doubt he reasoned that, if no one reads Plato, no one will have the least interest in Derrida. A conservative postmodernism, which plays idly with the Great Tradition while leaving it to politicians to manage a declining civilization, is also possible.[40] Postmodernism does seem to exclude some political philosophies, such as Russell Kirk's appeal to the "permanent things." But a thoroughgoing repudiation of the principle of contradiction would make even this sort of conservatism possible for postmodernists.

8. Postmodernism is, on the whole, quietistic in its political implications, though ad hoc alliances with the political Left or Right are possible.

Though neither Heidegger nor de Man can be called a man of the Left, conservative critics see the origin of deconstruction in Marxist politics and announce this fact as if they were digging up something hidden.[41] Such critics obscure one of the most troubling features of the contemporary intellectual-political scene: the invasion of the Left by Nietzsche.[42]

This phenomenon has many sources, but one of them is the inability of Leftists who no longer believe in Laws of History to answer the standard conservative criticism of their position, that they are proposing merely to replace one form of oppression by another. Another is a characteristically French confusion about the meaning of *bourgeois*—one sense opposed to "working class" and the other to "bohemian."[43] (There is no reason to suppose that working-class people are interested in rebelling against the concept of normality.) As a result, ideas that are on their face elitist, or imply a renunciation of any hope of a better society, have been enlisted to support egalitarian causes, without attention to the ensuing logical difficulties.

Postmodernists need a broadly Marxist conception of ideology, for they attempt to deconstruct not only individual fantasies, but also the system of ideas with the help of which powerful people exercise their power. But this side of postmodernism deconstructs itself. It is not possible, on postmodern premises, either for a group to agree on a common platform, or, supposing they could do so, to know whether they are succeeding in carrying out that program in practice. The effect of postmodern rhetoric is thus to unsettle all institutions and practices without distinction, including those that protect deviants from the wrath of the majority; and at the same time to cut the heart out of any possibility that the resulting confusions could be resolved in a progressive, or even a coherent, way.

9. Postmodernism leads, first, to rebellion against the existing order in all its aspects, and, then, to collapse in the face of the biological and social pressures that bear on each of us.

Postmodernists begin by celebrating the death of God; they go on to reject all God-surrogates including Progress, unmasking those who appeal to such notions as practitioners of the will-to-power. The result, however, is not liberation or empowerment, but rather that described by Joseph Heller: "There seemed to be no plausible connection between cause and effect, between ends and means. History was a trash bag of random coincidences torn open by the wind."[44] If so, there are no grounds to resist the pressures for conformity that bear on each of us. (This aspect of postmodernism was already present in Nietzsche, who despite his celebration of the *Übermensch* denied free will and responsibility, with the result that even the strongest of us are pawns of our heredity and our environment.)

10. Postmodernists are not to be understood as presenting philosophical theses, or as denying what Plato and Aristotle assert, for example.

A philosophy that undermines all distinctions between essential and accidental undercuts any attempt to discern what elements are central to postmodernism and what idiosyncratic positions are taken by a few postmodernists. The same is true of the distinction between an author's considered position and a view he might unguardedly advance on a particular occasion. The resulting lack of any fixed postmodern position makes both defense and refutation irrelevant.

11. Postmodernism is at every point parasitic on the "logocentric" tradition it affects to despise.

Postmodernism combines two views, inherited respectively from Christianity and from the radical Enlightenment. The first holds that without God reason is impossible, and the second that human reason necessarily asserts its independence even of God. Long ago, Donne stated the result:

> Who sees Gods face, that is selfe life, must dye,
> What a death were it then to see God dye?[45]

Read most charitably, postmodernism is not a set of doctrines, but a set of skeptical strategies and a description of the intellectual and cultural situation hospitable to such strategies. In such a situation, it is bluff to appeal to common sense, or in any other way to invoke supposedly unquestionable constraints on inquiry. But it is also bluff to dismiss an idea as "outmoded" or its advocates as "reactionary." For the metanarratives in terms of which such epithets make sense are now contested. There are intelligent and well-educated people who believe in witches, in the strict sense of women in commerce with the devil. Hence the effect of postmodernism on the liberal-academic consensus is, if anything, more devastating than that of PC.

The way is now clear for a form of postmodern traditionalism—"neotraditionalism" for short—which recovers forgotten ideas in a surprising way. In an earlier period the theology of Karl Barth would serve as a prime example of neotraditionalism. At present, the philosophy of Alastair MacIntyre will serve as an example.[46] So will the (very different) theology of John Milbank, who writes: "Christianity reveals that nihilism understands its ontology as another *myth*. The only possible social critique 'beyond' nihilism will therefore be theological."[47] We cannot decisively exclude even a fundamentalist interpretation of tradition, for which revealed standards are protected against rational examination (or even attempts at understanding).[48] But the tradition to which one returns need not be the one from which one's ancestors (or one's earlier self) departed, and even if it is, it will take a significantly different form.

FROM TRADITION TO HUMAN NATURE

I have interpreted the Right-Left cultural spectrum in terms of our liberty in the interpretation of authoritative traditions. As is often the case, the two ends of the cultural spectrum reinforce one another.[49] For both assume that once space has been created for what Richard John Neuhaus calls "hermeneutical legerdemain"[50] there are no limits to its operation. When all concepts have been deconstructed, we are left with the Void, onto which we are entitled to project highly traditional ideas if that is our inclination. It is in this encounter that we may discover that these ideas are even true.

That authority has a wax nose has been known to lawyers, theologians, and literary critics since the foundation of these disciplines. But we cannot cease to be human beings (except perhaps by dying, as Plato counsels in the *Phaedo*). Hence the central hermeneutical question is that of human nature. To what extent does our common humanity help us in deciding within which tradition to work, and in assimilating, interpreting, and applying that tradition? What, for example, is the range of possible good-faith disagreements about moral issues? At one end of the spectrum are those for whom standards for both individual behavior and social structure are dictated by our genetic structure; at the other end are those for whom it is the paradoxical nature of human beings to have no nature.

Thomas Fleming speaks the authentic language of the cultural Right:

The laws and decrees enacted by human government are mutable and sometimes tyrannical, but the laws of human nature, curled tight within the spiral of the genetic code, are unchanging and just. More than just, they are justice itself, in this sublunar sphere.[51]

But Fleming has a hard time explaining how injustice is possible, and how institutions and forms of behavior he regards as unnatural nonetheless exist (and survive, at least for a while).

At the other end of the spectrum are those many writers (call them "existentialists") for whom we are free to construct ourselves—whether as individuals or as groups—however we please. But there is no reason to suppose that I, and the group(s) to which I belong, will construct ourselves in compatible ways. Existentialists are driven to argue that individuals and groups who endeavor to limit their own freedom—say because they find it frightening—are in fact behaving unnaturally. The notion that there are things it is wrong to do to a person, even to bring about otherwise desirable forms of social transformation or to preserve desirable features of the *status quo*, requires a concept of human nature resistant to the radical redescriptions proposed by the existentialists.[52]

In the chapters that follow, I consider two answers each to two questions concerning human diversity:

1. What sorts of diversity do we take seriously?
    a. Are these limited to a relatively short list of differences that happen to be taken seriously at a given time or place?
    b. Or do they include all forms of human difference that we can imagine (and even those of which we are not aware)?
2. What do we understand the relationship between diverse outlooks to be?
    a. Are they radically incommensurable, so that communication across outlooks is impossible?
    b. Or is some degree of self-transcendence possible (however difficult it may be), so that dialogue among adherents of diverse outlooks can lead to increased understanding?

From these questions and answers arise four different possible concepts of diversity, which can be exhibited as shown in Figure 1, and to whose detailed discussion the rest of the book will be devoted.

Figure 1

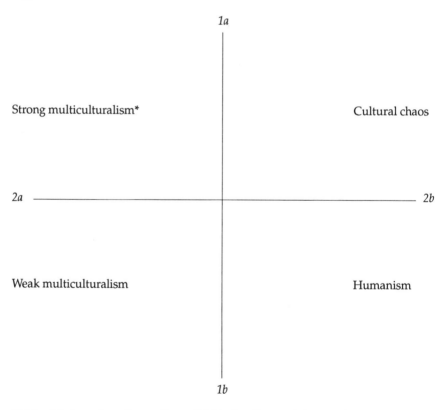

1a

Strong multiculturalism*   Cultural chaos

2a ——————————————————————————————— 2b

Weak multiculturalism   Humanism

1b

*I take this term from Steven Yates. "Multiculturalism and Epistemology," *Public Affairs Quarterly* 6 (October 1992): 435–456.

NOTES

1. See Peter Steinfels, *The Neoconservatives* (New York: Simon and Schuster, 1979).

2. Irving Kristol, "A Capitalist Conception of Justice," in Richard T. DeGeorge and Joseph A. Pichler, eds., *Ethics, Free Enterprise, and Public Policy* (New York: Oxford University Press, 1978). Roger Scruton, *The Meaning of Conservatism* (Totowa, N.J.: Barnes and Noble, 1980), pp. 86–90.

3. Allan Bloom, *The Closing of the American Mind* (New York: Simon and Schuster, 1987), pp. 277–278. See my article "Allan Bloom: Nihilistic Conservative," *New Oxford Review*, (October 1988), a slightly different version of which was reprinted in *Notes et Documents* (Rome), (January–August 1989). On the thought of Leo Strauss, which underlies Bloom's argument, see Shaida Drury, *The Political Thought of Leo Strauss* (London: Macmillan, 1988). The issues are spotlighted in Mark Henrie's review of Drury, *University Bookman* 32, 3 (1992): 17–23.

4. Roger Scruton, *The Philosopher at Dover Beach* (New York: St. Martin's Press, 1990), p. vii.

5. See Scruton's *The Meaning of Conservatism*, pp. 139–140. But Scruton now writes as if he is prepared to defend some form of Christianity, not just as socially useful, but as true. See *The Philosopher at Dover Beach*, ch. 1.

6. Michael Medved, *Hollywood vs. America* (New York: HarperCollins, 1992); quotations on pp. 27, 97. Medved cites Allan Bloom and Irving Kristol as his chief authorities.

7. Hilary Putnam, *Realism and Reason* (Cambridge: Cambridge University Press, 1983), pp. 238–239; quotation on p. 239.

8. Hilary Putnam, *Reason, Truth, and History* (Cambridge: Cambridge University Press, 1981), p. 128. He has since abandoned related claims about the incredibility of theism; see his *Renewing Philosophy* (Cambridge, Mass.: Harvard University Press, 1992). But he still speaks of "the reactionary move of trying to believe what people who lived two hundred or two thousand years ago believed." "Sense, Nonsense and the Senses," *Journal of Philosophy* 91, 9 (September 1994): 445.

9. Arlene W. Saxonhouse describes the program of Aristotle's political philosophy as follows: "The fear of diversity is the fear of disorder; if that diversity leads by nature into order, there is nothing to fear." *The Fear of Diversity* (Chicago: University of Chicago Press, 1993), p. 192. The difficulty, however, arises from the "ungraciousness of nature, which fails to clarify for us who is master and who is slave" (p. 193).

10. See, for example, David Wong, *Moral Relativity* (Berkeley: University of California Press, 1984). I criticize Wong in detail in my article, "Relativism, Abortion, and Tolerance," *Philosophy and Phenomenological Research* 48 (1987): 131–138.

11. See John Rawls, *Political Liberalism* (New York: Columbia University Press, 1993).

12. See John Rawls, *A Theory of Justice* (Cambridge, Mass.: Harvard University Press, 1971), and especially his subsequent statement: "that we have one conception of the good rather than another is not relevant from a moral standpoint. In acquiring it we are influenced by the same sort of contingencies that lead us to rule out knowledge of our sex and class." "Fairness to Goodness," *Philosophical Review* 84 (1975): 337.

13. Richard Rorty, *Contingency, Irony, and Solidarity* (Cambridge: Cambridge University Press, 1989), p. 59; "Thugs and Theories," *Political Theory* 15 (November 1987): 564–580.

14. For a defense of this position by a "moderately traditional Protestant of the Reformed theological heritage," see George M. Marsden, *The Soul of the American University* (New York: Oxford University Press, 1994), especially pp. 451–452; quotation on p. 7.

15. See Louis Montrose, "New Historicisms," in Sheldon Greenblatt and Giles Gunn, eds., *Redrawing the Boundaries* (New York: Modern Language Association, 1992), pp. 392–418; Brook Thomas, *The New Historicism* (Princeton, N.J.: Princeton University Press, 1991), especially pp. 35–36; and H. Aram Veeser, ed., *The New Historicism* (New York: Routledge, 1989).

16. Catherine Gallagher, "Marxism and the New Historicism," in Veeser, ed., *The New Historicism*, p. 38.

17. Stephen Greenblatt, *Renaissance Self-Fashioning* (Chicago: University of Chicago Press, 1980), pp. 113, 257.

18. For some of the implications of this fact, see Chapter 9.

19. Parenthetical references in this section are to Cornel West, *The Ethical Dimension of Marxist Thought* (New York: Monthly Review, 1991). I am indebted to James G. Devine and Violet Halpert for calling West's work to my attention.

20. Joseph Margolis, *The Truth About Relativism* (Oxford: Basil Blackwell, 1991), p. xvi.

21. Ibid., p. xv.

22. Cornel West, *Keeping Faith* (New York: Routledge, 1993), p. 133.

23. Ibid., p. 134.

24. Ibid.

25. Richard Rorty, "Putnam and the Relativist Menace," *Journal of Philosophy* 90, 9 (September 1993): 451.

26. James Davison Hunter, *Before the Shooting Begins* (New York: Free Press, 1994), p. 5.

27. For the debate on the reality of political correctness, see John Taylor, "Are You Politically Correct?" and Rosa Eherenreich, "What Campus Radicals?", both in Francis J. Beckwith and Michael E. Bauman, eds., *Are You Politically Correct?* (Buffalo, N.Y.: Prometheus, 1993), chs. 1 and 2.

28. Parenthetical references are to their book Jung Min Choi and John W. Murphy, *The Politics and Philosophy of Political Correctness* (Westport, Conn.: Praeger, 1992).

29. Fish's essay of that title is reprinted in Beckwith and Bauman, eds., *Are You Politically Correct?*, ch. 3. For a longer development of these ideas, see also his book with the same title (Oxford: Oxford University Press, 1994). Fish is quite candid: "Lately many of the liberal and progressive left have been disconcerted to find that words, phrases and concepts thought to be their property and generative of their politics have been appropriated by the forces of neoconservatism. This is particularly true of the concept of free speech. . . . The answer I shall give in this essay is that abstract concepts like free speech do not have any 'natural content' but are filled in with whatever content and direction one can manage to give them. . . . This is something the liberal left has yet to understand and what follows is an

attempt to pry its members loose from a vocabulary that may now be a disservice to them" (pp. 43–44).

30. John W. Murphy, *Postmodern Social Analysis and Criticism* (Westport, Conn.: Greenwood Press, 1988), p. 15.

31. Review of *Derrida and the Economy of Difference* by Irene E. Harvey, *Philosophical Review* 98 (April 1989): 273.

32. See David Harvey, *The Condition of Postmodernity* (Cambridge, Mass.: Blackwell, 1990).

33. I owe this point to Edith Black.

34. On the rejection of "humanism" implicit in the Nietzschean tradition, see particularly Jacques Derrida, *Margins of Philosophy*, Alan Bass, ed. and trans. (Chicago: University of Chicago Press, 1982), pp. 109–136.

35. David Hume, *A Treatise of Human Nature*, L. A. Selby-Bigge, ed. (Oxford: Clarendon, 1896), Bk. I, pt. iv, sec. 6.

36. Gary Wills, "Clinton's Troubles," *New York Review of Books* 41, 15 (September 22, 1994): 6–7.

37. See Charles Altieri, *Act and Quality* (Amherst: University of Massachusetts Press, 1981), pp. 29–31.

38. Paul Rainbow, ed., *The Foucault Reader* (New York: Pantheon, 1984), p. 385.

39. Christopher Norris, *Derrida* (Cambridge, Mass.: Harvard University Press, 1987), pp. 13–14.

40. For a postmodern conservative, see Tom Wolfe, *The Bonfire of the Vanities* (New York: Farrar, Straus and Giroux, 1987).

41. For example, Peter Shaw, *The War Against the Intellect* (Iowa City: University of Iowa Press, 1989), especially pp. 56–66.

42. A good example of the Nietzcheanism of the Left is Katharyn Pyne Parsons, "Nietzsche and Moral Change," in Robert Solomon, ed., *Nietzsche* (Garden City, N.Y.: Doubleday Anchor, 1973), ch. 9. Peter Berkowitz insists on an interpretation of Nietzsche that is not available for Leftist use in his "The Foundations of Nietzsche's Political Philosophy" (Ph.D. diss., Yale University, 1987).

43. I owe this point to a lecture by Roger Scruton at Providence College, fall 1994.

44. Joseph Heller, *Good as Gold* (New York: Simon and Schuster, 1979), p. 74.

45. John Donne, "Goodfriday, 1615. Riding Westward," in *Complete Poetry and Selected Prose*, Charles M. Coffin, ed. (New York: Modern Library, 1952), p. 246.

46. Despite his frequent statements to the contrary, MacIntyre is not a Thomist, at least of anything like the customary sort. For detailed discussion, see Janet Coleman, "MacInytre and Aquinas," and John Haldane, "MacIntyre's Thomist Revival," in John Horton and Susan Mendus, eds., *After MacIntyre* (Notre Dame, Ind.: University of Notre Dame Press, 1994), chs. 4 & 5.

47. John Milbank, *Theology and Social Theory* (Oxford: Basil Blackwell, 1990), p. 263.

48. In *Getting Saved from the Sixties* (Berkeley: University of California Press, 1982), ch. 2, Steven Tipton shows how many countercultural people naturally came to accept a strongly biblicist outlook.

49. But for an attempt to use deconstruction to criticize fundamentalism, ultimately in the interests of a moderate liberalism, see Kathleen C. Boone, *The Bible Tells Them So* (Albany, N.Y.: SUNY Press, 1989).

50. Richard John Neuhaus, *The Catholic Moment* (San Francisco: Harper, 1990).

51. Thomas Fieming, *The Politics of Human Nature* (New Brunswick, N.J.: Transaction, 1993), p. 231. Elsewhere, however, Fleming is well aware of the fluid character of the nature–convention distinction. "The border between nature and culture is as hard to fix as the border between two states divided by a river," pp. 68–69.

52. This sentence is directed specifically against Richard Rorty, who holds that "man is always free to choose new descriptions (for among other things, himself)." *Philosophy and the Mirror of Nature* (Princeton, N.J.: Princeton University Press, 1979), p. 362 n. 8.

PART II
FOUR VIEWS OF HUMAN DIVERSITY

For men and women are not merely themselves, they are also the region in which they were born, the city apartment or farm in which they learned to walk, the games they played as children, the old wives' tales they overheard, the food they ate, the schools they attended, the sports they followed, the poets they read, and the God they believed in.

W. Somerset Maugham, *The Razor's Edge*

I asked [my students] to look into the Abyss and, both dutifully and gladly, they have looked into the Abyss, and the Abyss has greeted them with the grave courtesy of all objects of serious study, saying: "Interesting, am I not? And *exciting*, if you consider how deep I am and what dread beasts lie at my bottom."

Lionel Trilling

3

Strong Multiculturalism

Louis Menand has observed that

> there is a very broad sense in which almost everyone today . . . is some kind of a multiculturalist. . . . In this most inclusive sense, multiculturalism means something like the following: a person's race, gender, or sexual orientation should be noticed when the difference noticing it would make is a positive one, but it should not be noticed when the difference noticing it would make is negative.[1]

But multiculturalism so defined, however popular, is incoherent for three reasons.

First, to treat one person's race as a positive trait is to treat someone else's race as a negative one: to prefer black people to white people is, inevitably, to regard white people as less valuable or less useful than black people. Second, most people do not believe in the unity of the virtues; hence the ascription of traits to some group will inevitably be double-edged. (The traits we value in a lawyer we may not value in a friend.) Third, even within the same sphere of evaluation, traits ascribed to persons on the basis of group membership are equivocal in their normative significance. If we think of Proust primarily or centrally as a homosexual, we will link our characterization to his aesthetic strengths and his aesthetic weaknesses.

But though simplistic multiculturalism does not adequately deal with the diversity of human beings and of their outlooks, human diversity remains. It is great enough if one limits oneself to the United States, and greater still if one takes into account the whole world. Each of the strategies for dealing with this issue implies or presupposes a different understanding of human nature, in some cases the paradoxical view that human beings are the sort of being whose nature it is to have no nature.

Strong multiculturalism (for the rest of this chapter, simply "multiculturalism") celebrates the diversity both of human individuals and of the cultures human beings create. Yet it also exhibits all the marks of a rigorous orthodoxy, including a penchant for shunning and shaming the opposition. More explicitly, I take multiculturalism to be the conjunction of the following twelve propositions.[2]

1. Human beings think, feel, act, and imagine in systematically differing ways, that reflect their differences in race, gender, class position, and psychology (among other things).

2. Human beings are social creatures whose ways of thinking, acting, and imagining are, in important ways, products of their social environments.

3. For that reason, human experience can be segmented into a plurality of differing cultures, representing the varieties of human types.

4. No adjudication—or even mutual understanding—is possible among these cultures: a person's adherence to his culture is a matter either of necessity or of unreasoned choice.

5. But some human differences, for example, those of race, gender, sexual identity, and (for some multiculturalists) class, are more important than others.

6. Hence it is possible both to identify particular cultures and to articulate their norms. A partial list of American "cultures" is as follows: Asian-American culture, black/African-American culture, Hispanic-American culture, male homosexual culture, lesbian culture, WASP culture, women's culture, and the culture of the "physically challenged." The result of such an enumeration is what Jean Bethke Elshtain calls a "politicized ontology—that is, persons are judged not by what they do or say but by what they are."[3]

7. Adherents of these and other cultures ought to be mutually tolerant.

8. Adherents of these and other cultures ought to accept and live by the norms of their cultures, as defined by their officially recognized leaders.

9. Acceptance of propositions 1 through 8 is essential to mutual tolerance among diverse sorts of men and women.

10. Hence all progressively minded men and women will cooperate with one another to create a world in which these propositions are universally accepted.

11. But the dominant culture of the West has neglected the canons of multiculturalism and represents only white, heterosexual males in leisured circumstances. ("Christian," though not, I think, in the religious sense, is sometimes added.) For that reason, it must be displaced in favor of the culture of a "Rainbow Coalition" of other groups. These other groups are said to be *empowered*.

12. The following sorts of individuals are not entitled to tolerance; on the contrary, they are open to every form of harassment:

    a. Those who reject the principles of multiculturalism, especially the relativist principle 4.

   b. Those who refuse—as required by 8—to accept the norms of their cultures, as defined by their officially recognized leaders.

   c. Those who identify, and attempt to uphold, a culture common to all members of a nation-state, or to the West generally.

   d. Those whose social identity, say as white (or WASP), heterosexual males, renders them suspect of violating the canons of multiculturalism, unless they prove their political acceptability by appropriate acts of penitence.

I comment on these propositions in reverse order.

POLITICAL CORRECTNESS

It is proposition 12 that gives multiculturalism its repressive face, from which the name "political correctness" is derived. The limits to tolerance asserted in this proposition do not arise from the personal limitations of multiculturalists, but are rooted in central features of their outlook. As relativists, multiculturalists are committed to holding that men and women who reject multiculturalism, or whose social identity disposes them to do so, are not wrong but only different. But this feature of multiculturalism does not preclude intolerance. Men and women with power have frequently concluded that those with whom they found it impossible to reason understood no language but force. Those without power still have tried to avoid or limit contact with those they find alien, and hoped for the day when they would have the chance to be the oppressors.

Clause d requires a bit more commentary. Whether white people, or heterosexuals, or males, are more or less likely to be relativists than the rest of the population I do not know; among other things, discovering the implicit philosophical commitments of the uneducated is a tricky business. But the leading representatives of the intellectual tradition of the West have been white and male (though St. Thomas Aquinas was a celibate and Plato a homosexual, but nonpracticing at least by conviction). Their views are imputed to other individuals resembling them in visible respects, without regard to the accuracy of the attribution. Multiculturalists are accustomed to thinking in terms of social identity rather than individual variation or a common human nature (see proposition 6). Hence they are led to ask what social identity is the bearer of the universalist tradition of the West, which is the primary object of their hostility. At the same time, members of the stigmatized group often attempt to free themselves of stigma by penitential exercises.

I have already cited Susan Sontag's denunciation of the white race as the cancer of history (see Introduction); some ecologists now extend this formula to the whole human race. Radical environmentalists claim that it is "anthropocentrist" to make a distinction between human beings and snail darters or ecosystems: they are, as Dave Foreman has put it, "more committed to Gila monsters and mountain lions than to people."[4] Other people have despaired of improving the lot of human beings, and consequently turn away from human problems to the claims of nonhuman nature. Peter Singer, for example, has written:

All reasonable people want to prevent war, racial inequality, inflation, and unemployment; the problem is that we have been trying to prevent these things for years, and now we have to admit that we do not really know how to do it.[5]

Members of every group that can plausibly portray itself as the victim of "patriarchy" have now opted out of the stigmatized class of antirelativists and celebrate a tribal culture all their own. One commentator, for example, writes quite happily of "the radical eco-movement [as a] . . . fairly diverse collection of different 'tribes' rather than a tightly organized social force."[6] The class of representatives of the patriarchy thus becomes exceedingly small (and in some contexts itself an oppressed minority by any standard).

THE RAINBOW COALITION

The intolerant clause 12 can be severed from the multiculturalist argument on the ground that multiculturalists lack the power to act on it, or out of an overriding commitment to tolerance. The connection between core multiculturalist beliefs and intolerance of their monoculturalist opponents, though deeply rooted in the multiculturalist outlook, is prima facie only. (By *monoculturalists* I mean those, however tolerant and open to dialogue, who believe in the existence of a culture-transcendent Truth to which one culture may be closer than any other.) It is harder, however, for multiculturalists to give up proposition 11, which analyzes the (undoubtedly many and severe) injustices of Western history as violations of the multiculturalist canon. That fascism was openly relativistic and that the abolitionists are nothing of the sort are discordant facts which multiculturalists must somehow explain (or explain away).

THE MULTICULTURALIST PROGRAM

It is even more difficult for multiculturalists to give up proposition 10, which calls on all right-minded men and women to help create a multiculturalist world. Even if multiculturalists are prepared to tolerate monocultural individuals, still the educational system (and cultural institutions generally) must be multicultural. At minimum, multiculturalists demand a stranglehold on public education and may not even tolerate monocultural private education (for example, church-related education), which they find insufficiently respectful of diversity. Thus multiculturalists hope that their views will prevail, if not in the present, then among future generations. In this respect at least, they follow one of their mentors, John Dewey.

But suppose multiculturalists elicit a crude tribalist response, say among poor white males.[7] On what grounds could a multiculturalist expect the eventual triumph of his vision? The maxim "great is truth and it will prevail" is doubly inapplicable: the (strong) multiculturalist does not believe in truth, except in the most narrowly honorific sense, nor does he believe in any "metanarrative" concluding with the triumph of his views. (The extent to which such views are actually held on the cultural Left I do not know, but there does seem to be some sort of congruence between multiculturalist theory and multiculturalist practice.)

In short, the multiculturalist must agree with Richard Rorty in rejecting the usual reasons for expecting victory

because, as Scripture teaches, Truth is great and will prevail [or] because, as Milton suggests, Truth will always win in a free and open encounter. . . . *A liberal society is one which is content to call "true" whatever the upshot of such encounters turns out to be.*[8]

If a liberal society decides to abolish liberal institutions, say out of fear of freedom, a liberal of Rorty's stripe is bound to endorse this result as "true." A multiculturalist caught in a society that decides to establish cultural uniformity is in the same position.

TOLERANCE

Proposition 9, linking multiculturalism and tolerance, is the core of the multiculturalists' social and moral program. Even if there is no reason to believe in progress toward a multicultural utopia, nonetheless multiculturalists believe that tolerance requires the acceptance of his program, and will defend policies designed as if his program were destined to prevail. Those who reject the multiculturalist outlook and policies based on it are risking civil war in the manner of Lebanon or Yugoslavia.

CONVENTIONALISM

Proposition 8, advising each of us to accept the conventions of our various groups, represents the conventionalism characteristic of most forms of relativism. It requires us, first, to discover the culture to which we belong; and, second, to discern its norms. In a world where many men and women are both literally and metaphorically polyglot, and in which most if not all communities are internally divided, these inquiries are at best very difficult. Appeal to the judgments of officially recognized leadership only postpones the problem, since many groups suffer from divisions in their leadership.

There are also communities for which the falsity of relativism is a cultural norm: these include the Islamic world, the Roman Catholic Church,[9] and (with some qualifications) the community of professional philosophers. (Relativism is regarded in philosophical circles as a charge, and some philosophers use considerable linguistic legerdemain to escape it—though a philosopher can defend relativism while remaining in good standing, provided he makes an effort to distinguish his position from the lazy relativism of students.) Rejection of relativism about questions of fact (though not about value or metaphysics) is central to the *mores* of the scientific community, some of whose representatives have been, for that reason, quite sharp with Thomas Kuhn and his followers. If multiculturalists are right, members of such communities are in a double bind: they are condemned to sin (and perhaps even predestined to damnation) by their very social identities.

RELATIVISM

As proposition 9 is the core of the multiculturalists' social program, propositions 6 and 7, linking social diversity to a tolerant form of relativism, are the core of their intellectual project. Yet there are three powerful objections to this extremely popular idea.

First, just as some groups reject relativism, so others reject tolerance. If one happened to find oneself a Nazi, propositions 6 and 7 would be inconsistent.

Second, relativism undermines two powerful arguments for tolerance: a relativist cannot hold, with Locke, that some truths must be assimilated by each individual himself. Nor can he hold, with Mill, that the discovery of truth in important part proceeds by dialogue among diverse standpoints.[10] On the contrary, a relativist can well conclude, with the most determined critics of liberalism, that war and conquest are the ultimate intellectual arbiters.[11]

Third, the "tolerance" that relativism in its more benign forms sanctions is limited and rather patronizing. If I could never convince you, and you could never convince me, however hard we tried to reach agreement, then our mutual tolerance is limited to issues neither of us regards as important. And this means that either our beliefs or our relationship cannot be very important, even if our relationship—say, marriage—is one that many people have understood in very different terms. It is sometimes right and proper to put up with harmless eccentrics, as it is sometimes right and proper to deal with sensitive topics by avoiding them. But these are not adequate models for dealing with the conflicts that occur in social life.[12]

IDENTITY POLITICS

Propositions 3 and 5 represent the multiculturalists' attempt to impose some order on the chaos their views otherwise entail. If one can identify, within contemporary America or the world at large, a fairly small list of "cultures," each with its own canons of judgments and official representatives, the life of the mind can proceed in a somewhat orderly way, despite the official relativism of the multiculturalist ideology. Propositions 3 and 5 also attempt to answer a crucial question posed by critics of multiculturalism: why are Milton's whiteness, heterosexuality, and maleness more important than his blindness, or why are the traits Dante shares with Kant more important than his experience as a political exile?

The notorious (and frightening) confusion between culture and race enters the argument at this point. Racial characteristics, real or alleged, are used to firm up otherwise shaky cultural identities, and the situation of persons of mixed heritage becomes precarious as a result. So Henry Louis Gates observes, of the alleged blackness of Cleopatra, "The belief that we cherish is not so much a proposition about melanin and physiognomy; it's the proposition that, through the mists of history, Cleopatra was a *sister.*"[13] But Cleopatra herself would have regarded all forms of contemporary culture, including our obsession with skin color, as alien. That she might have had to ride in the back of the bus, if by some miracle she had been translated into twentieth-century Alabama, is entirely irrelevant. It is, in short, a mistake to project contemporary American racial identities onto her and her world, whether or not some African genes found their way into her gene pool.

At this point, multiculturalists appeal to the judgments of a hostile society. As Gates has observed, "The conventional multicultural wisdom suggests that for every insult there is a culture; that is, if I can be denigrated as an X, I can be affirmed as an X."[14] This answer assigns the task of defining cultures to the enemy: it is, in fact, a philosophy of parasitism—a result that some of the postmodern side of the movement would in fact accept, but that has little to say for it otherwise.

Moreover, identity politics and the politics of liberation are in fundamental conflict.[15] For liberation includes liberation from an identity imposed, in part, by one's oppressors. And there does not seem to be any coherent way of defining the remainder. Thus feminists will have to decide, sooner or later, whether to affirm a feminine identity that implies a relationship to men, to advocate female separatism, or to work toward a society in which neither men nor women exist, except in the most narrowly physiological sense. In any case they will have to sacrifice something.

In short, despite its radical rhetoric, identity politics is conservative. For our various identities are always functions of existing attitudes, customs, and institutions.[16] It also has tragic implications, since our various identities—say, as Palestinian Arabs or Zionists, as Catholic Irish or Ulster Unionists—often bring us into deadly conflict with one another.

RELATIVISM AGAIN

Proposition 4 states the relativism underlying the multiculturalist program. Here we are dealing with relativism in a strict, and rather strong, sense. Not only is human thought characterized by a diversity of frameworks (paradigms, cultures); not only are there some disputes at present unresolved. Adjudication or even understanding across cultural lines is strictly impossible.

Relativism of this sort is inconsistent with another common multiculturalist theme: that the socially marginalized have a privileged epistemic position, since—at least when they have been properly awakened—they are not taken in by the illusions sponsored by the powerful. Near the core of the multiculturalist program is a demand for discursive affirmative action:[17] since the perspectives of white, heterosexual males of the leisured classes have heretofore dominated academic discourse, we need to give other perspectives a privileged position at least for the time being. The call to take into account the perspectives of the marginalized has considerable merit even within an antirelativist perspective. Nonetheless, care is necessary: being marginalized may carry with it its own quota of illusions, and severe poverty usually precludes theoretical reflection.[18]

In any event, the multiculturalist conception of human diversity, and consequently of marginal status, is formulaic, almost stereotypical. People of color, women, usually homosexuals and the "physically challenged," less commonly poor and working class people, and occasionally Jews exhaust the diverse groups whose perspectives multiculturalists invoke to correct the errors of the mainstream. When the multiculturalists have done their work, the perspectives of many kinds of people remain as marginal as ever. Such epistemically marginalized groups include untenured academics (and especially those not on a tenure track). They also include creation scientists, Jehovah's Witnesses, and impoverished Southern whites—those who are called "rednecks" by people who otherwise scrupulously refrain from derogatory language for groups of people. The working criterion for admission into the multiculturalist canon is fragmentation and social deviancy (rather than, say, poverty); representatives of living communities with standards different from those of the academic establishment are not welcome in elite intellectual circles. As Wendell Berry has bitingly put it, "the social and cultural pluralism some now see as a goal is a public of destroyed communities."[19]

The most fundamental difficulty with the multiculturalist program cannot, however, be expressed in terms of groups. Each individual in the contemporary world is a nexus of many different cultural identities, a fact that resists assimilation into a multiculturalist framework. Richard Rodriguez has memorably complained: "I'm not a Catholic to them, I'm Hispanic. And I'm not gay to them, I'm brown. And I'm not Indian to them, because they know who the Indians are—the Indians live in Oklahoma."[20]

To be sure, one might attempt to rank a person's cultural identities, at least on a case-by-case basis.[21] If a very dark, left-handed, heterosexual, African-American woman from the North is allowed to choose her own identity, she is likely to prefer the one that best advances her interests (or, if she is young and idealistic, the one that suits her present mood). If, on the other hand, an institution is prepared to say that race is more important than handedness, generally or in this case, some sort of rationale must be forthcoming for doing so, and it will be difficult to avoid highly questionable racialist theories (which, in any event, multiculturalists by their own standards have no business asserting).

THE REALITY OF HUMAN DIVERSITY

I shall be further questioning propositions 4 and 5 in the chapters that follow. Propositions 1, 2, and 3 seem, however, to be roughly true. (Proposition 3 is in fact questionable, but I shall let it pass for the time being.)[22] The diversity of modes of human life—and of the ways in which we act, think, feel, and imagine—is the starting point for the most central practical issues, and consequently also of the most central philosophical inquiries, of our day.

NOTES

1. Louis Menand, "The Culture Wars," *New York Review of Books* 41, 16 (October 6, 1994): 16.

2. For another critical analysis of the strong multiculturalist position, see Jerry L. Martin, "The Postmodern Argument Considered," *Partisan Review* 40, 4 (1993): 638–654.

3. Jean Bethke Elshtain, *Democracy on Trial* (New York: Basic Books, 1995), p. 53.

4. Dave Foreman, "Earth First!" Peter C. List, ed., *Radical Environmentalism* (Belmont, Calif.: Wadsworth, 1993), p. 189.

5. Peter Singer, *Animal Liberation* (New York: New York Review of Books, 1979), pp. 245–246.

6. List, ed., *Radical Environmentalism*, p. ix.

7. Elshtain reports that "the suicide rate among young white males jumped over 200 percent in the past decade" (p. 7)—in other words, during the decade when multiculturalism was most visible. Such violence could easily be directed outward.

8. Richard Rorty, *Contingency, Irony, and Solidarity* (Cambridge: Cambridge University Press, 1989), p. 52.

9. The rejection of relativism is central to John Paul II's encyclical, *Splendor Veritatis*, published in *Origins* 23 (October 14, 1993): 297–336. But this teaching is not even faintly new.

10. I am indebted to Robert J. Rafalko for emphasizing to me the role of antirelativist assumptions in the traditional case for tolerance.

11. Sir James Fitzjames Stephen, *Liberty, Equality, Fraternity*, R. J. White, ed. (Cambridge: Cambridge University Press, 1967), p. 165: "Force, in the widest sense of the term, must decide the question."

12. I am once again indebted to Rafalko.

13. Henry Louis Gates, "Beyond the Culture Wars," *Profession* 93 (1993): 6.

14. Ibid., p. 8.

15. See ibid., pp. 8–9.

16. Compare the concept of the situated self, as deployed in Michael J. Sandel, *Liberalism and the Limits of Justice* (Cambridge: Cambridge University Press, 1982).

17. I owe this phrase to Naomi Scheman, "Feminist Epistemology," American Philosophical Association, Eastern Division, December 29, 1994.

18. See further Chapter 7.

19. Wendell Berry, *Sex, Economy, Freedom, and Community* (New York: Pantheon, 1993), p. 169.

20. Richard Rodriguez, interviewed by Virginia Postrel and Nick Gillespie, "On Borders and Belonging," *Utne Reader* (March–April 1995): 79.

21. Joel Wilcox informs me that this is the practice of Xavier University in Louisiana.

22. For the views of one anthropologist, see Clifford Geertz, *After the Fact* (Cambridge, Mass.: Harvard University Press, 1995).

4

Weak Multiculturalism

The most troubling feature of strong multiculturalism is its relativism. The denial of communication across cultural boundaries implies either mutual avoidance or permanent civil war. Not surprisingly, therefore, academics otherwise impressed by the multiculturalist case have attempted to detach it from its relativistic elements.

Henry Louis Gates, Jr., has broken with multiculturalist orthodoxy for this reason. In his own words, "If relativism is right, then multiculturalism is impossible."[1] And he rejects the intolerant edge of strong multiculturalism in favor of an acceptance of pluralism of the sort proposed by Isaiah Berlin.[2] Similarly, the President's Task Force on Campus Diversity and Multicultural Education (California State University, Long Beach) tries to defend multicultural education by appeal to the common good:

A person who has benefited from a multicultural education will be able to communicate with others in spite of the differences brought by diversity of culture, race, gender, etc., and to negotiate with others and to interact with them for mutual benefit and the common good.[3]

The theoretical foundation for education conducted in this spirit has been laid down, from different angles, by Gerald Graff,[4] Alasdair MacIntyre,[5] and Charles Taylor.[6] We also require the philosophy of Michael Oakeshott to supply some important nuances.[7] Limitations on our psychological and material resources—and the need to keep dialogue from turning into a brawl—imply that any program of multicultural dialogue must confront three questions, each one of which creates considerable difficulty:

1. What cultures are entitled to participate in the dialogue?
2. What writers or texts are to be taken as representative of these cultures?
3. What should be the rules of debate among representatives of diverse cultural traditions, each of which has its own conventions of civility?

WHAT CULTURES ARE ENTITLED TO PARTICIPATE IN DIALOGUE?

MacIntyre proposes a system of higher education in which colleges organized around specific outlooks—in his version, Thomism, the Enlightenment, and "genealogy"—develop richly and finely crafted versions of their shared understandings. After conversations among themselves, the representatives of these philosophies then come together for debate. Two quick objections to this proposal are that the contending traditions need to be found in the actual social world, not excogitated in the philosopher's study, and that one of the contending traditions identified by MacIntyre cannot participate in an educational institution of any sort. A prospective *Übermensch* cannot be a colleague.

Even apart from these objections, MacIntyre's proposal only solves part of the question. Let us suppose, for the sake of argument, that we can identify a multitude of reasonably homogeneous "cultures" within contemporary America. Some such cultures may be objectionable in themselves, entitled to bare tolerance perhaps but not to the kind of recognition implied by an invitation to take part in civic dialogue. We have to decide whether small Bible colleges, colleges dominated by an Afrocentric educational philosophy, scientific institutions engaging in forms of research we regard as unethical, research institutes serving as lobbies for the avocado industry, or educational institutions promoting survivalism or Holocaust denial fall into this class. Resource constraints imply that we cannot even find a place for every "legitimate" point of view in any cultural forum. And even if we had limitless material resources, the limits on the human mind mean that one person could only assimilate and evaluate so many possibilities.

In dealing with questions of tolerance, some distinctions are useful. Parents whose children adopt ways of life alien to their own sometimes decide to break relations with them (and in some traditions erring children are mourned as dead). If they refuse this course, the choice is between approval, acceptance, affirmation, toleration, and acquiescence, each of which has different implications for the way they deal with their children.

The concept of *acceptance* is very important in contemporary popular morality, but the confusions surrounding it are almost as great as its importance.[8] We are frequently asked to accept disagreeable facts about ourselves, about other human beings, and about the world. Expressions like "What's done is done" and "That's all water under the bridge" express acceptance of facts beyond the power to change. But some facts, we are told, can never be accepted. Acceptance means something short of approval, but something more than mere acknowledgment of a fact, toleration of it, or even abandonment of any attempt to change it. One cannot make it the case that the Holocaust never occurred, yet many men and women are unwilling to accept that it happened. And the student who told me that she was "uncomfortable sharing a country" with Evangelicals did not accept them, though she showed no signs of active intolerance toward them either.

Probably the best reading of the concept of acceptance is that one should not only cease to struggle, in a practical way, against a given fact, but should also abandon an attitude of protest or rebellion against it, even in the privacy of one's thoughts. The antonym of acceptance is *repugnance*, with emphasis on the underlying Latin sense of "fighting against."[9] (There is no precisely corresponding verb, but *refuse, resist,* and *repudiate* are useful approximations.) I may disapprove of an act, say, Nero's murder of his mother, while feeling no repugnance toward it.

All of us have traits of character we regret having. What may be called the resigned view[10] of such traits counsels us to accept them. This means not only that we should stop trying to change these facts about ourselves, but also that we should abandon any attitude of protest or rebellion against them. In other words, we should decide not to feel guilty.

Besides the difference between approval and acceptance, we need also to understand the difference between acceptance and tolerance, acquiescence, or condonation. Tolerance maintains an attitude of protest but sharply limits the ways we express it—renouncing both coercion and the sharper forms of social pressure. Acquiescence merely registers the conclusion that one is, at least for the moment, unable to change an undesirable fact. (Acceptance is close to permanent acquiescence.) Condonation—roughly feigned approval—involves dishonesty in a way that excludes it from consideration here. *Affirm* probably means *approve,* although there remains a possibility of some stronger or weaker meaning, whose content is unclear.

No one is limitlessly tolerant, let alone infinitely accepting: pretending to be so is an unhealthy form of self-deception. And I am unaware of any useful formula for setting the limits of tolerance: Mill's harm principle is hopelessly ambiguous, and the private-public distinction, though we cannot do without it, is extremely porous. Nor is there any rule about what practices constitute approval, what constitute acceptance, and what mere tolerance; nor about the proper role of emotion and intellect in these decisions. This is not to say that prudential decisions are impossible, though how we make them depends on our larger moral, political, and religious assumptions.[11] The question at present is not altogether suppressing some point of view or form of activity, or refraining from doing so, but rather giving it the recognition and support implied in an invitation to take part in dialogue.

Limits on material and resources raise the issue of priorities. First, serious education for multicultural dialogue *must* include the study of at least one foreign language.[12] Access to a serious body of literature, and usefulness for business or travel, are desirable side-effects of foreign language study. But study of any foreign language—be it Swahili, Spanish, or classical Greek—achieves the same educational purpose: it requires the student to see the world through alien categories, or at least the appearance of such categories. Although linguistic relativism may not be true, the experienced world of those who distinguish between *tu* and *usted* (or *ser* and *estar*) will differ from that of those who do not.

Second, an understanding of the religious outlooks that underlie alien cultures is essential to any but the shallowest cross-cultural understanding. I deal with the secularism that underlies rejection of this proposal in Chapter 11.

Third, the "dead European white males" of the multiculturalist polemic are mandatory subjects for a number of reasons. They represent a family of cultural traditions of great importance for many men and women. Moreover, Western civilization, often in a debased form, is now that of the entire world—as those who hate the fact themselves acknowledge. The most memorable protests against the dominant forces of our civilization—those of the Slavophil Dostoevsky, the ultra-Protestant Kierkegaard, the radical Marx, and the militant atheist Nietzsche—have all been enrolled in the Western "canon." Other claimants, to make a reasonable claim on our attention, or pose a serious challenge to the view of life we accept, must first meet the criteria of excellence inherent in their own tradition, whether ancient or emerging; then they must make enough impression on us to gain our attention. (This proposition does not mean, as Saul Bellow thinks, that the Zulus have to produce a Tolstoy: African dance and music may have a great deal to say to us, though I lack the competence to discuss the relevant aesthetic issues here.)

Finally, marginal men and women, including those displaced from positions of power and influence, have made important contributions to the development of the Western tradition. Oppressed men and women both within and outside the West have seized on elements of the core Western tradition in order to protest the injustice done them, to convince both themselves and others that it is injustice and not just hardship, and to rally support for programs designed to better their lot. But the culture of the oppressed may serve as an opiate, serving only to perpetuate their oppression. (Let us not be too hasty, however: American slave revolts invariably failed, and black people had somehow to preserve a sense of their own dignity under conditions of servitude.) The worst kinds of oppression deprive their victims of the capacity either to protest their oppression or to console themselves for it.

The claim that some individual or group has been oppressed presupposes a standard of justice transcending the usages of society, whose existence and character are in question in cultural debates. Strong multiculturalists combine a theoretical commitment to relativism with a naive belief in the capacity of the word *equality* to resolve controversial questions of social justice; the rest of us must examine questions of justice with a bit more care.

WHAT WRITERS OR TEXTS ARE TO BE TAKEN AS REPRESENTATIVES OF THEIR TRADITIONS?

Each of us will promote the study of those ideas that we take to be true, or at least the best approximation to truth available. We need also to study those ideas that, in our view, represent the most serious challenge to the truth. We need to study ideas that are in fact influential, however weak their inherent claim to be accepted as such. I have put this issue in cognitive terms, but literary and artistic works can be judged on both the merits and the influence of the world-picture they project, as well as on their aesthetic qualities. A rough consensus as to the list of classics is still available; judgment of which contemporary writers are likely to be of continuing importance must of necessity be left to the individual instructor.

It is now necessary to examine the resulting issues a bit more closely. One problem for intercultural dialogue is the pressure to stereotype the representatives of the contending traditions. Once a scholar has been labeled a radical feminist, a liberal Catholic, or a neoconservative, he will be expected to defend, against all comers, the appropriate party line. In the process, nuances will be lost, and the professional judgment of academics will suffer considerable strain.

A state university[13] appoints a distinguished liberal Protestant scholar to teach "Christian Origins" (its euphemism, designed to quiet secularist scruples, for the New Testament). A group of Evangelical students, deeming him a heretic, decides to protest by denouncing him on the final exam rather than answering the questions, thereby forcing him to fail them.

A Roman Catholic school decides to offer a course in Basic Judaism and needs to decide what sort of rabbi—Reform, Conservative, or Orthodox—to appoint to teach it. Should it use numerical criteria, try to decide who is most authentically Jewish, or choose according to who most closely resembles some preferred form of Catholicism?

An American university desiring to teach Islam must try to find an authentical Islamic scholar who is prepared to deal on civil terms with the infidel. But willingness to deal civilly with the infidel will disqualify a scholar in the eyes of many Muslims.

That male homosexuals have written great literature is beyond doubt. And that Proust and Whitman are great writers, and the author of some scabrous work of homosexual pornography is not great, is only slightly more controversial. But is Proust a representative of the homosexual tradition—to be judged by some criteria special to homosexuals—or is he simply a greater writer than some pornographer?

In short, the most questionable assumption of weak multiculturalism is its focus on group membership. True, human beings are essentially social. But each one of us is nonetheless unique, among other things, in the network of social relations in which we participate. No one is simply a woman, a black person, or a male or female homosexual, just as no one is simply a man, a white person, or a heterosexual.

It is a commonplace of contemporary philosophy that meaning is somehow social. But the precise relationship between individual meaning and social practice has by no means been established. Is language to be understood as a collection of idiolects, or are idiolects to be understood as (correct or deviant) variations on some sociolect?[14] For the purposes of my arguments, the precise resolution of these debates does not matter. Publicity is essential to language, but each idiolect represents a unique nexus of sociolects. Similarly, each person represents a confluence of a different set of cultural traditions.

Except perhaps in theology, we must avoid reifying traditions. Theology is different only because the authentic voice of tradition is also understood as representing a tradition-transcendent Truth. An accurate account of the influences on any writer will include a wide variety of sources, in most cases including the core tradition of the West. Although placing a writer historically and culturally helps in the understanding of his writings, it does not replace confrontation with those writings in themselves and the insights of permanent value they may contain.

RULES FOR DEBATE

"The university," it has been well said, "sponsors moral conflict but in an atmosphere in which ideas can be tested short of mortal conflict."[15] To make this possible, rules of civility are needed, as are shared standards of good argument. Hence arises, among other things, the vexing question of speech codes. I limit myself to the questions of what the rules of debate should be, avoiding the difficult question, Who is to enforce them and how?

First, the rules of debate should not be designed to favor one side of the argument. (This principle is seldom if ever honored in practice.) A partial exception to this principle occurs in religiously affiliated institutions, or other institutions in which some ideas are given a conventionally protected position, as long as everyone involved has given his consent to the institution's character. These are entitled to protect the sensibilities of believers more than those of others. But even in such institutions, if it is forbidden to call someone a "nigger," it should also be forbidden to call someone a "kike" or "honky." Similarly, if it is forbidden to call a person a "faggot," it should be also forbidden to call him a "male chauvinist pig."[16] (And, in both cases, vice versa.)

Second, one task of the university is to teach students to distinguish between supporting one's judgments by reasons and mere sounding off. No relevant consideration should be silenced on the grounds that mentioning it constitutes "insensitivity," but nonreasons should be identified as such. If, for example, students in affirmative action programs do less well than other students, the fact needs to be known, so that the merits of such programs can be discussed intelligently. But unreasoned expressions of dislike for other members of the university community are to be discouraged.

We must, however, give the widest possible scope to considerations of an informal (and often emotion-laden) sort. At least some relevant considerations can be expressed in slogans (for example, during the Persian Gulf War, "No blood for oil!"). Despite their emotion-laden character, pictures of wartime atrocities and of the mangled bodies of fetuses present considerations relevant to moral and political judgment, even though they do not decide any issues. For when it is customary to cloak unpleasant decisions in euphemisms, at least a hearing must be given to those who present them in unvarnished terms.

The sorting out of various sorts of considerations, and the assigning to each its appropriate probative force, belongs to a later stage of inquiry. Nonetheless, weak multiculturalism requires us to assume that there are intellectual standards to which all reasonable men and women have access and to which they therefore may be held. Only on such an assumption can we dismiss, as no reason at all, such remarks as "I don't like you because you have black (or white or yellow) skin, and I hope that my fellow white people (or black people, or Chinese) will share my feelings."

In short, although weak multiculturalism provides a useful framework for dialogue, it collapses in four different directions. Since each person represents the meeting point of a slightly different family of cultural traditions, weak multiculturalism collapses into individualism. The same is true of strong multiculturalism, since each individual can be seen as the bearer of a unique culture. (The logical extreme of pluralism is atomism.) Because common standards of rational discourse are necessary if dialogue among diverse men and women is to be possible, weak multiculturalism collapses into humanism.

The most common form of collapse, however, has been the neglect of the fact that rival cultures contain mutually incompatible pictures of how things are and ought to be. Some people take as their model for understanding cultural diversity experimentation with exotic cuisines. Academic discussions of religion often speak the language of preferences and market shares rather than competing claims to truth. If we adopt either of these approaches, we will be crippled when we begin to think about practices that offend the moral sense of nearly all participants in the Western tradition, or about tensions within the Western tradition itself.[17]

Finally, we may take the claim of incommensurability with radical seriousness. Extended from the cultural tradition to the individual, this means that, like Leibnizian monads or angels in Thomistic theology, each of us has a unique perspective on the world and that (as Leibniz and St. Thomas would never say) there is no way of adjudicating the conflicts that result. In other words, we end up with a radical individualism, which has no place for shared moral or intellectual standards. Cultural chaos is therefore the inevitable result.

NOTES

1. Henry Louis Gates, Jr., "Beyond the Culture Wars," *Profession* 93 (1993): 11.

2. Ibid., p. 11. See ch. 1 of this book under "Pluralism" for a discussion of Berlin's position.

3. "The Challenge of Diversity and Multicultural Education," in Francis J. Beckwith and Michael J. Bauman, eds., *Are You Politically Correct?* (Buffalo, N.Y.: Prometheus, 1993), p. 77.

4. Gerald Graff, *Beyond the Culture Wars* (New York: Norton, 1992).

5. Alasdair MacIntyre, *Three Rival Versions of Moral Enquiry* (Notre Dame, Ind.: University of Notre Dame Press, 1990).

6. Charles Taylor et al., *Multiculturalism and "The Problem of Recognition*," Amy Guttman ed. (Princeton, N.J.: Princeton University Press, 1992).

7. *The Voice of Liberal Learning: Michael Oakeshott on Liberal Education*, Timothy Fuller, ed. (New Haven, Conn.: Yale University Press, 1989).

8. These confusions are faithfully reproduced in Richard Wollheim, *The Thread of Life* (Cambridge, Mass.: Harvard University Press, 1984), ch. 9, especially pp. 261–262, 264–265, 275–283.

9. Witness: "Our learned forebearance and cultivated sensibility lie at the root both of acceptance of abortion and repugnance to it" (see Benjamin DeMott, Review of John Irving, *The Cider House Rules*, in *The New York Times Book Review*, May 26, 1985, p. 25).

10. For a sophisticated presentation of this view, see Jonathan Harrison, "Be Ye Therefore Perfect," *Religious Studies* 21 (1985): 1–19.

11. For an effort by a conservative Protestant to address the question of tolerance, see Richard J. Mouw, *Uncommon Decency* (Downers Grove, Ill.: Intervarsity, 1992), especially ch. 10.

12. The (Cal State Long Beach) President's Task Force's Recommendations (sec. IX), like many other programs for multicultural education, contain no proposal for improved education in foreign languages, even in Spanish.

13. I do not here distinguish between colleges and universities. And much of what I have to say applies to other cultural forums.

14. For a sophisticated defense of the primacy of idiolects, see Akeel Bilgrami, *Belief and Meaning* (Oxford: Blackwell, 1992), ch. 3. But Bilgrami makes moral

responsibility essential to self-knowledge (ibid., Appendix), and moral resposibility requires a public criterion.

15. Manfred Stanley, "The American University as a Civic Institution," *Civic Arts Review* (spring 1989): 6. Quoted in Dinesh D'Souza, "Final Thoughts on Political Correctness," Beckwith and Bauman, eds., *Are You Politically Correct?*, p. 251.

16. At least where these expressions are understood as derogatory. I have seen (in Rhode Island) vanity license plates reading "MCP," in an apparent attempt to be simultaneously macho and cute.

17. James Davison Hunter well expresses this concern in his *Before the Shooting Begins* (New York: Free Press, 1994), ch. 7.

5

Cultural Chaos

It is impossible, or so we are told, to look either at the Sun or at death. But that wisdom requires confrontation with the Abyss is a recurrent theme in the discourse of our civilization from Homer to Heidegger.

Many people retain some lingering hope of an afterlife, but even the most zealous believers also find it necessary to mitigate the prospects of death by identifying with family lineages, national and religious communities, cultural traditions, and political movements that will continue in existence after they die. In order to confront death in its fullest sense, we must therefore consider the possibility that nothing we value will be transmitted to anyone who lives after us. The extermination of the human species (or the violent destruction of our civilization) is one version of this prospect. But limitless cultural decay also provides us with a useful diminished similitude.

Another name for death in its fullest sense is chaos. It is not possible to think about a world to which none of our present concepts apply (we could not even call it a world). The space between conceptual schemes, where confusion alone remains, is beyond the scope of literal discourse. Yet all philosophers use metaphors (for example, the "web of belief") and other nonliteral expressions. Even *clarity*, which describes one goal of philosophical reasoning, involves a metaphor. Hence we can use oblique discourse to confront a prospect that cannot be described directly.

One important form of oblique discourse is a narrative, in this case a narrative of decline from an earlier stage of coherence (or else of a preexisting chaos on which order has been imposed). Another is the use of a "limit

concept" (*Grenzbegriff*), in this case one pointing to an ideal limit to disintegration. We can thus project from present experiences of disintegration—
say, of Liberal Protestantism, New Deal Liberalism, or our students' writing
styles—to a notional situation in which the entropic tendencies we observe
in our world are given their fullest scope, and no order of any sort can be
found. So Michel Foucault spends considerable energy on the loving recon-
struction of a system of conceptual order, founded on resemblance, that his
readers are certain to find alien,[1] on the way to suggesting that the forms of
order that obtain in our experience are also destined to disintegrate.

At present, those who insist that "America is not over" speak with
defensive truculence,[2] while those who claim that our culture is in transi-
tion to something better and unspecified give the impression of whistling
in the dark. I speak of perceptions here, since it is difficult either to identify
a past Golden Age or to articulate criteria of health and decline that are
anything more than the reiteration of evaluations made from a position
within contemporary debates. Yet the perception of decline that is one
central feature of the contemporary cultural scene cannot be just dismissed
either.

God is dead, or so Nietzsche and his followers proclaim; whatever traces
of His existence remain in our theory and practice are nothing more than
what George Steiner has called a "vacant metaphor."[3] With God's death
comes the end of all God-substitutes, such as Care, Culture, Democracy,
Duty, Human Nature, Language, Law, Reason, Science, and Truth. A consistent follower of Nietzsche would also avoid giving a transcendent position to Power, a phenomenon that had a very different meaning in the
French intellectual world after the Second World War, in the late Roman
Empire, and in the antebellum South.

The Nietzschean world-picture may appear radically individualistic, but
it is, in the last resort, resigned—among other things to social pressure. Each
man and each woman is entitled to attempt to become an *Übermensch*, who
reshapes first him- or herself, and then the natural and social world, in
accordance with whatever vision happens to appeal at a given moment. But
those who have been liberated in this fashion are also deprived of any
resources wherewith to resist the biological and social pressures that bear
down on each of us. They are even deprived of a concept of a stable self,
which will enable them to dismiss their conformist impulses as not authentically theirs.

Advocates of cultural diversity often have very little idea of what culture
is, going so far at times as to expect people simultaneously to inhabit
incompatible cultures.[4] But "culture," James Davison Hunter has written,
"is nothing if it is not, first and foremost, a normative order by which we
comprehend ourselves, others, and the larger world and through which we
order our experience."[5] Men and women need a shared conceptual and
normative framework, including a sense of the limits on what victorious

opponents are likely to do, if they are to deliberate about common problems without killing each other. Even the most enthusiastic democrat cannot be expected to tolerate a party whose program implies genocide, at least if he himself is among its intended victims. The threat of genocidal "solutions" is never far from the surface of contemporary cultural controversy.[6]

But the need for common standards does not, of itself, produce them: in fact, cultural confusion seems now to be the order of the day all over the world. The emergence of culture is on any account mysterious, but when new cultural traditions arise, they usually at least owe their existence to charismatic figures like Marx, Moses, or Mohammed. Hunter expects strengthened democracy to create a common culture:[7] he seems to believe that attempts at cooperation among people holding contradictory views will, however slowly,[8] generate the normative framework required to sustain it.[9] He draws inspiration for this hope from the Jeffersonian tradition,[10] but he does not—at least in his book—avow the belief in a Creator God that held Jefferson's outlook together. Instead, he endorses Adam Seligman's conclusion that such Enlightenment beliefs "are no longer ours to share."[11] He concedes that his remedies are not adequate to his diagnosis: "As a sociologist I am professionally inclined to accept such [pessimistic] determinisms, but as a citizen I see no choice but to hope against them."[12]

The cultural Right is above all interested in protecting an inherited way of life from erosion; it identifies Truth, and in particular the truth about human nature, with those opinions authoritative within the relevant community (or authoritative there until some recent disruption). The cultural Center is interested in discarding what is bad in our culture while preserving and extending what is good. It allows a space between official opinion and Truth, and between our conception of human nature and the correct one—though it affirms that our tradition is at least heading in the right direction.

The cultural Left attempts to create a world in which the voice of the Father is never heard. (The "Father" here is a quasimythical personage, not God exactly but not quite the same as any particular person's actual father either.) It includes a rage against the concept of human nature, and in particular against those aspects of our nature—such as the fact that women give birth—involved in the transmission of humanity from generation to generation.

But the attack on human nature is not limited to its biological dimension. Foucault has provided the despair of the future central to the cultural Left with an intellectual basis:

As the archeology of our thought shows, man is an invention of recent date. And one perhaps nearing its end. . . . One can certainly wager that [if the structure of knowledge changed] man would be erased, like a face drawn in sand at the edge of the sea.[13]

But if even *man* is a construct, who did the constructing? (Foucault surely does not mean that we are constructed by God.) What Foucault means by *man* is also far from clear:[14] at least he does not mean "human beings."[15]

Man in Foucault's thought appears to be the liberal individual whose character was codified by Kant. Such an individual's autonomy includes, in equal measure, rational self-discipline and freedom from external restraint.[16] No one has produced a plausible account of what alternative conception might emerge from the "ocean of other possibilities to thought."[17] Many versions of life after "humanism," including the way of life adopted by Foucault himself,[18] are destructive by any known standard, though even these, we need to remember, are human possibilities.

Above all, the cultural Left rages against the very concept of truth, which it identifies with entrenched social power. As Foucault puts it,

Truth isn't outside power, or lacking in power. . . . Truth is a thing of this world: it is produced only by multiple forms of constraint. . . . Each society has its régime of truth, its "general politics" of truth; that is, the type of discourse which it accepts and makes function as true; the mechanisms which enable one to distinguish between true and false statements, the means by which each is sanctioned; the techniques and procedures accorded value in the production of truth; the status of those who are charged with saying what counts as true. . . . The political question, to sum up, is not error, illusion, alienated consciousness, or ideology; it is truth itself.[19]

There is, on such premises, no possible distinction between truth and power: might does not merely make right; it is right. Hence the liberation of scientific research from the demands of monopoly capitalism, as demanded by the radicals of the sixties "will never be more than a slogan."[20] Any attempt to distinguish between liberation and the succession of oppressors is flawed in its foundations.

Many people have an emotional commitment to defining themselves as men and women of the Left, and to rejecting at least traditional forms of religion. At one time such people were Marxists and especially adopted Marx's belief in laws of history capable of vindicating one political program as "progressive" and condemning another as "reactionary." They believed in a common human nature, though one concealed under capitalism, which would enable human beings to thrive in mutually supportive ways, once socially entrenched obstacles to its realization were removed. Guided by these premises, they undertook to expose the ideological defenses of the status quo, and to support the working class as privileged agents of social change.

But they came to see the belief in a common human nature, and even more so in the existence of laws of history, as matters of faith and hope, incapable of surviving the sort of debunking they directed against traditional religious and moral ideas. Hence they were driven to the view that power politics necessarily pervades social life, even in its most intimate aspects. In this respect they followed St. Augustine, though they could not accept the saint's belief in the overriding power of divine grace. Hence they devoted themselves to power politics, usually of a petty sort. The result was the invasion of the Left by Nietzsche, though in what sense the result was still Leftist is worth inquiry.

In light of these developments, let us further examine the prospect of a world in which multiculturalism has given birth to aculturalism—a world in which there is no such thing as culture in the normative sense, only each individual and group's idiosyncratic and temporary adaptations to circumstance. We may call such a world a "postmodern" world, or with important reservations, "radically relativist." For not everyone in a postmodern world is a relativist, and it is sheer bluff to suppose the *Zeitgeist* somehow forces anti-relativists to change their positions.

It is as much contrary to the character of a postmodern world to regard relativism as culturally normative as to claim this status for Eastern Orthodoxy. Groups making assertive claims for the truth of their positions, or even their privileged access to such truth, are as much a part of the postmodern scene as are those who implicitly or explicitly accept relativism. We must in any case deal with a variety of groups whose material interests and ideals of life both incline them to conflict with one another. In a cultural climate in which neither the Bible nor the Scientific Method nor anything else enjoys unquestioned hegemony, the interaction of rival views of life constantly produces cacophony and chaos.

In such a world, we may appeal to tolerance to protect ourselves and our allies: this is always possible even in the most antiliberal social climate. But tolerance in a postmodern world is the result of a temporary balance of forces, or else of contingent features of some particular outlook. Mill's argument for tolerance, which rests on optimistic assumptions about the ability of inquiry to uncover truth and bring about agreement, is irrelevant in such a world. When we are asked to tolerate those whose attitudes and beliefs we find deeply offensive, we are likely to conclude, with Stanley Fish, that

All affirmations of freedom of expression are . . . dependent for their force on an exception that literally carves out the space in which expression then can emerge. . . . When the pinch comes (and sooner or later it will always come) and the institution (be it church, state, or university) is confronted by behavior subversive of its core rationale, it will respond by declaring "of course we mean not to tolerate _____, that we extirpate," not because an exception to a general freedom has suddenly and contradictorily been announced but because the freedom has never been general and has always been understood against the background of an originary exclusion that gives it meaning.[21]

This is not merely a denial of First Amendment absolutism. Views that Fish regards as outside the pale—arguably those of most Americans—are for him no more to be tolerated than acts of overt violence.

Mussolini provides the most lucid expression of the outcome of Fish's argument:

> From the fact that all ideologies are of equal value, that all ideologies are fictions, the modern relativist infers that everybody has the right to create for himself his own ideology and attempt to enforce it with all the energy of which he is capable.[22]

But Fish's thought has not—not yet at least—found the constituency that makes for a genuine fascist movement.

What distinguishes fascists from Nazis is that Nazism involves not just a generalized intolerance of outsiders, but also a virulent form of racism. Some racialists claim scientific warrant for their positions. Their opponents argue that there is no one thing called "intelligence" and no reason to believe that the many things called by that name are causally linked with skin color and the like (or perhaps even with each other). They also point to the many ways in which the scars of slavery persist, both in the black and the white populations, with the resulting bad effects on the performance of black people. Indeed, the bad effects of slavery on the character of slaves were recognized in antiquity. As Homer put it: "Zeus who views the whole world takes away half the manhood of a man, that day he goes into captivity and slavery."[23] We may also add, slavery is morally injurious to women, though perhaps not in exactly the same way.

We can admire the ability of men and women to maintain a sense of human dignity under adverse circumstances. We should not make ability to compete in a highly individualistic economy the sole or sovereign measure of virtue. Nonetheless, we all have to live in the world as it is, and a disadvantage overcome is still a disadvantage. Moreover, that an effect is cultural rather than biological does not make it easy to remove it.

My argument does not require me to go over these familiar questions in detail. Some racialists—for example, Alfred Rosenberg[24]—have defended their position in ways entirely congruent with a relativistic epistemology. In America Revilo T. Oliver argues that the human species is divided into a number of "races" or "nations" having incommensurable modes of thought and ways of life. Like Peter Singer, though with very different consequences for practice, Oliver draws a close analogy between our treatment of other races and our treatment of other species.[25] He concludes, not that members of other species have the rights of human beings, but that members of other races lack the rights of white people. Oliver's position does not quite imply that it is impossible to treat members of other races unjustly. He maintains, for example, that it is unjust to force Indian children to attend white schools.[26] Nonetheless, he speaks quite frankly of "the right

of a superior people to seize the country of an inferior people and extermi-
nate them."[27] That we may find such views frightening or even abhorrent
does not excuse us from examining their logic.

Oliver's position does not require support from science or pseudos-
cience; a relativistic epistemology will serve his purposes just as well, one
differing from those popular among mainstream intellectuals only because
tied to differences in skin color and other bodily traits.

To be sure, he appeals to biological facts and claims that his views are
the only ones that recognize reality as it is rather than as we might wish it
to be. But this is a stock problem for relativists: they persistently hold that
they are somehow right and their "Platonic" opponents somehow wrong.
It remains the case that, on radically relativist premises, we can construct
the world however we choose. Oliver's construction in terms of race is
no worse, intellectually at least, than any other. It is morally abhorrent,
but in saying this I am merely reiterating my own antiracist moral
commitments.

Oliver's views imply endless war, and among smaller and smaller
groups. On radically relativist premises this may be an inevitable (and
perhaps even a welcome) conclusion. The first step toward a deeper refutation is to apply relativism to itself: a sort of argument that unsympathetic
thinkers are likely to regard as fraudulent, though on what grounds I am
not sure. (One commentator dismisses self-referential arguments as "the
sleaziest weapon in the philosopher's arsenal.")[28] Nonetheless, a relativist
is committed to the conclusion that the antirelativist is not wrong, but only
different from himself. At this point, the antirelativist is entitled to affirm
the existence of truth, and indeed of Truth, without troubling himself about
relativistic alternatives.

But *Truth* has an honorific use that is available even to the radical
relativist, for whatever assertions one wants to endorse. (Oliver, for example, writes, "Persons who are not capable of objectivity or are unwilling to
disturb their cortical repose by facing disturbing facts, should never read
pages that cannot but perturb them emotionally.")[29] Even if one has no
criteria of judgment, or these criteria frankly rest on individual or collective
decision alone, one can still speak of one's assertions as "true" (or even
"objectively true"). Sometimes the pragmatic meaning of talk of truth is
something like this: I will not change, however much pressure you may put
on me. To validate talk of truth, of Truth, or even of God, is therefore only
to complete part of the task.[30]

Nor is it sufficient to argue for a privileged epistemological position for
one's community of discourse, whether it be the Church or the scientific
community. Such language can easily serve as a mask for collective egoism.
Our task, which can only be performed in detail, is therefore to connect the
notion of truth to public discourse: the citadel of transcendence cannot be
taken by storm, but the danger remains of its succumbing to siege. Yet if we

do manage to give life and substance to our claims to truth (or to a pursuit of truth not entirely hopeless), then we need not worry further about relativistic claims.

NOTES

1. Michel Foucault, *The Order of Things* (New York: Pantheon, 1970), especially ch. 2.

2. Rush Limbaugh, *See, I Told You So* (New York: Pocket Books, 1993), ch. 3.

3. George Sterner, *Real Presences* (Chicago: University of Chicago Press, 1989), p. 3. This, of course, is not Steiner's point of view.

4. "Rather than forcing all students into the majority culture mold, the educator, with great care and sensitivity, *can help students live in more than one culture.*" Donna M. Gollink, Frank Klassen, and Joost Yff, "Multicultural Education and Ethnic Studies in the United States" (Washington, D.C.: American Association of Colleges for Teacher Education, 1976), p. 13. Quoted in James Davison Hunter, *Before the Shooting Begins* (New Haven, Conn.: Free Press, 1994), p. 202. Emphasis in the original.

5. Hunter, *Before the Shooting Begins*, p. 200.

6. See the passages from Walker Percy and Laurence Tribe, cited in ibid., pp. 6–7.

7. See ibid., especially ch. 9.

8. Consider his citation of T. S. Eliot on the slowness of cultural development. "You must wait for the grass to grow to feed the sheep to give the wool out of which your coat will be made." *Christianity and Culture* (New York: Harcourt Brace Jovanovich, 1977), p. 200, as quoted in Hunter, *Before the Shooting Begins*, p. 20 n. 4

9. Hunter, *Before the Shooting Begins*, pp. 231–234.

10. For the most explicit statement of Hunter's indebtedness to Jefferson, see ibid., p. 245 n. 3.

11. Ibid., p.254 n.54, quoting Seligman, *The Idea of Civil Society* (New York: Free Press, 1992), p. 205.

12. Hunter, *Before the Shooting Begins*, p. 226.

13. Foucault, *The Order of Things*, p. 387.

14. James W. Bernauer, *Michel Foucault's Force of Flight* (Atlantic Highlands, N.J.: Humanities Press International, 1990), secs. 3.1–3.3, and Charles E. Scott, *The Question of Ethics* (Bloomington: Indiana University Press, 1990), ch. 3, sec. 4, reproduce the obscurity of the original.

15. See Foucault, *The Order of Things*, p. 318.

16. See Allesandro Pizzorno, "Foucault and the Liberal View of the Individual," in Timothy J. Armstrong, trans., *Michel Foucault, Philosopher* (New York: Routledge, 1992), pt. 3, ch. 6.

17. Bernauer, *Michel Foucault's Force of Flight*, p. 81.

18. See James Miller, *The Passion of Michel Foucault* (New York: Simon and Schuster, 1993). Foucault's defender Wendy Brown, in her review of this book, *differences* 5 (summer, 1993): 140–149, argues in effect that as a heterosexual Miller could not understand Foucault. (I am indebted to Matt Carlos for this reference.)

19. Michel Foucault, *Power/Knowledge*, Colin Gordon, ed., Colin Gordon et al., trans. (New York: Patheon, 1980), pp. 131, 133.

20. Ibid., p. 52.

21. "There's No Such Thing as Free Speech and It's a Good Thing, Too," in Francis J. Beckwith and Michael E. Bauman, *Are You Politically Correct?* (Buffalo, N.Y.: Prometheus, 1993), pp. 44–45.

22. Quoted in Henry B. Veatch, *Rational Man* (Bloomington: Indiana University Press, 1964), p. 41.

23. Homer, *Odyssey*, Bk. XVII, lines 373–375; Robert Fitzgerald, trans.

24. See Mark W. Roche, "National Socialism and the Disintegration of Values," *Journal of Value Inquiry* 26 (1993), especially pp. 370–373.

25. Revilo T. Oliver, "Postcripts," *Liberty Bell* 18 (July 1991): 31 n.16. I am indebted to Reverend Ronald Tacelli, S.J., for introducing me to Oliver's writings.

26. Ibid., p. 39 n.24.

27. Ibid., p. 27.

28. David L. Hall, *Richard Rorty* (Albany, N.Y.: SUNY Press, 1994), p. 115.

29. Revilo T. Oliver, *America's Decline* (London: Londinum, 1982), p. 4.

30. Philip E. Devine, *Relativism, Nihilism, and God* (Notre Dame, Ind.: University of Notre Dame Press, 1990) is open to objection on this ground.

6

Humanism

Human beings, and more narrowly Americans, are an extraordinarily varied lot, as both our philosophy and our literature inform us. It is also important to understand the differences among various sorts of difference: race is not gender is not sexual orientation is not class position. Yet a keen sense of the many different ways of being human is the best preparation for the recovery of belief in our common humanity.

The word *person* is often used to signal a moral and metaphysical claim, both by those who accept the claim that all human beings are persons[1] and by those who reject it.[2] Nonetheless, the concept of a human being is not quite morally neutral, as a word like *humane* testifies. The concept of a person remains tied to the human paradigm: if we think of God as a person, or even of the three persons of the Trinity, we do so by analogy with human persons.

In this chapter, I use *human being* to refer to all living members of the human species, without thereby intending to beg any moral or metaphysical questions. This seems the most appropriate way of responding, at the conceptual level, to human diversity.

HUMAN DIVERSITY AGAIN

Let us now look more closely at the ways in which human beings differ.

1. Human beings differ in age, from conception or birth[3] to death. Young people see the world in ways different from those of old people or people in middle age.

2. Human beings are male and female, and there are also some anomalies, both physical and psychological.

3. Except for identical twins (or, to be precise, monozygotic multiple births), each one of us has a unique genetic endowment.

4. There are six major "racial" groups in America: white people (European Americans), black people (African Americans), Hispanic Americans, Asian Americans, Polynesians, and American Indians/Native Americans. Each racial group is internally diverse; they seem far more homogeneous to outsiders than to their own members. In any case, racial differences are to a large extent social constructs that imperfectly reflect even bodily traits.

5. There are also a variety of other bodily traits, some of which, such as hairiness (or breast or penis size), are socially sensitive. Some men and women are attractive, and others plain or ugly.[4] Some physical traits are genetic in origin, while others, such as a circumcised penis, pierced ears, and bound feet are socially imposed.

6. Quasiracial ("ethnic") groups such as Jews and WASPs are quite as important as officially racial groups such as black or white people. Matings between men and women of diverse origins—which take place even when the *mores* strenuously discourage them—muddle both our racial and our ethnic categories. Ethnic groups are descent-based, and are distinguished to some degree by both physical appearance and cultural baggage, which accounts in part for the notorious confusion between culture and race. Groups not defined by descent, ranging from deaf people to lesbians, are sometimes treated as if they were ethnic groups, but this usage makes no sense.

7. Moreover, the cultural influences that bear on each of us are not limited to our physical ancestors. When asked, in an early ethnic census (about 1970) to specify the ethnic traditions in which he stood, the author correctly included both Greek and Jewish traditions, although he has, so far as he knows, ancestors of neither sort.

8. Even if linguistic relativism should be in error, our ways of seeing the world and responding to it are influenced by the language we speak. Different humans have different first languages, and different dialects within these languages. The distinction between a dialect and a language is itself largely political.

9. Human beings come from a wide variety of religious backgrounds, including backgrounds in which a religious tradition has been partly suppressed. Some people continue in the religion in which they were brought up, some leave it, and some take up other forms of religion. Both the traditions we assimilate and the ways in which we assimilate them are affected by other sorts of difference such as gender and class position. It is too quick to say that the differences between Evangelicals and Roman Catholics, or between Mormons and relatively conventional Christians, have ceased to be important. But the religious differences most important for contemporary life correspond at best roughly to denominations defined in another cultural epoch.[5]

10. The line between culture and religion, though of importance to missionaries among others, is difficult to draw. Consider, for example, the sense of Jewish-

ness which is a feature of the consciousness of many Jewish people, even those raised in unbelief.

11. What we once believed is as important a fact about us as our present convictions. We make different "gut" moral judgments, which are often more important to us than the beliefs we are able to articulate and defend. Such judgments are never wholly transcended, however much we may reflect on moral and social issues.

12. Human beings are brought up and live in different regions that need not correspond to political boundaries. Some American states—Illinois and New York, for example—do not have a noticeable local culture, but the various states of New England do. Some American regions—most conspicuously the South, but also the Great Plains[6] and New England—have cultural traditions exclusive of outsiders.[7] These regions are neither homogeneous nor able to exclude all "outside" influences, but neither are any of the other cultures studied by anthropologists these days.

13. Some of us are first children, some of us are middle children, some of us youngest children, some of us only children. Some of our parents were divorced, others stayed together with varying degrees of concord. Some of us were conceived or born out of wedlock. Some of us have had abusive parents; others have parents who killed themselves.

14. Each of us has his own limits, not just of approval or tolerance, but of capacity even to understand other men and women's motives, desires, and enjoyments. There is also a variety of prejudices, ranging from those based on skin color to such things as a propensity to dislike Episcopalians or women named "Hilary." We differ not only in our beliefs, but also in the range of positions we are able to take seriously enough to evaluate them.

15. Class position is transmitted from generation to generation in ways that are nonetheless reliable for not being genetic. Class remains important in a society in which everyone pretends to be middle class (though class differences are in fact becoming wider).[8] Some class differences are stark: some people must risk their lives to earn a living, while others need not. Others represent the status seeking that is so much a part of the life of all societies. Claims to superior taste and to more enlightened attitudes are one justification frequently given for privilege. In some circles, it is considered a mark of social superiority to be above the distinction of genders.

16. Men and women suffer from a variety of disabilities, ranging from allergies to incurable life-threatening illnesses. No one is free of physical or psychological limitations. Others are gifted, either physically or mentally.

17. People are more or less averse to risk. Rawls's theory of justice fails in part because, under conditions of ignorance, one has to decide whether to play it safe with his "maximin" strategy or risk extreme poverty for the sake of a chance at big winnings. A decision on this point requires either knowledge of one's personal attitude toward risk or appeal to an ideal of life favorable or hostile to gambling. People are also more or less desirous of placating others, and thus are more or less responsive to the rhetoric of guilt common in contemporary politics. Some people have expensive tastes derived from their

upbringing, which lead them to make larger claims on resources than do those brought up in more modest circumstances. Others may have sensitivities arising from childhood traumas that may have the same effect.

18. *Different* is sometimes a euphemism for *homosexual*. (*Diversity* has the same euphemistic use.) But there are also other men and women with varying erotic inclinations: for example, bisexuals, sadomasochists, and people who prefer children as their sexual partners.

19. I have so far limited myself for the most part to differences which, as far as we can judge such things, are not chosen. But human beings at least appear to have some freedom of choice, and if this appearance is an illusion all proposals to change our ways of thinking (including proposals to adopt determinism) are futile. So we must add to our list of forms of diversity belief-systems and modes of life that have been reflectively adopted.

20. I have also limited myself here to forms of diversity found in the United States: if we take into account the kind of men and women found only outside America—tribal Masai, for example—the prospect of finding common ground among human beings becomes even more daunting. (Or compare traditional Hindu attitudes toward marriage with those that prevail in America or Sweden.) The search for cultural universals is frustrating: while there are plenty of near-universals, for example the social cultivation of virility, the exceptions, however rare, preclude simple biological determinism.[9] Knowing that all societies condemn sexual relations between mother and son (except under circumstances regarded as exceptional) is not very useful in resolving other moral issues.

21. Nor are the forms of diversity that obtain among human beings the only ones possible, as science fiction and fantasy writers constantly remind us. If we had to deal with actual extraterrestrials, the "ape-men" that may be found in many works of science fiction, or the sorts of diversity found in J.R.R. Tolkien's Middle Earth, we would face a forbidding problem in defining principles of justice to govern the resulting relationships.

Some philosophers would extend the moral privileges of humanity to nonhuman animals—what are sometimes called "beasts"—despite their many differences from human beings. It is not sufficient to respond that beasts lack reason and thus cannot claim their rights. For some human beings presently or permanently lack this capacity, and nearly all people believe that at least some such creatures have important rights, for example, the right to live. But the burden is on animal rights advocates to tell us where they would draw the line: to treat sagebrush as if it were human would to be to deprive human status (or it is sometimes called "inherent worth") of its moral weight. The question of animal rights, and the stronger moral claims brought forward by radical environmentalists, are discussed further in Chapter 10.

Some animal rights advocates abandon the case for chickens and pigs, and make a more modest claim on behalf of apes. Indeed, it does seem that chimpanzees and gorillas are owed better treatment than other nonhumans.

But the practical implication of treating apes as human is the acceptance of racism, although not in the form most racists now defend it. For the best position that could be gained for apes is that of beloved inferiors, as in sentimental portrayals of the role of "darkies" in the Old South.

It is a natural contingency that human beings are roughly equal in their natural capacities, just as it is a natural contingency that each of us has a certain array of gifts and limitations. There could be a world in which there was a multitude of more or less intelligent species, relations among which would be governed by principles we can barely imagine. Even believers in an immortal soul, or some other transcendent source of human dignity, cannot escape empirical questions, since it is an empirical question whether the creature before me is a human being with transcendent capacities rather than a beast.

But if there is something about human beings, however limited their capacities, that places limits on what we may do to them, then we need not be so apprehensive about statistics that tend to show that some groups, on the whole and for the most part, have greater capacities than others. There may always be environmental explanations of such phenomena, but our failure to find them will not throw our morality into disrepair. We can, for example, continue to affirm that human beings have a right to be treated as individuals rather than as members of races or other categories.

IMPLICATIONS OF HUMAN DIVERSITY

The fact of human diversity supports a powerful argument against imposing a conception of justice on human beings, without attending to existing practices and the debates they generate. All policies distinguish among those to whom they apply: hiring procedures distinguish between those well qualified for a job and those poorly qualified for it; criminal laws distinguish between men and women disposed to break the law and men and women disposed to keep it. Discrimination is thus not the making of any distinction, but the making of an unfair distinction on the basis of group membership. And the formulaic invocation of concepts modeled on *racism* to resolve complex social problems fails miserably.

Already implicit in the claim that a practice "discriminates" against some group is a background conception of justice, whether philosophical or customary. Defending this conception requires defending at least a rough understanding of human nature, in terms of which it is possible to weigh the case for and against social and legal distinctions. Rawls attempted to avoid this result by means of a veil of ignorance, but (as he subsequently has conceded) without success. In the absence of some shared conception of human nature, and consequently of some shared conception of justice, claims of discrimination are but one more weapon in the struggle among groups jostling for advantage. To avoid this implication, we need to know what purposes are humanly important and what human traits are relevant to such purposes.

Some views of human nature trivialize diversity, while others give it so much weight that war is the only possible relationship among unlike individuals and groups (and indeed among the various tendencies that exist within the same individual). The resulting perplexity haunts feminist thought, which sometimes portrays men and women as "persons," whose sameness has been obscured by a sexist or patriarchal society; and sometimes as so alien that the sex war is a permanent and inescapable reality.

In the first case, the culprit is an assumption that cultural practices are to be understood instrumentally, as outlets for independently specifiable needs (say, for food, for companionship, for sexual gratification, or for self-esteem). Hence the paradigm for appreciating difference is eating at exotic restaurants, and the same approach can be extended to alien sexual or religious practices as well. This approach leaves out the fact that cultures are constituted, at least in part, by differing beliefs, including differing conceptions of the sort of life appropriate for human beings; and that questions of truth and error are therefore involved in cultural encounters.

In the second case, the differences between Americans and Japanese (for example) are thought to be so large that we cannot understand them or they us. Hence attempts at diplomacy are doomed in advance, and conflicts between the two nations can be settled only by force (as has happened once already).

THE HUMANIST PROGRAM

The humanist tradition—whether secular, Christian, or other—invokes our ability to reflect on our beliefs and practices, however well entrenched these may be, and sometimes to modify them as a result of this scrutiny. In this way, it attempts to discover the essential facts about human nature, and at the same time, through dialogue on the basis of our shared humanity, the truth about justice and other crucial issues. Opposed to humanism are a false irenicism, which covers up disagreement with ambiguous formulas, and the sectarian approach, which discounts in advance the perspectives of outsiders.

Another source of humanism is the belief that other human beings, quite apart from the damage they can do us, make moral claims on us. The Jewish philosopher Emmanuel Levinas, writing in response to the Holocaust, puts it this way:

I cannot evade the face of the other, naked and without resources. The nakedness of someone forsaken shows its face in the cracks of the personage, or in his wrinkled skin; his being "without resources" has to be heard like cries not voiced or thematized, already addressed to God.[10]

As this quotation indicates, humanism does not exclude belief in supra-human sources of meaning and value, but insists only that belief in (say) Christ is not a necessary condition for participation in dialogue. I once attended an extremely intelligent student discussion between an atheist and an Evangelical on the relationship between religious belief and claims to knowledge. The atheist concluded that capital punishment was needed to exclude epistemic deviants from society, while the Evangelical found it hard to explain how non-Christians could know anything. Humanism attempts to avoid such conclusions.

Sometimes extreme positions are true, and sometimes common sense is ideologically corrupted. Common sense in Wichita, Kansas, is not the same thing as common sense in Cambridge, Massachusetts. What the humanistic ideal requires is therefore not moderation, but a willingness to examine all positions on the basis of the common humanity of those taking part in the discussion. The marks of the sectarian mind are an affinity for extreme positions and a corresponding disposition to neglect that somewhat amorphous body of habits or thought that one shares with one's opponents, and in which outsiders can find handholds. The sectarian, for example, assimilates all opposition to his views to the most extreme versions of opposing positions, in order to be able to dismiss all alien views together.

We frequently hear complaints that the academy has become excessively political, indeed that "politics has corrupted higher education."[11] Charitably interpreted, this complaint does not mean that academics address political issues, or even that one dislikes the political beliefs of one's colleagues. Instead, it means that politics has invaded fields remote from politics in the conventional sense in a destructive way. Even so, the notion that politics and literature are hermetically sealed against one another will not bear scrutiny. The truth contained in the complaint that the intellectual world has become too political is that issues are framed in terms of us versus them, and that militant groups refuse dialogue with outsiders. Historically, the conservatives have most often answered dissenters with anathemas, but refusal of dialogue is now a hallmark of the cultural Left.[12]

Thus Alison Jaggar calls for "a safe space for in-house discussion among feminists,"[13] in view of the many disagreements among them—in vision as well as in strategy and tactics. A "safe space" in this context means a space from which nonfeminists are excluded and in which it is therefore possible to avoid the most difficult and therefore also the most important questions for contemporary feminism. No doubt, in-house discussion has its place in the intellectual life, but if feminists disagree about as much as Jaggar says they do, perhaps what they need is discussion among human beings, men and women alike, without making ideological commitment a condition of participation. For the many differences among feminists reflect prior differences among women, of conviction as well as of temperament and social position. The humanity that women share with men is sometimes at least a sounder basis for discussion than the supposed common interests (or shared ideological commitments) of women as a class. To the extent that feminists following Nietzsche have become mistresses of suspicion, they have no justification for excluding suspicion of the sources of their position, say, as arising from a desire to lord it over both men and less sapient women.

Some pro-choice people have adopted a strategy of refusing to discuss the issue. It was liberal Democrats, so-called, who refused to let Governor Casey of Pennsylvania speak at the Democratic National Convention and disrupted a debate on the topic "Can a liberal be pro-life?" with chants of "Racist, sexist, antigay, Governor Casey go away."[14] In such a climate, vigilante justice against abortionists and the personnel of abortion clinics, however deplorable, is hardly surprising.

Nihilists also exclude themselves from dialogue. They are prepared to criticize other people's positions, but refuse to reflectively admit any premise, from which either a response to their criticisms or a modified position could be generated. Rather they are prepared, at any moment, to abort discussion by proclaiming the hollowness of the entire enterprise.

But self-exclusion of the kind just examined does not exhaust the obstacles to appeals to our common humanity. It is absurd to talk about how Latin Americans think, or how all women think, or how members of any other group think. It is, therefore, even more absurd (or so it seems) to talk about how all human beings think. If this argument is an example of the fallacy of composition, we need to know exactly why the class of all human beings is different from the class of women or Latin Americans.

Yet the consequences of this contention need to be faced openly. If there is no common humanity to which we can appeal in our arguments, or if this common humanity does not include a capacity to step back from appetite and social pressure, there is no reason to suppose that dialogue will produce agreement. Rather, there is considerable reason to suppose that, as the issues become clear, so disagreement among human beings will widen, and discourse will be more and more a matter of choosing sides and pressuring others to follow one's example. In other words, party (or tribal) conflict will reach all the way down.

Sartre and his followers, who deny the existence of human nature on *a priori* grounds, contradict themselves. For they are making a claim about human nature, that it is radically free in ways that exclude (other) claims about human nature. Thus we find, among Sartre's followers, flat-footed arguments such as: "There cannot be such a thing as a paradigm human being. The attempts to subordinate human reality to some necessary pattern, biologically, theologically, or morally prestructured, *fly in the face of facts.*"[15] If these facts are facts of human nature (and what other sort of facts might they be?), this argument undermines itself.

Yet a self-referential argument of the kind just given is unsatisfying because it tells us nothing about the nature of human beings, if indeed *nature* is the word of choice. If we are totally agnostic about the content of human nature, we might as well do without the notion altogether.

The existence of a common human nature is thus a moral (and political) postulate first and a theoretical insight only later. The utility of affirming our common humanity is evident, at least to those who wish to avoid the fate of Yugoslavia. For we now live in a society in which every form of human oddity is publicized. One strand of modern thought reads "postulate" as "pious lie," and either endorses that lie or attempts to destroy it as the writer's political perspective might dictate. For example, a cultural conservative might argue that sexual normality is a fiction, but one that is necessary to make sense of what otherwise would be the chaos of human sexuality—and especially so for young men and women facing a confusing world. If we are prepared to accept the postulate of a common human nature as a working hypothesis, the theoretical question is at least not hopeless. For the effect of the postulate is to shift the burden of proof, at a point at which considerations of burden of proof are all-important. Even among people whom one is disposed to find very strange, the bonds of common humanity may appear upon careful examination.

In our attempt to discover our common humanity, we need to avoid treating our own peculiarities as definitive of human nature, a failing to which the privileged are perhaps peculiarly subject. (Outsiders have other characteristic failings—for example, overvaluing worldly success.) But the attempt to take into account the perspectives of the marginalized runs into serious difficulties. If we attempt to include all the marginalized, from sadomasochists to displaced royalty, then nothing coherent will emerge. If we examine only the perspectives of those people whose exclusion we regard as unjust, then we have made no significant step toward escaping the limitations of our perspective. The same is true, even more emphatically, if we look to those of the excluded with whom we hope to form a political alliance.

Many attempts to invoke the marginalized fall afoul of these considerations. Richard Rorty, for example, calls for the study of works outside the canon, on the ground that "they help students learn what it has been like (and often still is like) to be female, or black, or gay."[16] But he shows no interest in helping students learn, say from Flannery O'Connor, what it is like to be an impoverished Southern white person. What most of us do is to take into account whatever perspectives may commend themselves to us by a mixture of sympathy and practical necessity—a perfectly acceptable procedure, but not one that promises radical insights.

TOWARD HUMAN NATURE

In a recent attempt to place limits on possible moral positions, John Kekes distinguishes between primary values, whose satisfaction is required for any reasonable conception of the good life, and secondary values, which are in some sense optional.[17] Primary values are, in his view, grounded in facts of three sorts.

First, there are facts of the self: "Our physiology imposes requirements on all of us: we need to eat, drink, and breathe in order to survive, and we need protection from the elements" (p. 39). Moreover,

we all know the difference between a state of nature characterized by doing what is necessary for survival and a civilized state where we have leisure, choices, and the security to go beyond necessity. And we all prefer the civilized state to the primitive one. (pp. 39–40)

Second, there are facts of intimacy:

We are born into small human groups, and depend on them for the first few years of our lives. We live in a network with our parents, our guardians, other children, and later with our sexual partners, and we extend our relationships when we enter the larger community of which the small one is a part. (p. 40)

Third, there are facts of the social order: "human vulnerability, scarce resources, and limited strength, intelligence, and skill force cooperation on us (p. 40), requiring forms of association beyond the intimacies just mentioned.

Religion is a secondary value in Kekes's account. Contrasting the nutritional meaning of bread with its religious significance, he writes,

Nutrition is a primary value, while religion is secondary. For nutrition is, and religion is not, among the minimum requirements of all conceptions of a good life. ... For if the claims of nutrition were not generally satisfied, there would be no one left to fast. (p. 50)

Against Plato and Rousseau, Kekes takes as unproblematic a preference for a civilized life over that of the noble savage. Against St. Thomas Aquinas, he omits reproduction from his list of basic human needs—though, to paraphrase Kekes's own argument, if men and women ceased to reproduce, there would soon be no one left to be childless. Against the partisans of sex without love, he regards sex as a need of intimacy rather than, say, a physiologically grounded craving, despite his use of the language of sexual partnership in preference to that of love. Similarly, he fails to examine the importance of sexual difference for our understanding of human nature. He ignores the fact that religious people make truth-claims: on theistic premises, if there were no God there would be neither bread nor human beings to eat it. If Buddhism is true, then our desire for bread has a very different position from what it has on Christian or naturalistic premises.

Moreover, his account of human nature sidelines the very reflective inquiry in which he is engaged. Human beings are at least creatures who can ask questions about their own nature. Even Heidegger is prepared to say, "This entity which each of us is himself *and which includes inquiring as one of the possibility of his Being,* we shall denote by the term 'Dasein,' "[18] although he would resist carrying this premise in the traditional Socratic direction. To ask about one's nature or condition is to have the capacity to reason in at least one (and very arguably the most important) sense of the term.

THE PROJECT CONTINUED

Whatever else human beings may be, they are rational beings. We have the capacity to reflect on our beliefs and practices, and sometimes to modify them as a result of scrutiny. Hence dialogue on the basis of our shared humanity is a more appropriate way of settling differences than the use of force. But athough human beings are rational, they are also aggressive and given to making alliances with like-minded men and women against common enemies. The advantages of rational discussion require no argument, but in particular cases discussion may involve concessions that members of some embattled group have strong reasons not to make.

To be rational is also to be free, in the sense of having the capacity to set aside biological and social influences, and to act instead for reasons. We need not address the issue here, whether this capacity is compatible with causal determination. But the attempt to deny our capacity for free choice is self-destructive, since it both invokes and asks us to set aside the way we spontaneously think about ourselves, and to adopt instead a view of ourselves alleged to be rationally superior.[19]

But we are not merely free and rational beings. We frame our questions, including the question of our own nature, in some language. Language requires organs of speech or writing—in other words a body. And particular languages are spoken among some men and women, and at some times and places, and not others. Hence, too, our nature is in part animal, social, and historical.

The "naked ape" view of human nature depends on the question-begging assumption that biology (and especially evolutionary biology) provides a sufficient source of data for understanding us.[20] But that is no ground for denying our partial kinship with nonhumans. The emotional side of our nature bridges the animal and the distinctively human: a cat can experience simple emotions such as fear but not more sophisticated emotions such as nostalgia.

There might be angels who examine the nature of angels using angelic language, but any man or woman who denies human animality will quickly be refuted by experience. Thus the etherealizing tendency of much contemporary bioethics, which among other things defines a privileged class of "persons" possessing rights denied mere human beings, rests on nothing more than the shared intuitions of its proponents—intuitions out of keeping with the moral responses of much of the rest of humanity.[21]

Our nature is also social and historical. We learn to be human within a particular society, with a particular heritage of shared understandings and conflicts. If by virtue of our reason we also participate in a transcendent order, this participation needs to be set alongside the animal, social, and historical aspects of our nature.

Our disputes about human nature have to do not with our character as rational, social, and historical animals, but with the relative importance of these aspects of our nature, and the precise relationship among them. Disputes about sexual ethics turn on our understanding of the relative roles of pleasure, procreation, personal union, and difference of gender in our sexual life, but that sex has these four aspects (and many others as well) has not, so far as I know, been seriously questioned. We may also add agreement on the fact that sexual emotion can cloud the mind, illustrating some tension between the animal and rational aspects of our nature.

Again, we are a two-sexed species whose two halves must somehow learn to live with one another. Those, on the one hand, who attempt to reduce sexual difference to the moral status of eye color and those, on the other hand, for whom war is the only possible relationship between the sexes, adopt positions contrary to the possibility of human social life. But there is a great deal of space between these positions.[22]

As social beings, we have, and sometimes follow, moral codes. Any account of moral judgment must include both rational and emotional elements. Moral beliefs could not motivate if they did not involve emotion, whereas gut responses without any underlying rationale do not even rise to the level of moral error. One cannot, however, use this fact to dismiss the moral convictions of people who are not philosophically trained, and for that reason are inarticulate about the grounds of their moral judgments.[23] (We can usually find an articulate spokesman for such people if we look hard enough.)

The sometimes bitter disputes about the relative roles of culture and biology in forming the human personality are difficult to understand, for these elements in our nature cannot be kept apart. We cannot observe an acultural human being, or a culture floating free of the human organisms that participate in it. Our cultural environment—for example, our clothing and our buildings—is adapted to our biology, whereas social practice affects mating and hence also the biology of future generations.

Much of the culture versus biology debate assumes that culture can be changed, perhaps even with relative ease, whereas biology is immutable. But neither of these propositions is true. Those who would bring about change in a culture, whether politicians or educators, themselves participate in it (or in some alien, say, imperial, culture, that limits them in its own ways). Xenophobia may have cultural rather than biological roots, but there is little evidence that it can be eradicated. In contrast, modifications of the human organism are the routine business of the medical profession, athletic trainers, and those who perform ritual practices such as circumcision. We may contrast those changes that are transmitted through the gene pool, because they arise from mutation and selection, whether natural or artificial; and those that are not so transmitted. But both biological and cultural transmission affect the kind of people we are, and both are afflicted with considerable uncertainty.

CONCLUSION

That we are all rational, social, and historical animals, and share moreover the particular biological features of the human species, at least provides a basis for conversation concerning justice, morality, and the good life. The conversation about the nature of humanity, the good life for human beings, and the institutions that contribute to it is not merely a philosophical but a political process. The need for participation by all varieties of human beings favors democracy.

In Hilary Putnam's words here (he follows Dewey),

the need for such fundamental democratic institutions as freedom of thought and speech follows . . . from requirements of scientific procedure in general; the unimpeded flow of information and the freedom to offer and criticize hypotheses.[24]

In particular, we should not rely on the allegedly privileged opinions of experts—whether philosopher-kings, priests, or social scientists—in disregard of the perceptions of the ordinary man or woman. Even the answer to the question, whether priests are speaking for God, are entitled to have their words accepted on His authority, or are merely responding to some secular or clericalist ideology, must rest with the common sense of ordinary folk— what Roman Catholics call the *sensus fidelium*. Scientists, too, though they claim a special understanding of nature, must in the end vindicate that understanding in terms of the perceptions of ordinary observers.

In Dewey's words,

All special privilege narrows the outlook of those who possess it, as well as limits the development of those not having it. A very considerable portion of what is regarded as the inherent selfishness of mankind is the product of an inequitable distribution of power—inequitable because it shuts out some of the conditions which direct and evoke their capacities, while it produces a one-sided growth in those who have privilege.[25]

This strand of Dewey's thought is in considerable tension with another strand that is particularly conspicuous among his contemporary followers:

the use of professional authority to impose a Deweyistic faith upon the multitude.

In furthering the needed conversation, lessons can also be drawn from history as well as from philosophy. Some experiments in individual or collective living prove disasters—and not just by my personal code or some preferred moral theory. It is attractive to speak here of constraints imposed by human nature (and by the larger world of which human nature is a part). Still, apart from divine revelation, the sustainability of a set of institutions can be resolved only by awaiting events. It is not just fools who need to learn in the hard school of experience. Thus Putnam gets the essential issues right when he states,

The notion that our words and life are constrained by a reality not of our own invention plays a deep role in our lives, and is to be respected. . . . [To understand it, we should look] at the ways in which we endlessly renegotiate—and are *forced* to renegotiate—our notion of reality as our language and our life develops.[26]

But five linked issues remain, even if we find the arguments so far persuasive. First, living with other human beings (and ourselves) does place limits on the theoretical and practical positions available for adoption, however difficult it may be to explain how. But we need to say something further about the reality check that human nature imposes on our propensity to metaphysical-epistemological-linguistic fantasy.

Second, we must ask whether (and if so how) all human beings—despite the many things that divide us and the unadmirable character of many of us—can continue to affirm one another's dignity in both theory and practice, however severe may be the conflicts our diversity engenders. Dewey's philosophy is of little help here, since on his premises, both civil libertarian protections and moral rules such as that against murder have only a provisional validity. Putnam writes that "the constitutional protections on the unlimited exercise of majority power, such as the Bill of Rights, are not a limitation of 'democracy' in Dewey's sense, but a protection of it."[27] But it is hard to see how much staying power these protections can have in Dewey's perspective, when they come into conflict with ideological imperatives perceived as "progressive." The pragmatic value of a nonpragmatic attitude toward some of our commitments has enormous practical and theoretical importance.

Third, epistemological democracy has an implication that secular intellectuals have generally failed to absorb. In the contemporary world, ordinary folk are more religious in outlook (and more conservative in culture) than are elites. Democracy is culturally conservative in more than a merely statistical sense: it relies crucially on the shared, often poorly articulated understandings of ordinary men and women to make political deliberation possible. There are, to be sure, powerful objections to settling cultural issues by popular vote. (As George Steiner puts it: "Given a free vote, the bulk of humankind will choose football, the soap opera, or bingo over Aeschylus.")[28] Nonetheless, the greatest literature—be it the Bible, the Dialogues of Plato, or the plays of Shakespeare—has considerable popular appeal, and we may hope to broaden the tastes of our students at least by education. There is, however, no excuse for argument from social to intellectual superiority, frequently masked by an egalitarian rhetoric, common in the academic world.

Fourth, what are we to say about those religiously based conceptions of human nature, widely held in our society, which some writers would bar from the forum of "public reason"? Is it legitimate to dismiss creation science, as secularly minded intellectuals are wont to do, despite its popularity among the population at large?[29] (I address this issue in Chapter 9.)

Fifth, is it correct to focus on human beings for the purposes of resolving the problem of diversity? In more technical language, are all and only human beings persons, or is the class whose interests and perspectives need to be taken into account in reasoning about justice and the good life larger or smaller than the human species (or both at once)? The abortion and animal rights issues are not merely politically difficult: they also have immense theoretical importance.

NOTES

1. Thus Karol Wojtyla (later John Paul II) writes: "The assertion that the human being is a person has profound theoretical significance. . . . It marks out the position proper to the human being in the world; it speaks of the human being's natural greatness." See *Person and Community*, Theresa Sandok, O.S.M., trans., (New York: Peter Lang, 1993), p. 178.

2. Mary Anne Warren advocates birth as a dividing line between persons and nonpersons, on the explicitly political ground that "There is only room for one person with full and equal rights within a single skin." See "The Moral Significance of Birth," in Louis Pojman and Francis J. Beckwith, eds., *The Abortion Controversy* (Boston: Jones and Bartlett, 1994), p. 441.

3. Those who believe that all human beings are persons discover ambiguities during the first fourteen days after fertilization. For a discussion of the status of the "pre-embryo," see Norman M. Ford, S.D.B., *When Did I Begin?* (Cambridge, Mass.: Cambridge University Press, 1988). For a critique of Ford's argument, see Germain Grisez, "When Do People Begin?" in *Abortion: A New Generation of Catholic Responses*, Stephen J. Heaney, ed. (Braintree, Mass.: The Pope John Center, 1992), ch. 1, pp. 15–19. But an unfavorable judgment on the personal status of the pre-embryo would not resolve all moral questions. After fourteen days, questions must be directed to the species principle itself rather than to its application.

4. Aristophanes anticipates contemporary political correctness, not only by repudiating "looksism," but proposing—humorously, of course—a program of affirmative action, in which the unattractive are guaranteed preferential sexual privileges. See the discussion of his *Ecclesiazusae* in Arlene W. Saxonhouse, *Fear of Diversity* (Chicago: University of Chicago Press, 1992), especially pp. 15–19.

5. Robert Wuthnow, *The Restructuring of American Religion* (Princeton, N.J.: Princeton University Press, 1988), explains how this change happened.

6. For an expression of Great Plains regionalism, see Anthony Herrigan, "A Moral Redoubt in the Heartland," *Touchstone* 7, 2 (spring 1994): 23–25.

7. George Kennan has suggested that the United States be divided into twelve relatively autonomous republics: New England, the Middle Atlantic States, the Middle West, the Northwest, the Southwest (including Southern California and Hawaii), Texas, the Old South, Florida plus Puerto Rico, Alaska, New York, Chicago, and Los Angeles. See *Around the Cragged Hill* (New York: Norton, 1993), pp. 149–151. Alan Buchanan discusses the normative questions in his *Secession* (Boulder, Colo.: Westview, 1991), but his criterion of "discriminatory redistribution" is too friendly to secessionists.

8. Paul Fussell, *Class* (New York: Dorset, 1983), is an indepensable though somewhat dated, portrayal of class relations.

9. See David D. Gilmore, *Manhood in the Making* (New Haven, Conn.: Yale University Press, 1990).

10. *The Levinas Reader*, Seán Hand, ed. (Oxford: Basil Blackwell, 1989), p. 181.

11. Subtitle of Roger Kimball, *Tenured Radicals* (New York: Harper and Row, 1990).

12. With the happy exception of Gerald Graff, *Beyond the Culture Wars* (New York: Norton, 1992).

13. "Introduction" to Jaggar's anthology *Living with Contradictions* (Boulder, Colo.: Westview, 1994), p. 2.

14. Quoted in John Leo, *Two Steps Ahead of the Thought Police* (New York: Simon and Schuster, 1994), p. 272.

15. Konstantin Kolenda, *Rorty's Humanistic Pragmatism* (Tampa, Fla.: University of South Florida Press, 1990), p. 15; emphasis added.

16. Richard Rorty, "Two Cheers for the Cultural Left," in Darryl J. Gless and Barbara Herrnstein Smith eds., *The Politics of Liberal Education* (Durham, N.C.: Duke University Press, 1992), p. 239.

17. John Kekes, *The Morality of Pluralism* (Princeton, N.J.: Princeton University Press, 1993), especially ch. 3. Parenthetical references in this section are to this book.

18. Martin Heidegger, *Being and Time*, John Macquarrie and Edward Robinson, trans. (New York: Harper and Row, 1962), p. 27 (H 7). Emphasis mine.

19. Here I follow Joseph Boyle, Germain Grisez, and Olaf Tollefsen, *Free Choice* (Notre Dame, Ind.: University of Notre Dame Press, 1976).

20. See Chapter 9.

21. For a forceful critique along these lines, see Jenny Teichman, "The False Philosophy of Peter Singer," *New Criterion* (April 1993): 25–30.

22. For further discussion, see my anthology with Celia Wolf-Devine, *Sex and Gender* (Boston: Jones and Bartlett, forthcoming).

23. Despite Ronald Dworkin, *Taking Rights Seriously* (Cambridge, Mass.: Harvard University Press, 1977), ch. 10, where he argues that objections to homosexual practices and pornography do not rise to the dignity of moral error.

24. Hilary Putnam, *Renewing Philosophy* (Cambridge, Mass.: Harvard University Press, 1992), p. 188.

25. John Dewey and James H. Tufts, *Ethics*, rev. ed. (New York: Henry Holt, 1932), pp. 185–186, quoted in Putnam, *Renewing Philosophy*, p. 189.

26. Hilary Putnam, "Sense, Nonsense, and the Senses," *Journal of Philosophy* 91, 9 (September 1994): 462.

27. Putnam, *Renewing Philosophy*, p. 225 n.23.

28. George Steiner, *Real Presences* (Chicago: University of Chicago Press, 1989), p. 67.

29. Ronald L. Numbers reports: "According to a 1991 Gallup poll, 47 percent, including a fourth of the college graduates, continued to believe that 'God created man pretty much in his present form at one time during the last 10,000 years.' " See *The Creationists* (Berkeley: University of California Press, 1993), p. ix.

PART III

IMPLICATIONS

The temples of the idols in [England] ought not to be broken; but the idols alone which be in them. . . . For if such temples be well built, it is needful that they be altered from the service of devils to the true God.

Bede

7

The Epistemic Superiority of the Oppressed

Some broader theoretical questions still need to be addressed before we move to questions of practice. One of these is whether a country like the United States can discover, or create for itself, a common identity sufficient to make possible reasoned discourse about difficult moral and political issues. The most important impact of the cultural Left is to throw this question into doubt, replacing *E pluribus unum* by *Ex uno plures* as our national motto. Multiculturalists regard this fragmentation as in some sense progressive.

One theme in the rhetoric of the cultural Left, noticeable especially in their critique of humanism, is the superiority of the oppressed, not only in morals, but also in ability to understand social facts (for example, the nature of the family, or what exactly happened during the sixties). Standard epistemology, such people maintain, is that of the privileged; oppressed people have different and better ways of knowing. (This contention is not the same as the claim that the test of the justice of our institutions is their effect on the most vulnerable members of our society. This maxim does not endorse their interpretation of their condition or otherwise suppose that different sorts of people have different ways of knowing.) One version of the supposedly superior epistemic standpoint of the oppressed is presented in feminist epistemology, an intellectual and cultural program controversial among both feminists and philosophers.[1]

Oppression is a contested concept with a strong normative component. Some people believe that welfare mothers exploit hard-working taxpayers to support an irresponsible mode of life, and are for that reason oppressors.

Smokers these days could easily be regarded as an oppressed group, since they (or their characteristic forms of activity) are excluded from many public places. Overt racists—no doubt rightly—are also systematically disparaged in contemporary America. In general, whether social deviants form an oppressed group depends on one's evaluation of the laws and customs that condemn their behavior. Our response to such claims will depend in part on our interpretation of the social facts into which the oppressed are thought to have a special insight.

In order to get a grip on the question of epistemic privilege, it is best to begin with arguments that do not put normative questions in the forefront of discussion. Moreover, more than mere oppression is required to generate a claim of privilege. Those who never had a chance in life—crack babies, for example—gain no wisdom thereby.

One concept sometimes invoked by the multicultural-feminist alliance is that of *invisibility*; they propose to make the invisible visible and in that way correct the distortions of the understanding of the Establishment. The invisible are presumed to be the best judges of their own situation and the change in our beliefs and practices that their problems require. But the least visible people—the institutionalized mentally ill or retarded—also have the least to say about social facts, except as they palpably affect their situation.

The most striking contemporary example of making the invisible visible is the exhibition of whole and aborted fetuses by the pro-life movement—a display that does not blend with the multiculturalist program (though it might harmonize with another sort of movement for social justice).[2] The same is true of the concept of being *silenced*: persons whose perceptions are unacceptable to feminist "orthodoxy," such as women who regret having had abortions,[3] need to break silence and have their voice heard. (Feminists have perfected the art of making an objector feel as if he has been guilty of an impropriety.) Taking such issues seriously is in any case lethal to the orthodox feminist ideology: ponder, in the light of the abortion issue, the following sentence from the reputed Bible of PC: "Racism and sexism are both comprehensive systems of oppression that deny individuals their personhood."[4]

Moreover, whether the criterion of oppression is lack of visibility/audibility, lack of wealth, lack of power, or lack of prestige, what Michael Harrington has called the "have-not, have-little" problem remains. Neither Rawls's division of society into the best-off and the worst-off, nor the Manichaean distinction between the powerful and the powerless favored by those who consider themselves more radical than Rawls, is convincing. What may appear to middle-class people, including middle-class radicals, as an abyss is in fact a highly structured world, in which child abusers rank below embezzlers and in which the police have both a protected and a stigmatized role. The inversion of such socially established hierarchies produces a bizarre world in which the greatest weight is given the perceptions of black paraplegic lesbians with AIDS (or whoever else wins the oppression sweepstakes).

According to Terri Elliot, the epistemic privileges of the oppressed arise from their perception of the recalcitrance of social reality—in Heidegger's jargon, they perceive social reality as present-at-hand.[5] In her words,

Oppressed people discover the unusability of aspects of the social order which appear to them as merely present-at-hand. They (we) see ways in which society is in need of repair; that is, we see manifestations of the oppression. For the most part the experiences that "throw a sudden floodlight on the ways we have been living, the forces that control our lives, the hypocrisies that have allowed us to collaborate with these forces, the harsh but liberating facts we have been enjoined from recognizing" are experiences [like that of a broken rather than a functioning bicycle].[6]

No doubt the first step toward recognizing the need for change is an experience of something wrong: witness the conservative maxim, "If it ain't wrong, don't fix it." There is, in fact, much wrong with the world. But to take the experience of wrongness as somehow privileged is massively to beg the question. For it is to condemn the status quo, not as unjust or otherwise bad, but just for existing, and thus to make social justice impossible by definition. Whatever the state of society, some people will persistently complain.

A social philosophy for which our options are being reliable or broken-down equipment has some disturbing implications. The resulting politics of sheer obstructiveness and of oppressed people turning oppressors as soon as they get the chance is undesirable by any standard.

Elliot remarks in a footnote:

In twentieth-century American patriarchy, women become wives, secretaries, nurses, prostitutes, that-which-puts-dinner-on-the-table-and-puts-the-kids-to-bed. Women become merely ready-to-hand to men, that is, we are perceived as having the being of equipment rather than the being of *Dasein*. Feminists, though, appear on the scene as problematic, throwing a wrench in the works. . . . feminists are merely present at hand for patriarchs. This signals feminists as *unusable*; this signals the break-down of patriarchy.[7]

On Elliot's showing this means that patriarchs, even apart from any further injury victorious feminists may do them, have become an oppressed group and for that reason epistemically privileged. A male who is punished or humiliated for borderline rape or sexual harassment, or who is denied career advancement by an affirmative action program, will have his epistemic privilege correspondingly enhanced.

The class of those who find social reality recalcitrant is not an intellectually or politically useful category of human being. For it is thoughtless to regard the experience of the recalcitrance of human life as somehow the preserve of oppressed groups. Both rich people unable to find adequate servants and servants who must deal with the irrational whims of their employers experience, in their own ways, the recalcitrance of social reality. There may be people who live in social wombs, protected against every frustration (though I very much doubt it), but they are more likely to be the petted favorites of the rich and powerful than the rich and powerful themselves.

What the epistemic privilege of the oppressed means, in its most defensible form, is that social outsiders see things that insiders do not. But being an outsider is not the same thing as being oppressed. A rich Jew in England between the wars, though privileged in many ways, was nonetheless an outsider. An unbelieving sociologist observing a fundamentalist service will enjoy many privileges his subjects will lack. A mammy in the Old South, while oppressed, was nonetheless well integrated into the institutions and practices of her society. And women as such, however oppressed feminists may think them, are not as such outsiders, though women who have rejected (or are unable to perform) the traditional roles of wife and mother may qualify as such. Outsiders are not limited to those on the official lists: "liberated" women, members of racial minorities, working-class people, the "physically challenged," male and female homosexuals, and so forth. Wallflowers—or what are now called the "socially challenged"—are outsiders for very different reasons. There are yet other kinds of outsiders, ranging from "rednecks" to Cambridge liberals, whose experience of the social world is sharply different from that of mainstream America (assuming for the moment that there is such a thing as mainstream America). Perhaps some white male Episcopalians are perfectly integrated into their society, though I very much doubt it.

The existence of many different outsiders will blunt the political lessons that the party of diversity may want to draw from outsiders' perspectives: a well-qualified white, male college professor who has spent twenty years in effectively terminal positions is unlikely to take seriously the pieties of the academic community, especially when they are invoked to support the affirmative action programs that are in part responsible for his situation. We are all of us both outsiders and insiders; a complete social outsider, say a feral child, would be incapable of insight into society.

What outsiders see, and insiders cannot, is the pointlessness of certain social customs—except as ways of keeping them outsiders. Excluding outsiders has two aspects: it deprives them of wealth and power, and it maintains hierarchies of esteem in which, for example, monogamy is more highly valued than promiscuity (and consequently monogamous people more esteemed than promiscuous ones).

Nonetheless, insiders are able to see, and outsiders cannot, the point of social customs: for example, the aesthetic and intellectual value of works that outsiders, until they become insiders in part, will dismiss as the work of dead white males. One important step in the liberation of oppressed groups has been their learning to use elements in their oppressors' culture, both to argue for their own freedom and to guide their actions in the struggle for emancipation and afterward. To prefer the knowledge of outsiders to that of insiders is to beg important questions in the direction of nihilism.

Once we embrace nihilism, we have no reason to accept the epistemic privilege of the oppressed or of anyone else. Perhaps the strongest source of support in the larger society for the ideas discussed in this chapter is Jewish and Christian: the stone that builders rejected has become the cornerstone. But total rejection of inherited ideas means the rejection of this idea as well.[8] In short, unless we have reason to suppose that all our social practices are mere masks for the will to power, we have no reason to privilege the perspectives of outsiders and dismiss those of insiders.

In its Hegelian-Marxist form, the principle of the epistemic superiority of the oppressed means that those engaged with material reality are in a better position to know the world than those who deal professionally with symbols or live lives of protected leisure. While the master lies around enjoying life, the slave, by struggling with recalcitrant material things, gains a knowledge, and even a power, his master lacks. It is true that engagement with the material world in all its recalcitrance does supply a reality check that is much lacking in contemporary theorizing. But too much immersion in practical tasks can also be debilitating, since it interferes with the imagination required to envisage new possibilities for thought and life. Hence the Hegelian-Marxist argument begs the metaphysical question in favor of materialism. Moreover, to the extent that the Hegelian-Marxist argument retains its persuasive force despite such considerations, it implies—contrary to the political intentions of the contemporary proponents of the idea of the epistemic virtue of the oppressed—that white, male plumbers and construction workers who are the sole support of their families are better able to understand society than are childless academic women.[9]

We need to evaluate each of our social norms, and the ideas that support it, on its own merits. And each of us, in our attempt to understand the social world, must take into account as many different perspectives as possible, and submit our results to those whose range of imaginative sympathy is different from our own. But it does not follow that just any fringe view (for example, denial of the Holocaust) has anything whatever to say for it.[10]

Similarly, if we are concerned about evaluating some controversial decision, such as the atom bombing of Hiroshima and Nagasaki, we ought to attempt to see how the decision looked both to the Japanese and to people of color who were not directly involved in the quarrel between the United States and Japan. But we ought also to enter imaginatively into Truman's situation and into that of his constituents.

Our task is to find a way of defining a community which, though inevitably excluding some people to some degree, will leave out as few people as possible and enable those at the center to treat the marginalized humanely. Only God can combine all perspectives in a coherent vision. Any religious tradition that claims to speak for God must establish its credibility by speaking to all sorts and conditions of people.

NOTES

1. For the controversy within both groups, see Susan Haack, advisory ed., "Feminist Epistemology: For and Against," *Monist* 77, 4 (October, 1994). Harriet Baber compares feminist philosophy with home economics, which secured jobs for academic women in a way that undermined the feminist program. See "The Market for Feminist Epistemology," ibid., especially pp. 419–420.

2. Barbara Duden, *Disembodying Women*, Lee Homacki trans. (Cambridge, Mass.: Harvard University Press, 1993) protests the emergence of the "public fetus" (ch. 7) and the "skinning" of women (pp. 7, 14, 26, 78) it implies.

3. See David C. Reardon, *Aborted Women: Silent No More* (Chicago: Loyola University Press, 1987), especially the Foreword by Nancyjo Mann.

4. Paula S. Rothenberg, *Racism and Sexism: An Integrated Study* (New York: St. Martin's Press, 1988), p. 1.

5. Terri Elliot, "Making Strange What Had Appeared Familiar," *Monist* 77, 4 (October, 1994): 424–433.

6. Ibid., p. 431. The quotation is from Adrienne Rich, *Of Lies, Secrets, and Silence* (New York: Norton, 1979), p. 215.

7. Elliot, "Making Strange," p. 413 n.21.

8. On "TOTALREJ" and its implications for feminism, see Daphne Patai and Noretta Kortege, *Professing Feminism* (New York: Basic Books, 1994), pp. 115–120.

9. See Christopher Lasch, *The Revolt of the Elites* (New York: Norton, 1995), for the practical and theoretical implications of this line of thought.

10. See Nadine Fresco, "The Denial of the Deed," Audri Durchslag, trans., *Dissent* 28 (1981): 467–483. Fresco makes no pretense of being above the battle, but her article contains sufficient quotations from Faurisson and his followers to enable one to reach a judgment.

8

Defining Our National Identity

Christopher Lasch has acutely questioned the assumption, shared by conservatives and radicals alike, that "academic radicalism is genuinely 'subversive.'"[1] The cultural Left has massively ignored important political issues, even when they directly affect higher education. It ignores the rising tuition costs that make higher education the privilege of the very few, to whom are added a limited number of colorful "minorities" to provide a semblance of diversity. Yet cultural issues are important in the world outside the academy, where they interact in complex ways with struggles over resources. No account of cultural diversity can ignore questions of wealth and power.

In America, diversity issues often take a racial form. African Americans, Asian Americans, European Americans, and Hispanic Americans all, it seems, dislike one another and are prepared to assert their identity at one another's expense. Other cultural groups, for example, homosexuals, are also demanding a place at the table. Moreover, each of these groups is internally diverse, and subject to internal conflict about both cultural issues and questions of material advantage. An "orthodox" feminism centered on the advancement of upscale women claims to speak for all women, but in fact neglects the material and moral interests of working mothers.[2]

When we think of human diversity, we should think not only of black people and male and female homosexuals, but also of Mormons, Jehovah's Witnesses, and followers of the Lubavticher rebbe. Next to differences of wealth and power, the form of diversity that is the most serious source of conflict is difference of outlook.

The resulting issues are muddled by the peculiar ways Americans use the word *minority*.[3] We confuse statistical questions with moral-political claims. Worse yet, we combine an ideology that legitimates the claims made by groups as groups, as long as they manage to get themselves recognized as oppressed, with deeper assumptions that imply that such groups should cease to exist—which sanction what militant representatives of these groups are likely to regard as a form of bloodless genocide. These conflicts are reproduced within each minority group: their members experience both an impulse to assimilate to the larger society, and an impulse to affirm those respects in which the minority differs from the majority (or appears to do so). Nor do representatives of minority groups necessarily accept their official designations. Richard Rodriguez says bluntly: " 'Hispanic' is not a racial or a cultural or a geographic or an economic description. 'Hispanic' is a bureaucratic integer—a complete political fiction."[4]

The possible (and actual) forms of intergroup conflict on diversitarian premises are staggering. Issues such as the school curriculum, the status of Tito as a public icon, and the willingness of the intelligentsia to accept nationalist ideologies, played important roles in the breakup of Yugoslavia.[5] All of these issues have parallels on the contemporary American scene.

Diversity, though currently celebrated on the Left, is a traditional conservative idea, usually opposed to equality.[6] On thoroughly diversitarian premises, there can be no question of equality among communities. A government having the power to redistribute wealth and power among them will end up invading their space in countless ways. Even the formal equality implicit in, for example, a scheme of proportional representation will survive only as long as no other stable way of apportioning power among communities emerges. There will be as much or as little equality within these communities as their governing principles allow. The result of proceeding in this way ranges from political quietism to fascism, depending on how bellicose a disposition informs our reasoning and how difficult we conceive the task of establishing order to be.

Any attempt to resolve the problem of human diversity in liberal terms will encounter a deadly ambiguity in the idea of self-determination of peoples. It is systematically unclear what entities count as "a people," entitled to determine its own destiny. (Need the people of Ireland include the inhabitants of the whole island of Ireland?) Some libertarians, for example, Thoreau, have resolved this problem by moving from group secession to individual secession, and have claimed the right to exist as "independents," ignoring the state within whose territory they live.[7]

The alternative to destructive diversity is the attempt to recover a common culture, at least within an existing nation-state. The building of a world civilization, however vital a project, will prove futile if its component national units dissolve into chaos. The attempt to cover up discord by imposing a code of gentility, or a conception of public reason manufactured in Cambridge, leads only to distortion and displacement—with results that are sometimes very ugly. Like every attempt to solve problems by repression, such efforts are fundamentally flawed.

In a postmodern cultural context, there is no obstacle in principle to the recovery of a common culture, although there are many obstacles to it in practice. For the remark "You just can't *do* such a thing" will be without force. Yet common early childhood experience, external threats, common religious heritage, and charismatic leadership are on any premises more important influences in cultural formation than is philosophy. Here I attempt the little a philosopher can be expected to do.

I understand Sheldon Hackney of the National Endowment for the Humanities (NEH) to be asking, not what *conclusions* Americans should reach about English-only legislation or other such issues, but what *premises* we can take for granted when we discuss them.[8] Once a fundamental consensus is established, it will be possible to discuss questions of relative detail, however painful. But without it we are doomed to progressively more intense and bitter controversy. For human beings are quite capable of stopping an argument at the first sentence, if is likely to support a threatening conclusion. And procedures are not sufficient to the needs of public discourse: those who are injured or offended by the results produced will act on the maxim, *If you're losing the game, change the rules.*

One ground for hope is that our very diversity will prevent the formation of a majority large and determined enough to repress minorities effectively. Another is a political tradition, widely admired outside the United States as well as within it, that begins with a ringing affirmation of the claims of our common humanity. "We hold these truths to be self-evident," the Declaration of Independence proclaims, "that all men are created equal; that they are endowed by their Creator with certain unalienable rights, that among these rights are life, liberty, and the pursuit of happiness."

The Declaration is as politically incorrect a document as one could hope to find. Radical relativists find Jefferson's reference to self-evident truths hopelessly outmoded; feminists are offended by his use of the generic *men*. Anti-egalitarians dislike his appeal to equality, and secularists are offended by his reference to a Creator God. Neo-Manichaeans, militant atheists, and legal positivists reject his earlier reference to "the laws of nature and nature's God." Some bioethicists reject a document that places the right to life over the right to die or even the right to choose. The New Right is offended by his lack of any specifically Christian (or even Judeo-Christian) references, and radical ecologists are offended by his "speciesist" limitation of rights to human beings. By "speciesism" is meant an irrational preference for one's own species, as racism is an irrational preference for one's own race. Yet it is difficult to see what other basis for national identity there might be.

Insisting on its specifically Protestant communalism of early America[9] would lose the allegiance of Roman Catholics and Jews, not to mention Hindus and Muslims—though many black people and women (and remarkably many Asian Americans and Hispanic Americans) might find such a result acceptable. And few people would want to revive the intrusive scrutiny that characterized social life in older communal societies.[10] Even Alasdair MacIntyre now "strongly" dissociates himself from the communitarian movement inspired in part by his writings, on the ground that communitarians "advance their proposals as contributions to the politics of the nation state."[11] But without common creed we are doomed to endless fragmentation. MacIntyre's repudiation of communitarianism makes it difficult to see how his philosophy could be socially embodied (as on his own showing it must be). A more modest civic republicanism is perhaps the best we can do.

In short, the Declaration remains, so far as ideas are concerned, our best bulwark against the fate of Yugoslavia and Rwanda. If we cannot find or create a consensus in support of a document of our nation's founding, other formulations are likely to prove even more divisive. The tradition that takes the Declaration as a central document sustains practices, such as resistance to injustice, and virtues, such as tolerance and respect for other persons. It enables us to place our actions within a narrative that began before we were born, and, we may hope, will continue after we leave the scene. The rich, concrete commitments involved in full-blooded communalism will find their place within families, churches, and informal social groups, which our polity should nurture indirectly but not attempt to create.

Along with many other writers,[12] I have been calling for a renewal of the idea of civil society—a relationship of mutual trust among human beings, prior to either law or private agreement. The philosophical underpinnings of the idea of civil society, as developed in the eighteenth century, cannot now be revived without change. The expectation that the interests and ideals of the members of society can be satisfied, at least enough to make it possible for society to continue to function without massive repression, is itself a matter of faith and hope.

In a postmodern intellectual climate, however, the claim that an idea is outmoded is very thin. Even what sophisticates consider the Declaration's quaintest feature—its appeal to a Creator God—is in fact essential to it. For it gives our human status a root outside our passions and wills, immune both to the self-hatred of some intellectuals and to the passions of neo-tribalist ideologues.

Believers in a transcendent God are better off than secularists when they undertake to criticize the status quo. For if one believes that human society is entirely a human creation, then there is no appeal possible to God or History or Nature to rectify the institutions of society when one finds them oppressive. As Foucault in effect argues, might does not merely make right;

it *is* right. Might here includes not only the army and the police, but also public opinion, childhood influences, the marketplace, and even the sentiments the weak are sometimes able to elicit in the strong. One of V. S. Naipaul's characters puts the result well: "The world is what it is; men who are nothing, or who allow themselves to become nothing, have no place in it."[13]

As Adam Seligman points out, in an informative though skeptical discussion of the concept of civil society, the pro-life movement is the most robust example of a call for the recovery of this ideal.[14] The pro-life movement, among the movements that compete for our allegiance, makes the most powerful appeal to the tradition of the Declaration of Independence, while at the same time getting most of its support from Catholics and Evangelical Protestants. The most disturbing implication of contemporary debates about abortion is that who counts as a "man" (in the preferred language of bioethicists, a "person") is not only a philosophical issue, but also one open to political manipulation (see Chapter 10). This is true long after the Thirteenth, Fourteenth, Fifteenth, and Nineteenth Amendments were thought to remove any ambiguity about the scope of the American community.

Nonetheless, the postulate of God-given rights has great appeal in American society and can claim universal relevance. And it is, so far as I can see, the only way of harmonizing the liberal conception of individual rights with the need to maintain a community capable of securing those rights. We need a vision of social life that combines an appeal to abstract right and a conception of a society protective of those unable to defend themselves in the world of politics and the market.

We need not, however, strictly require belief in God in the usual sense as a condition for taking part in the dialogue about American national identity. Whether agnostic Kantianism makes sense is an important question but is not one to be pursued here. What we need is shared belief in a nonempirical root of human dignity. It is natural to call such a root "God," but the matter of God's further attributes—whether, for example, "He" is in any sense personal—is one for debate within our national consensus rather than an article of national faith.

Nonetheless, the overwhelming majority of Americans believe in God "or a universal spirit." Sustaining this belief in the lives of Americans will require a richer context of faith, but on detailed issues of religious belief and practice we cannot expect a national consensus. Believers of a more full-blooded sort will rightly protest any attempt to reduce their faith to an instrument of national solidarity. I shall return to these issues, as well as to the secularism that would dispute my entire project, in the last two chapters.

NOTES

1. Christopher Lasch, *The Revolt of the Elites* (New York: Norton, 1995), p. 192. See the whole of his ch. 10.

2. Elizabeth Fox-Genovese made this point forcefully in a lecture at Providence College on March 23, 1995.

3. The American concept of a minority is adroitly deconstructed by Philip Gleason, "Minorities (Almost) All," *American Quarterly* 43, 3 (September 1991): 392–494.

4. Richard Rodriguez, *Days of Obligation* (New York: Viking, 1992), p. 69.

5. Mihailo Crnobrnja, *The Yugoslav Drama* (Montreal: McGill-Queens, 1994), pp. 108–109 (curriculum), p. 109 (Tito), and pp. 115–118 (intelligentsia).

6. See, for example, George F. Kennan, *Around the Cragged Hill* (New York: Norton, 1993), ch. 6. Jean Betke Elshtain elaborates this point in *Democracy on Trial* (New York: Basic Books, 1995), pp. 68–77.

7. I owe this point to Alan Buchanan, *Secession* (Boulder, Colo.: Westview, 1991), especially p. 13.

8. Sheldon Hackney "Toward a National Conversation," *Responsive Community* 4, 3 (summer 1994): 4–10.

9. See Barry Allan Shain, *The Myth of American Individualism* (Princeton, N.J.: Princeton University Press, 1994).

10. But see Susan Schechter: "in a socialist feminist world . . . family life would be open to community scrutiny, because the family would be part of and accountable to the community." *Women and Male Violence* (Boston: South End Press, 1982), p. 239.

11. Alasdair MacIntyre, "A Partial Response to My Critics," in John Horton and Susan Mendus, eds., *After MacIntyre* (Notre Dame, Ind.: University of Notre Dame Press, 1994), p. 302.

12. For example, Elshtain.

13. V. S. Naipaul, *A Bend in the River* (New York: Knopf, 1979), p. 3.

14. Adam B. Seligman, *The Idea of Civil Society* (New York: Free Press, 1992). Seligman's discussion of the pro-life movement is on pp. 135–136.

9

Creation and Evolution

Despite the bad reputation of the legal profession, law remains king in America. A highly diverse society relies on the laws (and especially the Constitution) to maintain a working sense of the dignity and inviolability of each individual. And a persistent element in contemporary debates is the fear that naturalistic theories of the human person will erode our belief that we have a dignity greater than that of other natural objects. Thus the endurance of the creation versus evolution debate is due less to the arguments of creationists, or to the continued influence of the book of Genesis, than to the reading of the evidence provided by Phillip E. Johnson of the University of California, Berkeley, Law School.[1]

Though not in the usual sense a man of the Left, Johnson uses the rhetoric of the avowedly Leftist critical legal studies movement[2] to challenge the biological establishment and to discredit its claims to a monopoly of public reason. We shall also discover important analogues between his position and that of the feminist theorists of knowledge discussed in Chapter 7. Creation scientists and religious groups such as Seventh Day Adventists that support them, are cognitively marginalized in our society if anyone is. Anyone who takes human diversity seriously must include such groups.

Creation scientists and their supporters raise the same issue that other marginal people do—to what extent we take seriously slogans about the fundamental equality and inherent dignity of all people, and to what extent biological Darwinism and social Darwinism are covert allies. Erosion of the moral boundary between man and beast, as proposed on evolutionary grounds by Peter Singer, is a particular threat to those human beings whose

lack of education and social graces lead their "betters" to understand them
as nearer the border than themselves. When Darwinism stops being a
narrowly scientific theory, and—as happened virtually at once—is turned
into a new paradigm for understanding human beings and their societies,
the specter of social Darwinism (including the collectivistic version called
"fascism") is difficult to dispel.

Thus Johnson combines a suspicion of elites with a penchant for understanding what appear to be intellectual questions, even questions of scientific fact, as questions of power. In his own words, "the 'fact of evolution'
is an instrument of cultural domination and it is only to be expected that
people who are being consigned to the dustbin of history should make some
protest."[3]

THE ARGUMENTS

The term *Darwinism* is unfortunate, though hard to avoid, since it con-
flates questions of scientific theory with questions of religion and metaphysics or even party allegiance. I will use the expression *Darwinian
evolution* to refer to the process of biological development described by
Darwin and his followers, while leaving open the question of design,
providential guidance, or occasional miraculous intervention.

For present purposes there are three possible positions. *Creationists* hold
that God created the various species of life, in such a way that the explanations offered by Darwin and his followers are impossible or illegitimate.
This group now includes highly intelligent people with good scientific
credentials:[4] they cannot be dismissed as Yahoos, even if we do not accept
all their arguments. (That they include few biologists may testify only to
the efficiency of the biological establishment in maintaining orthodoxy
within the profession.)

Naturalistic Darwinians, in contrast, accept evolutionary explanations
and understand them to exclude belief in a Creator God, or at least one Who
takes an active part in the affairs of His world. In its most sophisticated
form, it holds not that evolutionary biology directly entails the falsity of
theism, but that it has created an atmosphere in which religion is a quaint
anachronism, one in which—if religion is to be allowed to survive—it must
accept naturalistic direction concerning its doctrines and practices.[5] Believers are likely to find this superciliousness more offensive than straightfor-
ward unbelief. In any event, the advocacy of such views by prominent
persons makes it clear that, even if creationists are in error, their concerns
cannot be dismissed as unreal.

Theistic evolutionists hold that God created the world and takes an active
part in its affairs, but that Darwin's theory or something like it is still true
of those events that do not represent God's (presumably rare) direct interventions in the cosmos. Theistic evolutionism is a species of compatiblism:

other examples are soft determinism, the attempt to combine pro-life morality with pro-choice politics, and belief in merely procedural affirmative action. Whether such attempts to harmonize discordant forms of discourse are tenable must be decided case by case, but a certain kind of mind dismisses them without consideration. In their eagerness to fight one another, neither creationists[6] nor naturalistic Darwinians take theistic evolutionism seriously. Nonetheless, some defenders of evolutionary theory make a careful attempt to show that the theory of evolution need undermine neither religion nor morality.[7]

I here defend the coherence and pragmatic value of theistic evolutionism, though I do not present any direct argument for either theism or (broadly Darwinian) evolution. I distinguish between evolution as a scientific theory, however well established, and evolutionism as a religion or ideology. Underlying this distinction is the deeper distinction between methodological and metaphysical naturalism. (Briefly put, methodological naturalism holds that scientists should investigate only natural relationships among natural events, whereas metaphysical naturalism maintains that natural events are the only events there are.) My thesis is not centrally a scientific one, though I will have to examine scientific issues in the course of my argument. I am concerned, rather, to maintain theistic evolutionism as a genuine alternative in debates about science education and the public role of religion. (I assume that if the philosophical case can be made the interpretation of Genesis will present no further difficulty.)

Fallacious reasoning on both sides of the issue obscures the logical situation. Much of the debate consists in the attempt by creationists and naturalistic Darwinians to gerrymander theistic evolutionists into their respective camps. Thus naturalistic evolutionists equivocate shamelessly about the logical status of evolutionary doctrines. Michael Ruse, for example, speaks of Darwinian evolution both as a "fact, *fact*, FACT!" and as a "strong ideology," and "one to be proud of."[8]

Similarly, Johnson writes:

The most visible creationists are the Biblical literalists who believe in a young earth and a creationist in six, twenty-four hour days; Darwinists like to give the impression that opposition to what they call "evolution" is confined to this group. In a broader sense, however, a creationist is any person who believes that there is a Creator who brought about the existence of humans for a purpose.[9]

More disturbingly, Johnson dismisses theistic evolutionism as "an appealing rationalization if you want to be an orthodox member of two communities, one committed to a naturalistic understanding of reality and one committed to theism."[10] We may agree that creationists need not believe in a young earth and that theistic evolutionists cannot accept that evolution is a *complete* explanation of the human and other life. But the suggestion that theistic evolutionists are intellectual quislings has much rhetorical but little intellectual force.

Johnson is able to distinguish metaphysical and methodological naturalism, and hence also metaphysical creationism and creation science, when it suits his purposes.[11] But he persists in asking: "Is there any reason that a person who believes in a real, personal God should believe Darwinist claims that evolution occurred through a *fully* naturalistic evolutionary process?"[12] The answer is No, but not the No that Johnson wants.

Theists hold that nature observes its accustomed courses only because it is sustained in them by God's creative activity. But theistic scientists need not advance theological explanations when professionally engaged in evolutionary biology or other forms of scientific investigation. There are good *theological* reasons to be reluctant to let belief in God "enter into the very fabric and practice of science and the utilization of scientific methodology," as J. P. Moreland phrases the issue.[13] We cannot expect the kind of knowledge of God's purposes that a merger of natural theology and natural science would require. The effects of God's activity may be observable, even in the fossil record, but that they result from God's special intervention is not a scientific hypothesis. To treat this claim as a matter of observation or experiment is to put God to the test, in a way both the Jewish and the Christian traditions forbid.

Johnson, moreover, argues that "because Darwinism has its roots in metaphysical naturalism, it is not consistent to accept Darwinism and give it a theistic interpretation."[14] But that P is held along with Q, or even inferred from (or implied by) Q, does not imply that, if Q is false, P is either false or insufficiently established. (If Q implies P and P is false, then Q is false, but in terms of our present discussion this means at most that to refute Darwinism is to refute metaphysical naturalism, not that to refute metaphysical naturalism is to refute Darwinism.) If we reject metaphysical naturalism, we might have to reexamine the grounds on which we hold Darwinism, but these may turn out to be adequate independently of metaphysical naturalism. In American law, even perjury requires only a new trial, not outright acquittal of the defendant.

Johnson further complains that "theistic evolutionists [get vague when they] try to explain exactly what God had to do with evolution."[15] But believers cannot, on any account, explain God's way of working within the world with any sort of precision. Whatever its inadequacies, we cannot expect a radical improvement on the old-fashioned formula: that the human body arose naturally but that God created our souls specially. But we cannot expect to understand exactly how this happened either.

Yet these simple logical moves are not sufficient to refute the claim that Darwinism depends for its credibility on a naturalistic world-picture. One way of bridging the gap between evolutionary biology and such a total world-picture is to question the positivistic framework within which this distinction is often advanced. First, the logical independence of metaphysical propositions and historical claims concerning human prehistory is not sufficient, since there are relationships of evidentiary support weaker than entailment. A rich description of a massacre, for example, will carry with it a strong evaluative charge, even if we can discover no logical entailment between "fact" and "value." Pictures of human nature have a similar sort of evaluative impact: if Darwinian evolution implied that there was no qualitative difference between human beings and other animals (the so-called naked ape view), then (unwelcome) moral and political results would no doubt follow. But, in fact, many naturalistic evolutionists disavow any such reductive conception of human nature. Even those philosophers and biologists who do accept it can hardly claim that it has the hard-core factuality claimed for evolution. For biology is not our only source of data about human nature.

Second, some writers attempt to bridge the gap between methodological and metaphysical naturalism by way of the concepts of "scientific methodology" or "attitude." Ruse defines these as follows:

Commitment to the idea that the world is law-bound—that is, subject to unbroken regularity—and to the belief that there are no powers, seen or unseen, that interfere with or otherwise make inexplicable the normal workings of material objects.[16]

Ruse compares this methodology or attitude to one's political beliefs or to a preference for baseball over cricket[17] (comparisons that do not prevent him from using public education to impose it on the children of objecting parents). Nonetheless, he suggested that anyone who undertakes to engage in scientific inquiry must accept such an attitude.

William A. Dembski makes a similar argument from a creationist point of view.

Once one realizes that natural selection is precisely the vehicle needed to transform a theory of evolution into a *fully naturalistic* theory of evolution, the implication follows at once. Darwinism does implicate naturalism. The less God has to do, the more reason there is to adopt naturalism.[18]

He also argues that naturalism implicates Darwinism.

As Al Plantinga has put it, if you accept naturalism, Darwinism is the only game in town. . . . Naturalism manages to keep Darwinism afloat. Indeed, Darwinism needs more than scientific facts to keep it afloat.[19]

Both of these arguments—that Darwinism supports naturalism and that naturalism supports Darwinism—suppose that divine and natural causality are logically and metaphysically rivals, so that the more we have of nature, the less we can have of God.[20] The picture of a "God of the gaps," destined perpetually to retreat before the advance of science, is deeply ingrained in the rhetoric of both creationists and naturalistic Darwinians.

But theists believe that nature is orderly because God so created it. They also believe that as finite creatures, our capacity to know God's purposes is very limited. Hence theism authorizes scientific inquiry, while counseling modesty about the larger implications of our more extravagant hypotheses (and a willingness to revise them in the face of unfriendly experience). The order discovered by scientists can be understood as testimony to the Creator, as received by our limited human intelligences. Many scientists from Copernicus to the present day have in fact so understood them. Even miracles do not undermine the possibility of combining theism with science, as long as they do not happen so frequently as to interfere with the ordinary course of scientific investigation. St. Augustine, for one, would have found the post-Enlightenment debates concerning divine and natural causality unintelligible.

Third, there is no such thing as a brute scientific fact, wholly independent of the theoretical and evaluative framework (or, as it is now called, "the paradigm") in which it is placed. And who gets to establish the burden of proof is of great importance in cultural conflicts, including those over science education. Most, though not all, evolutionary biologists hold that nature does not make leaps, to which creationists add, "but God does." Thus both creationists and naturalistic Darwinians will argue that our *a priori* principles make a difference in the way we conduct scientific investigation, and hence also that it is appropriate to ask us to choose between their rival perspectives.

But the existence of an *a priori* element in science does not mean that we are free to defend any fantasy we please or which we can get other people to accept by coercion or propaganda. Nor are we forced, either while doing science or attempting science education, to view the natural world through the lens of either Biblical fundamentalism or dogmatic naturalism rather than through that of theistic evolutionism. Theistic evolutionists can propose their own version of the ground rules for cultural life: they need not (and should not) insist that God's existence be postulated as part of any scientific theory, but only that we make (a relative at least) distinction between religion and science that makes room for their position.

QUESTIONS OF DEMARCATION

Yet the creation–evolution debate continues to provoke deep worries. Contemporary philosophers of science have questioned the project of drawing a line of demarcation between science and nonscience (including religion), which underlies the conventional theistic evolutionary position.[21] To be sure, there are clear cases: Mendelian genetics is a scientific theory, and the doctrine of the Real Presence is a theological dogma. But outside such clear cases, demarcation is a matter of social convention—broadly speaking a political issue. Moreover, the legally and constitutionally important concept is not *science* but *religion*. (As Ruse frankly puts it, "The Constitution does not forbid the teaching of bad science.")[22] Hence a line of demarcation between science and religion had to be devised, however weak its intellectual credentials, so that creation science would turn out to be a form of religion. And a demarcation line created for such purposes seems highly questionable.

What most biologists believe, I suspect, is that creation science is such bad science as not to count as science at all. (Similarly, we might argue that Hitler's "law" retroactively authorizing the Night of the Long Knives was so unjust as not to count even as bad law.) But that does not mean that creation science is religion, either. The prominence of militant atheists within the biological profession might lead believers to treat their judgments of what is acceptable science with suspicion.

But we are entitled to resist the identification of politics with warfare that arguments along these lines suggest. That the line between religion and science is in large measure a matter of social convention does not mean that we can do without such conventions. Nor does it mean that we should reframe our conventions so as to force a choice between creationism and naturalistic Darwinism. We can still defend theistic evolutionism as not merely politic but reasonable—unless either theism or evolution is discredited on grounds other than its supposed conflict with the other. In accordance with this proposal, we can limit the scope of science to the natural properties of natural entities without prejudice to the claims of religious teachings to tell us about other sorts of realities.

One reason for taking this position is a desire to avoid sectarian science. Defenders of theistic science do not advocate Christian science (if only to avoid confusion with the views of Mary Baker Eddy). But they do hold that "Christians ought to use all that they know or have reason to believe in forming and testing hypotheses, explaining things in science and evaluating the plausibility of various scientific hypotheses."[23] It is hard to see how sectarian science—even science conducted in accordance with the canons of the synod of Dort—can be avoided on such premises.

There are, after all, clear cases for the natural–supernatural dichotomy. The existence and activity of a Creator God is supernatural if anything is. Thus the statement that God created all things, however true, does not amount to a *scientific* theory. Nor do the rhetorical invocations of Evolution, which begin to replace appeals to God in the nineteenth century, count as scientific explanations either.

Moreland, in his defense of "theistic science," invokes theological principles chiefly to solve conceptual rather than empirical problems.[24] He thus redraws the line between science and philosophy in the direction of the "natural philosophy" of Newton and Descartes, half-admitting that he does so in an effort to capture the cultural prestige of science for theological and philosophical arguments.[25] (One of his collaborators, Stephen C. Meyer, frankly acknowledges that "the question of whether a theory is scientific is really a red herring.")[26] It seems better to admit that we are dealing here with philosophy of a highly traditional kind, and to insist on its intellectual legitimacy, than to smuggle such considerations into a heavily empirical science such as biology.

Truth, to be sure, is more important than demarcation. But it remains useful to distinguish science from nonscience (among other things, to make clear what the standards for evaluating a theory are). Conventional science is oriented toward prediction and control, as opposed to (say) reverent appreciation; this fact about it means that not everyone will be prepared to endorse its methods.[27] But only those who are prepared to accept the large costs of holding that the prediction and control of natural processes are never legitimate can reject science as a whole for this reason. The rest of us can use science for prediction and control and invoke art, poetry, and devotional religion to express other attitudes. Metaphysics and dogmatic theology occupy a middle place on this continuum, and the rules of reasoning in these disciplines need to be articulated accordingly.

Here I am not arguing that "origins theories must be strictly materialistic,"[28] as Meyer phrases the issue. But, *insofar* as we address the origins of human and other life in natural-scientific terms, we should limit ourselves to naturalistic explanations, while honestly admitting those points at which these explanations appear to fail. At this point the philosopher and theologian will have their say.

DISTINCTIVELY THEISTIC CONCERNS

I have so far refuted the view of the Presbyterian theologian Charles Hodge (shared by naturalistic Darwinians) that Darwinism means atheism. But I have left open the possibility that Darwinism implies either deism or pantheism—both of which, like naturalism, deny the possibility of divine interventions in the course of history or prehistory. But theistic evolutionists also believe that God providentially guided the evolutionary process, so that, among other things, human beings would arise on the scene in the fullness of time.

Evolutionary biology does not exclude this position. For it is a historical discipline: it tells us not about regular processes such as the movement of the planets around the sun, but about how things happened a long time ago.[29] And it is not possible for historical explanation to be so logically tight as to exclude the discovery of new causal factors, say the influence of lead poisoning on the aristocracy of imperial Rome. Even agency from outside the historical process likewise cannot be excluded. Whether divine intervention in prehistory is a matter for scientific investigation is a separate issue; even human action belongs to the sphere of such investigation only insofar as human beings act predictably.

Evolutionary biology is incomplete in yet another way. Natural selection, rather than produce evolutionary change, only culls novelties incapable of surviving to reproduce. The mutations that fuel the evolutionary process, and especially those that are viable (let alone adaptive), are unpredictable and inexplicable at least in practice. Jacques Monod expresses Darwinian orthodoxy on this question when he writes, "chance alone is at the source of every innovation, or all creation in the biosphere. Pure chance, absolutely free but blind, is at the root of the stupendous edifice of evolution."[30]

The widely admired evolutionary writer Richard Dawkins denies that chance is the crucial actor in evolutionary development. For him, it is natural selection—what he paradoxically calls the "blind watchmaker"—that explains the appearance of design in living things. As we are told, it does so rather as a sufficiently large number of monkeys, given sufficient time, could produce the complete works of Shakespeare.[31] But the monkeys do not produce either the English language or the criteria by which we distinguish poetry from noise: similarly, the evolutionary process presupposes, and therefore does not explain, the transmission of genetic information from generation to generation. For that matter, we could not be said to have explained the works of Shakespeare if we said they were produced by the random behavior of a troop of monkeys. (Nor does it explain a puzzling event to say that it happened very gradually.)

Chance is not an explanation, but an admission that the event in question is unexplained (or even inexplicable), at least within our chosen framework. It may mean that, although each of two events is adequately explained, there is no further explanation of their conjunction—say, that Shakespeare and Cervantes died on the same day.[32] But a stronger sense of *chance* is now available: strict determinism no longer holds sway even in physics, so that there are now no scientific grounds for asserting that the natural world *must* be deterministic, even when appearances suggest otherwise. Even those philosophers and scientists who remain determinists can hardly hold their view on biological grounds alone.

In short, the theory of evolution does not provide, or even seriously promise, the sort of total explanation that would exclude a guiding role for divine Providence. As Gould has eloquently emphasized, the evolutionary path that led to the human species is beset with many contingent happenings.[33] God may have specially intervened to secure some of these, though which we could hardly ascertain on biological grounds alone.

Moreover, Ruse is prepared to admit that an adherent of the scientific world-view can believe in transubstantiation.[34] Even if a new species were to materialize out of thin air, this fact would not be discernible in the fossil record. A (more plausible) miraculous mutation at the outset of the human species would, like transubstantiaton, involve a conceptual or metaphysical transformation rather than an event within the empirical order, even if it should also have observable empirical effects, such as the solemn disposal of the dead.

None of this suggests that the sequence of observable events should not be exactly as Darwinists suppose or that it is possible to maintain the occurrence of prehistoric miracles on biological grounds alone. I am arguing only that Darwinian theories are incomplete and that theists are entitled to point out their incompleteness. How many miracles one should believe in, and of what sort, is a theological question, although there is an ill-defined point beyond which frequent miracles undermine the possibility of scientific investigation.

BROADER CONSIDERATIONS

The conflict between religion and science is not the result of narrow-minded religious people interfering with the work of dedicated scientists. On the contrary, scientists have as often as not been the aggressors (and this has been the case almost from the beginning). Dawkins, for example, writes: "Our own existence once presented the greatest of all mysteries, but . . . it is a mystery no longer because it is solved. Darwin and Wallace solved it."[35]

We have reasons for regretting, from a *scientific* point of view, the biologists' habit of using their science to attack Christianity (and sometimes also to support substitute religions). The resulting confrontations with traditional believers place enormous pressure on biologists to follow the party line, to the detriment of their ability to propose new hypotheses that may be in tension with it.[36]

Biological imperialism distorts the philosophy of science as well as the practice of biology. Larry Laudan's comment on the most recent "Monkey Trial" litigation is devastating: "The pro-science forces defend[ed] a philosophy of science which is, in its way, every bit as outmoded as the 'science' of the creationists."[37]

Moreover, biological imperialists cover up the anomalies that all scientific theories face, and by grappling with these anomalies, the scientific enterprise progresses.[38] In the case of evolution, these center on the existence of isolated and well-defined biological taxa, and the scarcity of plausible intermediate forms—facts that are difficult to explain by extrapolating empirically established microevolutionary processes.[39] In Gould's words, "The extreme rarity of transitional forms in the fossil record persists as the trade secret of paleontology."[40]

The most severe of these problems is that of the origin of language, which marks the difference between human and nonhuman. We do not carry our language in our genes, and it makes no sense to argue (as Darwin supposed) that the inventor of language went on to teach his invention to prelinguistic creatures.[41] Just outside the domain of Darwinian evolution lies the question of the origin of life, which has led one prominent scientist to observe that "[it] seems to be almost a miracle, so many are the conditions which would have to be satisfied to get it going."[42] Also outside Darwinism is the question of mechanism versus teleology in biology. Contrary to popular belief, Darwinism does not support the mechanistic position on this issue: it presupposes, and for that reason does not explain, the existence of determinate self-sustaining entities called "organisms" and the transmission of biological traits from parents to offspring.

At least until someone develops a better scientific theory to account for the observed facts, biologists are bound to use the best theory available.[43] But they should not use a theory accepted on such grounds as an instrument of antireligious polemic. We ought neither to block the path of scientific inquiry nor to make the demands for total scientific explanation that naturalistic advocacy requires.

That questions of human origins have from the outset been entangled with political and religious issues should surprise no one; one way we define who we are is by telling the story of how we came to be. Thus Gould writes of the fossils discovered in the Burgess Shale: "We greet them with awe because they are the Old Ones and they are trying to tell us something."[44] Hence differences of religious belief, metaphysical commitment, and political opinion will continue to influence the interpretation of ambiguous data. Yet it seems well to support a form of inquiry that attempts to minimize the effect of such broader disputes on the resolution on the professional discussions of scientists.

With regard to issues of educational policy, Johnson's concern about the arrogance of Darwinian scientists remains serious—though the exasperating character of their opponents makes this arrogance at least understandable. There is no reason why naturalistic Darwinians should be permitted to use public school classrooms to preach their creed, while invoking the law of church and state to deny the adherents of other faiths the same privilege. But it is surely possible to give students the best science available, without sanctioning scientific triumphalism. In Irving Kristol's words, "our goal should be to have biology and evolution taught in a way that points to what we don't know as well as what we know."[45] We know, for example, that evolution at least sometimes occurs and, consequently, that some species are descended from others. We do not, however, have a complete story of the origin of the species and the descent of man. Nor can we prove, on scientific grounds, that God did not intervene in this process, either providentially or miraculously.

A policy of intellectual modesty will make it easier to resist the erosion of belief in human dignity which many people on both sides of the debate have believed evolution to imply. It also will mean that vague appeals to the "atmosphere" created by Darwin, in which religion must either negotiate an unfavorable peace or be squeezed out of human society, will have considerably less plausibility. In short, traditional forms of religion, and their associated moral codes, remain as possible approaches to the question of human diversity, for anything the Darwinist might say.

In conclusion, I should specify clearly and exactly what I am arguing in this chapter. I have defended neither theism nor evolutionary theory: both seem to me altogether defensible, but the argument would take me too far afield. I have been arguing a compatibilist thesis and maintaining further that this form of compatibilism has desirable scientific and social implications (and at least should be recognized as an intellectually respectable position in debates about science education and the public role of religion).

Theistic evolutionism is scientifically desirable because it enforces a policy of intellectual modesty and willingness to revise existing paradigms, both of which are in tension with attempts to use Darwinism to undermine our cultural, moral, and religious traditions. It is also socially desirable inasmuch as the erosion of the sense of human worth, implicated by rejection of these traditions on Darwinist grounds, can lead only to disaster. Finally, my thesis entails the hope of peace on at least one front in the culture wars, which is not to say that universal peace is so easily obtained.

NOTES

1. See Johnson's *Darwin on Trial* (Washington, D.C.: Regnery Gateway, 1991).

2. On which see Roberto Mangabeira Unger, *The Critical Legal Studies Movement* (Cambridge, Mass.: Harvard University Press, 1986).

3. Phillip E. Johnson et al., *Evolution as Dogma* (Dallas, Tex.: Haughton Publishing, 1990), p. 13. (This pamphlet was originally published in *First Things*, October and November 1990.) But see p. 17, where he speaks the traditional language of truth.

4. For a high-quality collection of creationist writings, see J. P. Moreland, ed., *The Creation Hypothesis* (Downers Grove, Ill.: Intervarsity, 1994). The authors hold Ph.D.s from Cambridge, the University of Chicago, Harvard, the University of Texas at Austin, and the University of Toronto.

5. See Daniel C. Dennett, *Darwin's Dangerous Idea* (New York: Simon and Schuster, 1995), pp. 411–420.

6. See Moreland, ed., *The Creation Hypothesis*, Introduction, pp. 13–14 (pleading lack of space to discuss theistic evolutionism).

7. See Philip Kitcher, *Abusing Science* (Cambridge, Mass.: MIT Press, 1982), ch. 7 (with Patricia Kitcher).

8. Michael Ruse, *Darwinism Defended* (London: Addison-Wesley, 1982), pp. 58, 280.

9. Phillip E. Johnson, "Darwinism's Rules of Reasoning," in Jon Buell and Virginia Hearn, eds., *Darwinism: Science or Philosophy?* (Richardson, Tex.: Foundation for Thought and Ethics, 1994). (This book represents the proceedings of an academic conference on Johnson's claims, held at Southern Methodist University in March 1992.) Cf. Johnson's "Darwinism and Theism," ibid., p. 42.

10. Phillip E. Johnson, "Two Views: Science and the Christian Faith," *Touchstone* 8, 1 (winter 1995): 7. Worse yet: "Well-meaning theistic evolutionists end up running interference for the metaphysical naturalists when they try to reassure the Christians that the rulers of science don't really mean what they say" (ibid.).

11. Johnson writes: "The problem with scientific naturalism as a worldview is that it takes a sound methodological premise of natural science and transforms it into a dogmatic statement about the nature of the universe." *Evolution as Dogma*, p. 14.

12. "Introduction" to *Darwinism: Science or Philosophy?*, p. 2. "Darwinism and Theism," ibid., p. 44.

13. Moreland, ed., *The Creation Hypothesis*, Introduction, p. 13. Moreland uses the same language in his essay "Theistic Science & Methodological Naturalism," ibid., p. 42.

14. Johnson, "Darwinism and Theism," pp. 45–46.

15. Ibid., p. 41.

16. Michael Ruse, "Philosophical Preference, Scientific Inference, and Good Research Strategy," in Buell and Hearn, eds., *Darwinism: Science or Philosophy?*, p. 21.

17. Ibid., p. 22.

18. William A. Dembski: "Response to Arthur M. Shapiro," in Buell and Hearn, eds., *Darwinism: Science or Philosophy?*, p. 173. Dembski develops his position at length in "On the Very Possibility of Intelligent Design," Moreland, ed., *The Creation Hypothesis*, ch. 3.

19. Dembski, "Response," p. 174.

20. For a lucid portrayal of evolution and design as rival "scenarios," see Kurt P. Wise, "On the Origin of Life's Major Groups," *The Creation Hypothesis*, ch. 6.

21. See Larry Laudan, "The Demise of the Demarcation Problem," in Michael Ruse, ed., *But Is It Science?* (Buffalo, N.Y.: Prometheus, 1988), ch. 21. Laudan applies his argument to the case at hand in "Science at the Bar—Causes for Concern," and "More on Creationism," ibid., chs. 22, 24. For a discussion of the issue by a creationist, see Meyer, "The Methodological Equivalence of Design and Descent," in *The Creation Hypothesis*, pp. 72–88.

22. Michael Ruse, "The Academic as Expert Witness," p. 389.

23. *The Creation Hypothesis*, Introduction, pp. 12–13.

24. Moreland, "Theistic Science & Methodological Naturalism," *The Creation Hypothesis*, pp. 52 ff.

25. Introduction, ibid., p. 33.

26. Stephen C. Meyer, "The Methodological Equivalence of Design and Descent," ibid., p. 99.

27. Some such complaint underlies many demands for feminist science. Alan Soble shows that one important set of feminist arguments is self-undermining in his "Gender, Objectivity, and Reason," *Monist* 77, 4 (October 1994): 500–530.

28. Meyer, "The Methodological Equivalence of Design and Descent," p. 102.

29. Cf. Stephen C. Meyer, "Response to Michael Ruse," in *Darwinism: Science or Philosophy?*, ch. 3; Meyer, "The Methodological Equivalence of Design and Descent," especially pp. 88–98.

30. Jacques Monod, *Chance and Necessity*, Austryn Wainhouse, trans. (New York: Knopf, 1971), p. 112.

31. Richard Dawkins, *The Blind Watchmaker* (New York: Norton, 1986), especially ch. 3.

32. Peter van Inwagen's example, see his "Doubts about Darwinism," in *Darwinism: Science or Philosophy?*, p. 188.

33. Stephen Gould, *Wonderful Life* (New York: Norton, 1989).

34. Ruse, "Philosophical Preference," p. 22.

35. Dawkins, *The Blind Watchmaker*, p. ix. The rivalry between natural selection and belief in a "supernatural deity" pervades this book, especially chs. 1, 3, 11.

36. As Gould testifies, "Big Brother, the tyrant of George Orwell's *1984*, directed his daily Two Minutes Hate against Emmanuel Goldstein, enemy of the people. When I studied evolutionary biology in graduate school during the mid-1960's, official rebuke and derision was directed against Richard Goldschmitt, a famous geneticist who, we were told, had gone astray" (*The Panda's Thumb* [New York: Norton, 1989], p. 186). For some examples of the rhetoric of solidarity within the biological community, see Dawkins, end of ch. 9.

37. Larry Laudan, "Science at the Bar," p. 355. See the whole of *But Is It Science?*, Pt. IV.

38. For a discussion of the scientific problems evolutionary theory faces, see Michael Denton, *Evolution: A Theory in Crisis* (Bethesda, Md.: Adler and Adler, 1986).

39. The most famous "link" observed in life, the lungfish, does not quite work; "its fish characteristics such as its gills and its intestinal spiral valve are one hundred per cent typical of the same condition found in many ordinary fish, while its heart and the way in which the blood is returned to the heart from the lungs is similar to the situation found in most terrestrial vertebrates." Ibid., p. 109.

40. Gould, *The Panda's Thumb*, p. 181.

41. For a recent creationist account of the origins of language, which examines the question of ape speech, see John W. Oller, Jr., and John L. Ohmdahl, "Origin of the Human Linguistic Capacity," *The Creation Hypothesis*, ch. 7.

42. Quoted in John Horgan, "In the Beginning . . ." *Scientific American*, February 1991, p. 125. But scientists remain confident; as one of them puts it, "When we find the answer, it will probably be so damn stupid that we'll all say, 'Why didn't I think of that before?' " (ibid.).

43. On the absence of an alternative theory and its implications, see Denton, ch. 15, and the references to Thomas Kuhn and Paul Feyerabend found there.

44. Gould, *Wonderful Life*, p. 52.

45. In Johnson, *Evolution as Dogma*, p. 26.

10_____

The Politics of Personhood

Not only the creation–evolution dispute, but many other cultural issues as well, can (and must) be resolved through a mixture of mutual tolerance and pragmatic compromise. Even the United Nations can agree on a moment of silent reflection before beginning its business. Hence a moment of silence at the beginning of the public school day, during which each student may pray or meditate as his conscience (or that of his family) dictates, should meet the legitimate concerns of every party to the school prayer dispute—assuming for the moment that we retain enough of a common culture to render public schools workable institutions otherwise. Those who require more content should reflect on the difficulties of finding formulas that satisfy even all Protestants[1] (let alone Roman Catholics, Jews, and so forth). By adopting silence we run the risk of favoring Quakers over more doctrinally oriented traditions such as the Presbyterians. But families and religious communities can and should conduct fuller religious education at home, in church, or in voluntary after-school meetings. To them will fall the task of explaining to children the purpose of a moment of silence, thereby preventing pressure on children to conform to a state-sponsored theology.

Many cultural conflicts call for reciprocal norms of privacy and reticence, so that men and women can pursue diverse modes of life without invading one another's moral territory. Standards of dignity and courtesy, a shared sense that certain things are "not done" (at least in certain environments), and maxims such as *Good fences make good neighbors* and *Don't do it in the street and frighten the horses*, contribute much toward making life in a diverse society tolerable. A revival of the classical American pattern of a multitude of local communities, each with its distinctive conception of the good life, from which disaffected individuals are free to depart, could accomplish a great deal.[2] To be sure, there have to be collectively imposed limits on what such communities can be allowed to do to their members, especially to children (who will find it hard to leave their communities, however badly they are abused).

Our task is to define a framework of human rights that protects people against severe mistreatment, without being so intrusive as to foreclose the possibility of communal diversity. The range of the resulting communities would be far larger than in early America, and how they could co-operate to deal with shared problems such as health care and environmental degradation remains a severe problem. And the public-private distinction, however necessary, is both more porous and more problematic than liberal or even many communitarian writers recognize.[3] Privacy may be of supra-conventional value, as a way of protecting the possibility of intimacy (as Charles Fried has argued).[4] But how it is protected—under what circumstances, *don't ask, don't tell* is an acceptable policy—is very much a matter of local convention and prudential judgment. A concept such as *vulgarity*, though it may have supraconventional roots, depends for its application on the circumstances and traditions of local communities.

The resolution of cultural conflicts requires more than anything else a recognition of the shared humanity of everyone involved. At one time nationalism provided a sufficient bond among the citizens of the same nation-state. But the nation-state has now become vulnerable, both to transnational influences and to regional separatism, as well as to forms of nationalism that do not support its boundaries. A conspicuous feature of contemporary political life has been a revived tribalism, which "orthodox" liberalism has found itself unable to combat effectively,[5] of which moral and conceptual relativism are the intellectual correlates. No one has ever come up with a definition of who counts as a nation capable of resisting the forces of political opportunism. The simplest and best response to tribalism is that underneath our differences we are all human beings, and as such we have a common core of rights and duties (and can aspire to practice a common core of virtues).

Thus only our common humanity is a reliable basis for discussion, at least in the contemporary world. But as long as the question "who is human?" is a point at issue between different groups of people, appeal to our common humanity will be divisive rather than uniting. Who is to count as a human being—or, in technical language, as a person—is what is centrally at issue in disputes about abortion (and embryo research). Hence the abortion issue resists localistic and irenic solutions, and by common consent is of all issues most resistant to mutual tolerance and pragmatic compromise.[6]

Here I do not address all possible pro-choice or pro-life arguments. In particular, I omit the finer points of the when-does-life-begin question, hard cases, and the pragmatic aspects of legal regulation. I limit myself instead to consideration of three arguments that are closely connected with the theme of this book, which have not to my knowledge been adequately addressed in the literature (and to which I did not give adequate attention in my earlier work on the ethics of killing).[7]

The abortion issue is usually cast in terms of the moral status of the fetus or unborn child. One answer to this question is that, to use the language preferred here, all human beings are persons. Hence the fetus, being un-doubtedly human biologically, is a person as well. A somewhat narrower criterion—the potentiality principle—invokes the long-term capacity of the unborn to do characteristically human things, and for that reason accords most fetuses personal status. A key issue in the abortion debate is whether any narrower criterion than these is intellectually and politically defensible.

We begin with people arguing about abortion and other issues. Fetuses do not take part either in political bargaining or in philosophical dialogue. Hence, there is apparently no need to grant them even preliminary recognition. And so it might be, if the parties to the discussion were angels. All of us, however have periods of weakness—of sickness, say, or unconsciousness—concerning which we want our interests recognized. The most obvious grounds on which we demand recognition, during such periods, are that we are members of the human species and will, in due course, recover and be able to take part in the dialogue once again.

Formulas such as Rawls's "veil of ignorance" suppose, at least on one reading, a remarkable degree of culture on the part of the parties to the original position, and thus threaten us with a perverse analogue to the doctrine of the philosopher-king. For only the very sophisticated will be able even to pretend not to know who they are. Taking the interests of small children into account, as we must to apply Rawls's philosophy to the family, strains Rawls's description of the original position beyond the limits of our imagination. But if we move beyond considering the interests of those presently able to assert their rights, or argue for them philosophically, the boundaries of the human species provide the natural stopping place. Fetuses are members of the species as much as grown humans.

Here I consider three arguments, which in their adherents' belief require us to override or neglect the species and potentiality principles, at least for purposes of law and public policy. These are (1) the claim that access to abortion is required to give "life and substance" to the right of women to participate equally with men in public life; (2) the claim that the species criterion is too narrow, that a tenable criterion for moral standing must include nonhuman animals or the ecosystem; and (3) the claim that opposition to abortion rests on a religious basis, that (as Justice Stevens put it), "unless the religious view that a fetus is a 'person' is adopted, . . . there is a fundamental and well recognized difference between a fetus and a human being."[8]

THE FEMINIST ARGUMENT

Many women, often women who regret having had abortions, are pro-life.[9] Sometimes, too, they oppose abortion for feminist reasons.[10] Moreover, the feminist case for abortion is in tension with an important strand of feminism: the argument that our social practice has unduly neglected the "feminine voice" virtues—in particular, care for those particular others whom circumstance has placed within one's sphere of action, and the search for nondestructive alternatives in difficult cases.[11] Nonetheless, feminist "orthodoxy," defended by anathemas both more venomous and more effective than those issued at Rome,[12] supports an unlimited right to choose abortion.[13]

A crude version of the feminist argument is that women are made less able than men to compete in the marketplace by their liability to become pregnant. Hence abortion is necessary for the liberation of women. An employer might well be frustrated by the pregnancy of a valued female employee, and by her decision to quit or ask for leave to give birth and care for the child. But while abortion under such circumstances might be useful from the employer's perspective, it is hard to see how giving him the power to demand it might be in the interests of women. To be sure, the choice to abort would continue to rest with the woman, but employers would be able to so structure the employment relationship as to generate financial and other pressure against the decision to give birth.

A common theme in feminist argument is that women, because they are oppressed, are morally privileged and may exempt themselves from moral judgment when they elect to terminate unwanted pregnancies. In an article employing heavily feminist rhetoric, Caroline Whitbeck defends abortion as a "grim option."[14] But there is nothing specifically feminist (or feminine) about this argument: gritting one's teeth and doing the dirty deed is a core feature of masculine ideology. In fact, "grim options" is the standard male justification for injuring and deceiving women. If feminism means that women may treat men (and children) the way some men have treated women, then feminism continues the history of replacement of oppressor by oppressor, which is so frustrating to people with progressive aspirations.

Perhaps the best-known feminist argument for abortion is Judith Jarvis Thomson's: that a woman has a right to expel an "intruder" from her body, even at the cost of the intruder's life.[15] But—at least if we set aside the special case of pregnancy arising from rape—the picture of pregnancy Thomson's argument implies is so eccentric that it cannot stand alone as a defense of abortion. In fact, an abortion does not merely expel, but rather kills, the unborn child. The arguments to be considered here attempt to give

Thomson's idea greater credibility by appealing to the distinctive experience of women.

Catherine MacKinnon complains that "abortion's proponents and opponents share a tacit assumption that women control sex." In her view, both pro-life and pro-choice advocates fail to realize that rape is not an exceptional case, but rather a paradigm of heterosexual intercourse, so that every pregnancy can be treated as having been imposed on the woman. She thus argues "that the abortion choice must be legally available and must be *women's,* but not because the fetus is not a form of life."[16] This argument assimilates adult women to children and the mentally retarded, who cannot be held responsible for the consequences of their own actions. Such an evaluation of women is inconsistent with feminist politics—except of course in its starkly Leninist form, in which the definition of women's interests is the prerogative of a supposedly more enlightened vanguard.

Sally Markowitz[17] is also looking for a defense of abortion that does not require her to refute the claim that fetuses have a right to live. She is unwilling to appeal, as other feminists have done, to the conception of autonomy, which she finds objectionable on the grounds that it is capitalist or male-biased or both. She thus proposes two principles:

1. The Impermissible Sacrifice Principle: *When one social group in a society is systematically oppressed by another, it is impermissible to require the oppressed group to make sacrifices that will exacerbate or perpetuate that oppression.*

2. The Feminist Proviso: *Women are, as a group, sexually oppressed by men, and this oppression can neither be completely understood in terms of, nor otherwise reduced to, oppression of other sorts.*

In her view, together, these principles "justify abortion on demand for women *because they live in a sexist society.*" In a nonsexist society, the ethics of abortion would presumably be different.

Markowitz's argument addresses the situation of women as a group rather than as individuals. Even the wealthiest and best educated women can claim oppression to escape the sacrifices involved in pregnancy.[18] Moreover, in releasing women from one sacrifice, she is imposing another, that of life itself, on fetuses, whose right to life, let us remember, she does not deny. If the Impermissible Sacrifice Principle allows some oppressed people to improve their situation at the expense of others without moral restraint, it is a recipe for endless war and ever deepening injustice.

Markowitz's response to the fetus question is two-fold. First, she argues that "the fetus has a serious right to life does not imply that it is the sort of being that can be oppressed, if it cannot enter into the sorts of social relationships that constitute oppression." But why being unjustly killed does not amount to oppression escapes me. Perhaps what she means is that the unborn child is not alienated, in the sense that he is not enlisted into his own oppression. (If the enemy kills me, I am oppressed; if they make me dig my own grave, I am alienated.) But it is hard to see why the difference between oppression and alienation should make a significant moral and political difference for Markowitz. (Remember that she plays down the argument from autonomy.)

Second, Markowitz distinguishes between "two different ways of respecting the fetus's right to life. The first requires women to sacrifice while men benefit. The second requires deep social changes that will ensure that men no longer gain and women lose through our practices of sexuality, reproduction and parenthood." But restrictions on abortion do not benefit men who are trying to free themselves of responsibility for the woman with whom they have sexual relations and the children that result. Nor would all women lose by such restrictions. As Markowitz herself acknowledges, "many women in traditional roles fear the immediate effects on their lives of women's liberation generally and a permissive abortion policy in particular."

To dissolve an innocent individual's right to life into a program of social change is to warrant any atrocity, as long as its perpetrators manage to convince themselves that their program is "progressive." One could equally well defend the murder of Alexei Romanov, a hemophiliac child, on the ground that his family were oppressors. Markowitz needs, at minimum, an argument that the radical feminist program is destined to succeed and will do enough good to redeem the lives sacrificed on the way to utopia. Since the demise of the Marxist belief in our ability to discover the laws of history, no one to my knowledge has credibly suggested such an argument.

Mary Anne Warren defends birth as the cutoff point between persons and nonpersons, and consequently a radical discounting of the claims of fetuses, on the ground that "there is only room for one person with full and equal rights within a single skin."[19] She adduces conflicts between the interests of women and those of fetuses arising in medical practice, which have led physicians, in her view, to treat women as less than persons. But I see no reason why such conflicts as Warren adduces could not be handled without discounting the rights of the unborn child. The principle of double effect permits, for example, giving a person dying in great pain adequate morphine, even if he should die somewhat sooner as a result. This principle also implies that therapies designed to heal the woman may be legitimate even if they injure the child. In cases where there is nothing we can do for the woman—let us say because she is in a persistent vegetative state—the interests of the child naturally take precedence, though the principle of double effect forbids direct killing of the woman in such cases.

In any case, to allow political imperatives to govern ascriptions of personhood in this way is to open the door to endless redefinitions of the scope of the moral community. Such a tribalization of human life is hardly in the interests of women. Nor is it, I should think, in the interests of anyone, except perhaps a handful of *Übermenschen*.

Underlying many feminist arguments about abortion is the assumption that personhood is a social construction and that its boundaries are consequently a matter of utilitarian calculation or even partisan advantage.[20] The *conventionalist principle* holds that the boundaries of personhood are established by implicit or explicit agreement among those entities articulate and powerful enough to make their voice heard.

In fact, no convention defining the limits of personhood exists, except within some extremely homogeneous groups. Even if such a convention existed, its contours would reflect the power relations among various individuals and groups, and thus steeply disfavor those—small children, for example—who are unable to vindicate their claims by force (or guile). One advocate of this approach puts it frankly: "Any being with the capacity to pull the trigger on a gun, and to refrain from doing so out of respect for moral rules, deserves our equal moral respect."[21] Such a philosophy of "might makes right" is offensive to conventional morality itself, one whose clearest tenets is that black people and Native Americans were persons even when the laws and customary morality of white America treated them as less than human.

Nor is conventional morality sentimental in its rejection of "might makes right." Power relations are capable of changing abruptly, as when a member of the elite finds himself in a lonely place surrounded by members of the lower orders. Only a few professors of English, writing from a position of protected powerlessness, are likely to embrace such a philosophy openly. Those who wield real power are likely to realize how much their power arises, if not from right, then from the opinion of it. Since differences of opinion concerning the boundaries of the human community persist, there remains a role for supraconventional principles concerning who has rights and of what sort. Women in particular require, and frequently invoke, principles forbidding violence that cannot be sustained on grounds of power in the conventional sense alone.

To be sure, power in the conventional sense is not the only influence on conventional morality; the word *power* is in fact systematically ambiguous. Compassion for the vulnerable—say, for children and (cute) small animals—also influences its tenets. But human sympathies are at least as variable as power relations. We continue to require supraconventional principles to help us decide how much compassion for what sort of entities is appropriate.

ANIMAL RIGHTS/ECOLOGICAL ARGUMENTS

Some philosophers would dismiss the argument of this book—limited as it is to *human* diversity—as "speciesist," or "anthropocentric." Such philosophers might also oppose abortion, for if one opposes the taking of any life, that principle would include the taking of the lives of unborn humans as much as that of baby seals. (An exception for those in extreme and incurable pain, such as Gandhi was prepared to make, does not much affect the abortion debate.) Nonetheless, the animal rights/ecological contentions challenge the conventional framework within which the conventional bioethical argument about abortion as well as about euthanasia or experimentation proceeds.

Werner Pluhar[22] and L. W. Sumner[23] have advocated a principle of demarcation between persons and nonpersons that owes more to the utilitarians than to Kant. (Let us call it the *sentience principle*.) In their view, an entity is a person, merely if it has some sort of consciousness, however poor. On the abortion issue, the sentience principle leads to a line somewhere in the middle of pregnancy—exactly where must be left to the embryologist. It also leads to vegetarianism, since (with the possible exception of shellfish) all the animals whose flesh human beings eat have some sort of consciousness.[24]

As an argument in defense of early abortion, the sentience principle has serious deficiencies. We are sometimes so deeply asleep or comatose as to lack even simple consciousness—precisely how often is a difficult empirical question. Sometimes this condition is temporary. Surely we remain persons, whom it is wrong to kill, during such periods. Nonetheless, we could regard all sentient life as personal while still opposing abortion.

Animal rights advocates, and even more so ecological philosophers who mistrust the ethical tradition of the West as "anthropocentric," pose serious difficulties for the argument of this book. (Here I do not refer to the position that nonhuman nature has some moral claims, for example not to be destroyed without reason. I mean the rejection of the morally privileged position of human beings.) Such writers create obstacles to one popular pro-life argument: that when there is any case that what we are proposing to do is murder, we ought to abstain; and, for the sake of peace and justice, the laws of our society ought to protect what any coherent segment of public opinion regards as a person.[25] Such questions turn on the fortunes of public opinion, rather than on some deeply entrenched philosophical or political principle.

Those who argue for a personal status for nonhuman animals, the natural environment, and so forth must take as their premise a similarity (or other link) between such entities and paradigm humans.[26] The simplest attempt to accomplish this result appeals to the sentience of nonhuman animals (and in particular their capacity for pleasure and pain). But this argument fails to do the trick. For human beings undergo periods of deep unconsciousness and subsequently emerge. There is no reason why the way we evaluate pleasure and pain should not depend in part on the nature of the sufferer, as long as the differences we invoke are not arbitrary.

Borderline cases will exist for any criterion, although if membership in the human species is our criterion these cases will be few in number. The further we go beyond the human species, the more acute the question of borderline cases will be. One prominent animal rights advocate, Tom Regan, has written:

[My] argument . . . does not logically preclude the possibility that there are humans and animals who fail to meet the subject-of-a-life criterion and nonetheless have inherent value [in the Kantian sense]. . . . This incompleteness does not infect the adequacy of the subject-of-life criterion, when this is understood as a sufficient condition . . . nor does it undermine the claim that normal mammalian animals, aged one or more, as well as humans like those animals in the relevant respects, can intelligibly and non-arbitrarily be viewed as having inherent value.[27]

Read restrictively, and contrary to Regan's intentions, the clause "aged one or more" is a bit of special pleading for abortion and infanticide. But without some such restriction, Regan's position quickly becomes unmanageable.

If we press the skeptical questions that borderline cases provoke and demand rights for plants, rivers, and other features of our natural environment, the task of establishing priorities among moral claims will become impossible. An economy of scarcity is at work here: the wider the range of entities that are accorded full rights, the weaker these rights must be. If sagebrush has rights comparable to those of human beings, then the rights of human beings, even born human beings, cannot count for much. To expect human beings to follow the counsel of "deep ecology" and admit that penguins have a right to life as fundamental as our own,[28] when they have a hard time even recognizing one another's humanity, is to strain the motivational basis of morality beyond its strength. The unity of the human species has been preached for centuries with only mixed success; many men and women have difficulty subordinating their own interests to those of their own children.

Morality has three possible sources: (1) the need of human beings to live together in peace and to cooperate for shared ends; (2) an individual's conception of his own perfection, or the sort of person he wants to become;[29] and (3) a transhuman source of obligation, capable of adjudicating the rival claims of self and society. (Kant, I think, equivocates between bases 2 and 3.) Without a transhuman source, we are left with a moral dualism, for which there is no principled, or even stable, way of adjudicating conflicts between my conception of the good life and the needs of social order.

Basis 1 does not support strict animal rights or deep ecology, although it allows some room for compassionate feelings toward nonhuman animals and for protection of the natural environment for the sake of human beings. Even taking into account the interests of future generations is a problem for basis 1, since posterity is unable to take part in the process by which we define the rules of the social game. Nor does basis 2 provide a stable basis for deep ecology, except insofar as a person might take more or less anything as defining his perfection. Some men and even a few women take ruthlessness as a character ideal.

Hence a deep ecological ethics must be a religious, though not necessarily a Christian, one, and in fact ecologists invoke a variety of spiritual bases for their affirmations.[30] But it remains to be seen whether this grounding for ecological ethics can prevent lowering the moral standing of human beings rather than raising that of sagebrush and penguins. The religious basis that provides the greatest hope of doing so, since it has the deepest roots in our way of life, is the Christian and Jewish belief that we human beings are stewards of the natural order, responsible to God for the way we use or abuse it. This view involves the very anthropocentrism deep ecologists reject.

There are so few radical animal rights advocates that most of the time, their positions can be safely neglected in political contexts. The same is true, and even more so, of deep ecologists. But we need some principled ground for regarding animal rights (and deep ecological) claims as peripheral to the moral understanding of our society. In the last resort, the answer must be that we are heirs of a moral tradition that treats all and only human beings as morally privileged entities, and that places the burden of proof on those who would expand, and even more so on those who would contract, the protected class.

THE RELIGIOUS FREEDOM ARGUMENT

The moral tradition referred to at the end of the last section is historically associated with Christianity and Judaism, although there have been many attempts to assert it on nonreligious grounds. Hence the issue arises whether reliance on this tradition, in the sphere of public policy, is consistent with our understanding of religious freedom and the nonestablishment of religion.

Moved in part by such considerations, the United States Supreme Court has attempted to impose a relativistic consensus on the abortion issue. In a well-known passage, Justice Blackmun wrote:

We need not resolve the difficult question of when [human] life begins. When those trained in the respective disciplines of medicine, philosophy, and theology are unable to arrive at any consensus, the judiciary, at this point in the development of man's knowledge, is not in a position to speculate as to the answer.[31]

One would expect such an avowal of ignorance to lead to deference to the state legislatures (which were debating the subject even as Blackmun wrote). Instead, Blackmun used this argument to require permissive abortion laws throughout the United States. The most plausible defense of this employment of judicial agnosticism is an analogy with the American regime of religious freedom, which makes beliefs concerning the existence and nature of God a matter of private choice.

Many people who treat abortion rights as a species of religious freedom take Roman Catholic authority as their principal polemical target. But many of the most militant religious opponents of abortion, including the sponsors of Operation Rescue, are Evangelical, and other pro-life people are entirely naturalist in their approach.[32] Nor is opposition to abortion exclusively Western: a text in the Hindu scriptures treats abortion as akin to the killing of one's mother or father.[33]

Moreover, the pro-life argument on abortion is secular, at least on the surface. To be sure, one version of the crucial premise of the case against abortion is to be found in Scripture: that all human beings, men and women alike, are created in the image of God. Few people will, however, reject the affirmation of human dignity as somehow sectarian. The application of the idea of human dignity to the unborn child proceeds most persuasively without explicit appeals to religious authority. In contrast with bribery or homosexual practices, abortion is not expressly forbidden in either Testament. Writers such as St. Thomas Aquinas developed their position when people knew far less about embryology than we know today, so that it is not possible to apply their conclusions directly to our present situation.

Peter Wenz nonetheless argues that "personhood becomes a secular matter, and so a fit subject for legislation, sometime between twenty and twenty-eight weeks."[34] His reason is that protection for older, but not younger, fetuses can be derived by good arguments from widely shared "secular" beliefs. But that is exactly what pro-life people deny, for reasons set forth extensively in the literature. Wenz himself may find the moral arguments persuasive only for older fetuses, but this fact has nothing to do with the secular or religious character of the relevant considerations.

Moreover, Wenz assumes that "preserving the environment for future generations of human beings is a secular value" and that "suffering [even of nonhuman animals] is a secular disvalue wherever it occurs." But we know that we are neither nonhuman animals nor members of future generations—and it makes no sense to don a veil of ignorance concerning these facts. We cannot treat future generations as actual persons existing "downstream" in time, for their very existence depends on reproductive and other decisions made now. Even if we do not decide to cease reproducing, which particular individuals make up the humanity of the future depends on our family structure and sexual *mores* (and indeed on such contingencies as power outages).

Environmental and animal rights legislation thus requires a basis outside the usual course of secular politics, at least on one understanding of the secular. If, on the other hand, we follow Kent Greenawalt and define as secular those ends that are "comprehensible in nonreligious terms,"[35] then the protection of fetuses is as much a secular aim as are the protection of the environment, the interests of future generations, and the claims of nonhuman animals.

Furthermore, demands for permissive abortion laws, insofar as they arise from a desire to eliminate gender differences, have a religious, though of course not a Christian, basis. Radical feminism is a religion, one of whose central themes is, in Mary Daly's words, the "exorcism of the internalized Godfather in his various manifestations."[36] Both gender-blending and the war against the masculine are metaphysical demands made on the natural world, rather than proposals capable of receiving a conventional secular justification.

In truth, a person's views on any sensitive issue will reflect his outlook, and if this outlook is in any sense religious then religion will have an impact on the result. The politics of a democratic society requires that we find as wide a base as possible for our positions, whether on abortion or nuclear power or free trade, and not attempt nakedly to impose the outlook of a small group on the larger society. To deny a hearing to religious views—whether traditional or not—either disenfranchises believers or favors those sophisticated enough to conceal their presuppositions, perhaps even from themselves (see further Chapter 11).

CONCLUSION

I have attempted to consider selected pro-choice arguments in adequate detail, but my principal interest is in a larger issue: whether the very boundaries of humanity can be adjusted to serve the ends of some distressed individual or militant political movement.

Our society has been called "the republic of choice," but it is also one in which choice has become oddly trivial. I know a restaurant that advertises itself as "the restaurant that gives you a choice," as if other restaurants did not; and a radio station that advertises itself as "a world of choice," as if it did more than offer the same sort of choice that every other station did. The ideology of radical choice—whether individual or collective—that underlies defense of abortion is inconsistent with the presuppositions of liberal (or indeed of any civil) society. For the philosophy of every man (and woman) his or her own *Übermensch*—entitled to define a set of "rights" fashioned to suit whatever agenda his or her peculiarities might dictate—cannot be accepted in any society. It implies a war of each against all, without even the restraints that Hobbes's minimalist conception of human nature imposes.

Neotribalism implies endless war among tribes. Since nothing prevents the formation of a new tribe out of a minority group within an existing one, it implies endless war within existing tribes as well. Moreover, since most of us suffer from some sort of divided allegiance, war breaks out in our inner life as well. But appeals to human nature to resolve human conflicts remain intensely controversial.

The outlook I have been defending in this book is universal in its claims, and its adherents hope to win for it universal acceptance. Yet it has a history of growth—or at least phenomena like the rise of democracy and the enfranchisement of women suggest so—and is open to future development as well as decay. It is the result of the merger of Hebraic and Greek elements, consummated in the first thirteen centuries of our era, though without prejudice to the subsequent inclusion of Germanic, Asian, and African elements. It is possible that it will come to recognize the claims of earth-worms, although this remark should not be understood as either prediction or advocacy.

The Catholic Church has had a strategic role in this fusion. Hence the Church's opposition to abortion is of more than routine importance, even to those outside its boundaries. For the Church identifies with those on the margins of society, whether or not they find themselves on the official list of oppressed minorities. Nor are Catholics in America unfamiliar with prejudice and discrimination, or with hostility to their ideas and way of life. Yet the Church also speaks for the core commitments of our society, commitments that cannot be discarded while leaving the larger structure intact.

Some Catholic writers find the language of natural (or human) rights questionable, as tainted by anticlerical or even antireligious ideology. The present Pope takes a nuanced position:

The Gospel is the fullest confirmation of all of human rights. Without it we can find ourselves far from the truth about man. The Gospel, in fact, confirms the divine rule which upholds the moral order and confirms it, particularly through the Incarnation itself.[37]

NOTES

1. For a vigorous statement on this issue by a conservative Protestant, see Patrick Henry Reardon, "Classroom Chaos," *Touchstone* 8, 1 (winter 1995): 9.

2. See Barry Alan Shain, *The Myth of American Individualism* (Princeton, N.J.: Princeton University Press, 1994), ch. 3.

3. See, for example, Jean Bethke Elshtain, *Democracy on Trial* (New York: Basic Books, 1995), ch. 2.

4. See Fried's book *An Anatomy of Values* (Cambridge, Mass.: Harvard University Press, 1976), ch. 9.

5. An informative, though unfortunately self-advertising, discussion is Daniel Patrick Moynihan, *Pandaemonium* (Oxford: Oxford University Press, 1993).

6. The literature is immense; a good start is Louis P. Poijman and Francis J. Beckwith, eds., *The Abortion Controversy* (Boston: Jones and Bartlett, 1994).

7. See my *Ethics of Homicide* (Ithaca, N.Y.: Cornell University Press, 1978; paperback ed., Notre Dame, Ind.: University of Notre Dame Press, 1989). An up-to-date discussion, including questions not considered here, is my " 'Conserva-

tive' Views of Abortion," forthcoming in a volume of *Advances in Bioethics*, ed. by Rem Edwards.

8. *Webster* v. *Reproductive Health Services*, 492 U.S. 490, 568 (1989) (dissenting opinion), as quoted in Peter S. Wenz, *Abortion Rights as Religious Freedom* (Philadelphia: Temple University Press, 1992), p. 88.

9. Women Exploited by Abortion (centered at Venus, Texas) claims 60,000 members. The National Women's Coalition for Life (Oak Park, Illinois) claims 1.3 million members, 250,000 of whom regret having had abortions (information supplied by the National Women's Coalition for Life). Concerned Women for America, a conservative pro-life organization centered in Washington, D.C., claims 600,000 members.

10. The organization Feminists for Life (733 15th Street, N.W., Suite 1100, Washington, D.C. 20005) publishes *The American Feminist* and *Studies in Prolife Feminism*.

11. Juli Loesch Wiley, "Why Feminists and Prolifers Need Each Other," *New Oxford Review* 60 (November 1993): 9–14; Celia Wolf-Devine, "Abortion and the Feminine Voice," *Public Affairs Quarterly* 3 (1989): 81–97.

12. One of the stranger features of the present cultural-political scene is the existence of two organizations dedicated to the proposition that women need not follow a party line. They are the Womens' Freedom Network (4410 Massachusetts Avenue, N.W., Suite 179, Washington, D.C. 20016) and the Independent Women's Forum (131 18th Street, N.W., Washington, D.C. 20028), These groups should not be confused with Women for Freedom, founded by Larisa Vanno, which brings an overtly conservative voice to campus debates.

13. An extreme position is that of Barbara Duden. She maintains on feminist grounds that life, at least that of the unborn, is an "empty word" regardless of the scientific facts. Thus, she argues, "one can speak an unconditional NO to life, recovering one's autonomous aliveness." *Disembodying Women*, Lee Homacki trans. (Cambridge, Mass.: Harvard University Press, 1993), pp. 104, 110.

14. Caroline Whitbeck, "Taking Women Seriously as People—The Implications for Abortion," in Poijman and Beckwith, eds., *The Abortion Controversy*, ch. 25.

15. Thomson's "Defense of Abortion" originally appeared in *Philosophy & Public Affairs* 1 (1971), and has been frequently reprinted thereafter, for example, in Poijman and Beckwith, ch. 8. The best critique of Thomson is John T. Wilcox, "Nature as Demonic in Thomson's Defense of Abortion," *New Scholasticism* 73 (autumn 1989): 463–484.

16. Catherine MacKinnon, "*Roe* v. *Wade*: A Study in Male Ideology," in Poijman and Beckwith, eds., *The Abortion Controversy*, ch. 6; quotations, pp. 111, 110.

17. Sally Markowitz, "A Feminist Defense of Abortion," ibid., ch. 24; quotations, pp. 378, 378–379; 379, 381, 382, 383 n.16.

18. For example, a woman from a rich family is pregnant by, and engaged to be married to, a man of lower station. She agrees to an abortion to please her father, who is jealous of her new love, and resents her decision to marry a social inferior.

19. Mary Anne Warren, "On the Moral Significance of Birth," in Poijman and Beckwith, eds., *The Abortion Controversy*, p. 441.

20. Social constructionism is now all-pervasive on the cultural Left; see Daphne Patai and Norette Koertege, *Professing Feminism* (New York: Basic Books, 1994), pp. 135–147, 166–167.

21. Ronald Green, "Conferred Rights and the Fetus," *Journal of Religious Ethics* (spring 1974): 61. Why "equal"?

22. Werner Pluhar, "Abortion and Simple Consciousness," *Journal of Philosophy* 24 (1977): 159–172.

23. L. W. Sumner, *Abortion and Moral Theory* (Princeton, N.J.: Princeton University Press, 1981).

24. Cf. Peter Singer, *Animal Liberation* (New York: New York Review of Books, 1977).

25. See, for example, Germain Grisez and Joseph Boyle, *Life and Death with Liberty and Justice* (Notre Dame, Ind.: University of Notre Dame Press, 1979).

26. For further discussion, see my article, "The Moral Basis of Vegetarianism," *Philosophy* (October 1978).

27. Tom Regan, *The Case for Animal Rights* (Berkeley: University of California Press, 1983), pp. 246–247.

28. See the articles by Arne Naess, "The Shallow and the Deep," and "Identification as a Source of Deep Ecological Attitudes," reprinted in Peter C. List, ed., *Radical Environmentalism* (Belmont, Calif.: Wadsworth, 1993), pp. 19–38.

29. These correspond to Nietzsche's "slave" and "master" moralities, but I do not accept Nietzsche's evaluation of the two types of morality. Nor do I assume that anyone presents a pure case.

30. Two advocates of "deep ecology" put the matter plainly. "Many people have cultivated ecological consciousness within the context of different spiritual traditions—Christianity, Taoism, Buddhism, and Native American rituals, for example." See Bill Devall and George Sessions, "Deep Ecology," in List, ed., *Radical Environmentalism*, p. 39. For an explicit statement of the religious roots of ecological politics, see Elizabeth Dodson Gray, "We Must Re-Myth Genesis," ibid., pp. 55–69.

31. *Roe v. Wade*, 410 U.S. 113 (1973), as reprinted in Poijman and Beckwith, eds., *The Abortion Controversy*, p. 27.

32. See, for example, Michael Wreen, "In Defense of Speciesism," *Ethics and Animals* 4, 3 (1984): 47–66; Wreen, "The Power of Potentiality," *Theoria* 5 (1986): 16–40; D. Marquis, "Why Abortion Is Immoral" and "A Future Like Ours and the Concept of a Person" in Poijman and Beckwith, eds., *The Abortion Controversy*, chs. 20, 23; B. Nathanson, "Operation Rescue: Domestic Terrorism or Legitimate Civil Rights Protest," ibid., ch. 28.

33. *Kaushitaki Upanishad*, 3.1, quoted in G. Parrinder, *Sex in the World's Religions* (London: Sheldon, 1980), p. 12.

34. Quotations from Wenz, pp. 177, 187, 188.

35. Kent Greenawalt, *Religious Convictions and Political Choice* (New York: Oxford University Press, 1988), p. 22.

36. Mary Daly, *Gyn/Ecology* (Boston: Beacon Press, 1990), p. 1.

37. *Crossing the Threshold to Hope*, Vittorio Messori, ed., Jenny McPhee and Martha McPhee, trans. (New York: Knopf, 1994), p. 197.

11

The Case against Secularism

This chapter is not about God, but about human beings. Whether there is a God, if so of what sort, and whether and how He has communicated His intentions to humanity are questions beyond the scope of the present discussion. I assume only that belief in God is not so irrational that it can be excluded from public discourse on these grounds alone. It seems unlikely that a position defended by otherwise intelligent people in a wide variety of historical contexts should be so utterly without merit as to permit such summary dismissal. Nietzsche's proclamation of the death of God, and the positivistic labeling of religious claims as "cognitively meaningless," both amount to no more than bluff that the clearheaded believer can set aside.[1]

When we turn from abstract philosophy to political reality, the absurdity of proposals to dismiss religion from public discourse becomes even more evident. Sometimes religious issues are front and center in the culture wars—for example, in the conflict between Roman Catholics and advocates of an often explicitly anti-Catholic "religion of democracy" that followed World War II.[2] Religion is always at least a silent partner in cultural debates, including those conducted among people who share a common secularist commitment (and perhaps little else).

Consider the use of the pseudoreligious expression, the "canon," to describe the most important works of the Western tradition, including the works of militant atheists such as Nietzsche and Marx. True, an education that does not include a familiarity with the Bible (and Plato, Shakespeare, Nietzsche and Marx) is woefully incomplete. But these works do not comprise a "canon" in the sense that the Old and the New Testaments do.[3]

In fact, the uncritical secularism and the aesthetic pseudoreligion that pervade academic cultural debates both seem to me equally questionable.

THE VARIETIES OF AMERICAN RELIGION

Nearly all Americans believe in God ("or a universal spirit," as George Gallup puts it), and during the writing of this book there was a resurgence of belief in angels.[4] As of 1984, 81 percent or 92 percent of Americans accord the Bible some sort of religious authority, depending on how the question is put.[5] Thus the penetration of politics and culture by religion is deep, in America as much as in ancient Israel.[6]

Americans are individualistic in theory (though conformist in practice) about religion as about all else.[7] This combination of individualism and conformity helps account for the popularity of philosophies of cultural pluralism which, although they celebrate tolerance and diversity, imply intense pressures to conform within each cultural group.[8] Whether American individualism is good or bad depends on the presence or absence within the individual of an active and well-informed (even if sometimes erroneous) conscience. In any event, it creates special problems for the Roman Catholic Church, and even more so for the Jewish people, for whom descent is the primary principle of membership.

Our diversity guarantees the continued importance of our individualistic tradition, since only a very limited nationwide consensus is possible. Defining some individuals or groups as unacceptably deviant, religiously or otherwise, is always difficult. America has in fact provided a home for an extraordinarily rich variety of religious groups, ranging from Mormons to Unitarians to believers in Magick.[9]

American religion also suffers from a weak sense of transcendence, reflecting a continuing rebellion against Jonathan Edwards's proclamation of God's hatred of sinful humanity. Thus Americans treat religion as a consumer good, marketed in the same way as baseball or the movies.[10] Many Americans object to the fact that religious traditions have moral and other standards of their own, that may come into conflict with those of the secular order: such people define "attitudes of conflict with science/hospitals/schools" as symptoms of religious abuse.[11] In many communities, including the Catholic Church, "music ministries" take an unholy delight in waging war on awe.[12]

One manifestation of a weak sense of transcendence is the rhetorical use of religion to promote political programs deemed progressive on entirely secular grounds or to stabilize family structures and reinforce ancestral codes. Many "conservative" religious writers appear, in fact, to be in search of a Throne to which to subordinate the Altar, insisting only that the Throne be occupied by Republicans rather than Democrats.

Of the many reasons for regarding American religion as decadent, the least controversial is intellectual: religion has been banished from the mind of America, however powerful a place it may retain in its heart.[13] An avowedly secular writer sums up the result well: "Americans . . . can buy and read vast numbers of religious books, yet survey after survey suggests that they are stupefyingly dumb about what they are supposed to believe."[14] A weakness of theological background is not merely an intellectual deficiency. For on any account false prophecy is very common, and familiarity with a developed religious tradition is necessary to reject even its crudest varieties—and indeed to become aware of the problem.

We must not assume that religion as such is a good or a bad thing. (Neither historical nor sociological data can distinguish authentic faith from shallow acceptance of conventional religiosity.) Religious faith has inspired a belief in the unity of the human species. But all religion—and indeed all forms of socially embodied belief—has a communal aspect, since its adherents find it necessary to sustain a context in which the faith is nurtured, applied, and transmitted to future generations. Hence it is not surprising that religion has sometimes generated a virulent tribalism in which outsiders are regarded as less than human.

Religious beliefs, including the residues of belief that may remain in unbelievers, influence moral and political judgment in complex ways, which few if any people are able to sort out.[15] Even when a dispute among religious people looks like a mask for some secular conflict, we should hesitate to accept a reductionist view of the situation.

The dispute between Moderate and Fundamentalist Southern Baptists looked like a conflict between Democrats and Republicans. Or perhaps it was a question of marketing strategy: the Fundamentalists argued that, if the denomination "went liberal," it would lose the ability to hold and attract members—an argument to which the Moderates had no adequate reply.[16] But the Republican (and ultimately Emersonian) ideas about self-reliance, which have a great influence on American religious conservatives, have a discernible Pelagian coloration. One crucial issue in the Moderate-Fundamentalist dispute concerned human nature: to what extent is ambiguity in the rules governing our belief and conduct tolerable?

Contemporary American religion is shaped by the collapse of ("mainstream" or "oldstream") liberal Protestantism, in large measure as a result of its loss of resources for interpreting those aspects of human experience troublesome to the secular mind.[17] Among the many movements that have moved into the space so created are the ideology of the Cold War, radical feminism, the ecological movement, and (sometimes explicitly religious) nationalism.

Americans during the Cold War were governed by an ideology—sometimes called "hard anticommunism"—that enabled us to play the part of a Great Power while preserving an understanding of ourselves as morally pure. This ideology divided the planet into two worlds: a "free world," even when parts of it were ruled by dictators; and the "Evil Empire" or "focus of evil"—which some Catholics called "the incarnation of Satan within the historical process."[18] To admit that the Soviet elite was moved by the ordinary motives of the powerful, such as fear of losing their power, was in this view a heresy to be punished as such. To point to this ideology is not to defend the Soviet system, or to deny that it posed a challenge to the American way of life; it is only to observe that American responses to this challenge were shaped by a questionable framework of interpretation. The other religion-substitutes to be considered later in this chapter also reflect realities, though through a (sometimes seriously) distorting lens.

The radical feminist Mary Daly advocates Gnosticism with signs reversed. For traditional Gnostics the flesh was evil and the transcendent spiritual principle good. For Daly, the evil principle is the "Godfather," or the personification of traditional "patriarchal" culture. The Good God is the "Background," that is, "the realm of Wild Reality; the Homeland of women's selves and all the Others; the TimeSpace where auras of plants, planets, stars, animals, and all Other animate beings connect."[19] Her way of life is an "Outercourse," a spiralling away from "the imprisoning mental, emotional, physical, emotional, spiritual walls of patriarchy, . . . [and] surrounded and aided by the benevolent forces of the Background."[20] Thus she claims to have chosen herself as both a woman and a lesbian, at least before birth and possibly before conception,[21] and her initiation into overt lesbian sexuality produced, in her words, "an intuition of Elemental integrity."[22]

Nationalism is always at least partly a religious movement, and sometimes very heavily so.[23] A nation involves a solidarity, not merely with the present generation but with the dead and those yet unborn, neither of which can enter into contractual relations with presently existing people. (That we can pray for the dead, and they for us, is not the sort of thing most political theorists have in mind.)[24] The continued importance of nationalism, even in liberal democracies, is concealed by the cool way in which secular political theorists take the existence, legitimacy, and stability of the nation-state for granted.

Scholars of American religion tend also to neglect the ecological movement.[25] But though lacking the formal structure of either Christianity or Judaism, ecology now provides both an outlet and a focus for the venerable pantheistic strain of American spiritual life. It fosters a partial deification of the Earth, and includes as well a rich array of myths, symbols, and rituals—for example, the myth of an Arcadia in which Native Americans "lived in peace with the land" before the arrival of Europeans. Like all fighting faiths, it has sought and gained influence on both public policy and public opinion, happily disregarding secularist conceptions of public reason in the process.

If secularist individualism is self-evidently the correct social philosophy, then the fact that American practice persistently falls short of it is no argument for rejecting it (though getting it adopted might prove difficult). But if the philosophical question is open, however, our practice is relevant, for the attempt persists to dismiss a religious presence in politics as somehow "un-American." In practice, this usually amounts to giving a moral monopoly to pliant religious movements, excluding from public dialogue Catholics, Evangelical Protestants, and Orthodox Jews. But unless the America so invoked is an entirely mythical society, such attempts are without foundation.

THEOCRACY AND SECULARISM

The notion of the secular, like those of harm and tolerance, only appears to stand outside and above rival world-views. To say this is not to assert relativism, but only to point out that the phenomena that relativists describe as the "clash of competing paradigms" affect all of our moral and political concepts, so that relativism cannot be refuted by isolating one of them from the web of beliefs and practices in which it is located.

We might stipulate that the political practices of liberal democracy define the secular, and we might ask what legitimate place the religious convictions of citizens and officials may have in these practices.[26] In the present work, I take a slightly broader perspective and inquire into the role of religion, not only in the political, but also in the cultural and intellectual, life of the West, where these are not conducted under churchly auspices. We should not expect those whose traditions do not support our distinction to acknowledge their transcultural validity.

We can define religion substantively, as belief in superhuman entities on whose favor we depend, and the secular as what does not involve belief in such entities. Or we can define religion functionally, as a set of pictorial representations by which people attempt to provide a unity to their way of life, and the secular as involving the various elements of that way of life, taken in isolation.[27] In neither case ought we to follow George M. Marsden in defining the "secular" as "that which is not controlled by formal, organized, religion."[28] Such a definition is particularly disastrous for a country, like the United States, with a strong anti-institutional tradition.

The liberal tradition is often interpreted as a struggle against theocracy (which is not the same thing as a struggle against Christianity or against religion).[29] Any world-view with totalistic claims will pose a similar problem: for example, the slogan that "the personal is the political and the political is the personal" implies that no sphere of life is immune to the demands of feminist ideology. But here I state the question of theocracy in Christian terms.

Since God created all things, theocrats argue, there are no religiously neutral questions, and, similarly, no religious sphere immune to civil politics. If we have right on our side, our political adversaries are enemies of God; conversely, there can be no political union with God's enemies. In one version of this idea, the Pope or a private spokesman for God like John Knox has the power to depose civil rulers. In another, the king or majority ruling by divine right determines the religion of its subjects (and the clergy are for that reason civil servants).

Critics of theocracy must, in the last resort, take issue with the theocrats' theology. If a New Rightist tells me that it is God's will that the domestic federal budget be reduced, and I disagree, I have to respond either that there is no God, that He is indifferent to the details of our political arrangements, or that His will for us is something different from what the New Rightist supposes (say that the government use its financial leverage to support family and communal structures, or that fiscal issues be decided by democratic procedures). But dogmatic theology lies outside the present discussion: I limit myself to philosophical and political objections to tight linkages between theological and political allegiances.

The objections to theocracy from the standpoint of public peace are very powerful; the specter of the Inquisition, and of the Thirty Years' War, haunts even such bloodless controversies as those over school prayer. But such considerations are in the nature of the case indecisive. Secular, or supposedly secular, societies have their full share of conflict, intolerance, and bloodshed, and the practical impossibility of theocracy cannot be taken as a permanent feature of our political situation. If the price of civil peace is widespread damnation, no believer can be expected to accept the bargain. Even if we cannot save heretics by coercing them to accept orthodox doctrine, we might at least keep them from corrupting the rest of the population.

The moral and spiritual effects of religious pluralism are incalculable, however, and the evaluation of these effects poses questions of incommensurable value. We do not know whether a larger percentage of the population was saved in the thirteenth than in the twentieth century, or even whether thirteenth-century people were morally better than we are—whether by their own lights or by those of some objective standard. The costs of religious war are moral as well as material: theologically motivated hatred is at least as spiritually corrosive as is any other kind.

In the face of uncertainty about the relative effects of religious pluralism and imposed uniformity, it is our obligation to make the best of our circumstances, including the age in which we find ourselves. This age is hostile to theocracy, or at least to theocracy on behalf of any religion a reasonable person might accept. Yet the rejection of theocracy in no sense implies that religious believers should forsake or abandon their faith when they make decisions as citizens, or even (though their case is more complex) as officials. It only means that they should so far as possible conform their political activity to the conventions of liberal democracy, unless, of course, these conventions are manipulated to impose silence on them.

In its most militant forms, seldom found in America, secularism holds that religion is a public evil, to be extirpated by all the power of the state. Such secularists are committed to asserting, and claiming either exclusive legitimacy or eventual supremacy for, something that occupies the same logical space in their minds as traditional religion does in the minds of traditional believers. They are, in short, theocrats without God.

The form of secularism most common in America holds that religion is a tolerated vice, like prostitution in many societies, to be indulged out of the earshot of the squeamish and under no circumstances to be taken seriously. Secularists consider it sufficient to reveal the religious underpinnings of an argument to discredit it, and support a judicial veto on "religiously entangled" state and federal legislation.[30] Some of them may entertain the hope that men and women will eventually outgrow their religious "crutches."[31] But, at least for the time being, they are committed to a politics of accommodation within a diverse society.

A minor manifestation of secularism in the cultural sphere is the exclusion of sales in religious bookstores when compiling the list of best sellers.[32] A more serious example may be found in Sir Isaiah Berlin's recently published book on J. G. Hamaan.[33] In his account of a writer for whose historical importance, though not whose intellectual merits, he makes large claims, Berlin dismisses his "theology and religious metaphysics," while admitting that it is "the heart of his vision."

THEORETICAL PERSPECTIVES

Rawls

Rawls begins his *A Theory of Justice* with a ringing declaration of faith:

Justice is the first virtue of social institutions, as truth is of systems of thought. . . . Each person possesses an inviolability founded on justice that even the welfare of society as a whole cannot override.[34]

"No doubt [these propositions] are expressed too strongly," he observes on the following page. In subsequent writings he has based his views on justice on an appeal to "overlapping consensus," which undercuts his invocation of the peremptory claims of truth.[35]

Crucial to Rawls's finished argument is his conception of "public reason"; that is, a form of reasoning to which we are constrained at least when we discuss central constitutional issues. In fact, Rawls discusses unessential as well as essential issues in terms of "political values" (p. 229), that is, values determined by his conception of public reason. Accordingly, this conception of reason limits not only the deliberations of legislators and judges, or the public dialogue among citizens, but even the private reasons on which an individual citizen votes (p. 215). This doctrine amounts to a gag rule, keeping out of political debate propositions that, for all Rawls is able to show, are both rationally held and important. They may even be truths the community neglects at its peril.

By *pluralism* Rawls means the coexistence of a multitude of "comprehensive views" such as Christianity, Judaism, and agnostic Kantianism. He insists that, in his view, "pluralism is not seen as a disaster but rather as the natural outcome of the activity of reason under enduring free institutions" (p. xxiv; see also pp. 3–4, 36–37, 55, 128–129). He gives every appearance of believing that his position is a tolerant one, insofar as it does not require universal acceptance of agnostic Kantianism. But the effect of his theory is to prohibit many of the views of life whose coexistence he celebrates from bearing fruit in speech and action, well before their expression threatens the social order. In short, he holds that pluralism is a good thing, as long as the adherents of most of the competing creeds do not take their convictions seriously.

Underlying Rawls's arguments is an appeal to the concept of reasonableness, which he distinguishes from both rationality (Lect. II, sec. 1) and truth (pp. xx, 94). As he puts it, "Being reasonable is not an epistemological idea (though it has epistemological elements). Rather, it is part of a political ideal of democratic citizenship that includes the idea of public reason" (p. 62).

In its social aspect, reasonableness is defined in terms of a person's "willingness to propose and abide by fair terms of social co-operation" (p. 94). He explains "fair terms" as follows: "In recognizing others's views as reasonable, citizens also recognize that to insist on their own comprehensive views must be seen by the rest as simply insisting on their own beliefs" (p. 128). He elaborates his appeal to fairness as follows:

> Since the exercise of political power itself must be legitimate, the ideal of citizenship imposes a moral, not a legal, duty—the duty of civility—to be able to explain to one another on those fundamental questions how the principles and policies they vote for can be supported by the political values of public reason. (p. 217)

In short, Rawls defines reasonableness as a willingness to set aside one's moral convictions when addressing political issues, rather than, for example, as the willingness to support our views by reason and defend them when criticized, and to listen to those whose positions may require us to modify even our conception of reason. More is at stake here than the requirement that one's moral convictions be reasonable in the customary sense: Rawls is demanding that "reasonableness" be defined in terms of one particular political perspective—his version of liberalism.

There are some perspectives which any civilized society will somehow have to fence out. But even in the clearest case, that of the Nazis, we need to understand that economic collapse, cultural fragmentation, lack of political leadership, and low national morale helped bring about their victory, and we should not view it as a demonic invasion of a world otherwise progressing toward justice. It is sheer provincialism to suppose that all things that lie outside Rawlsian public reason are of the Nazi variety. To be sure, some of them will be, but they will also be outside the pale of every understanding of reasonableness at work in contemporary American life—which is why the Nazis have the role they do in our discourse.

There is no reason to believe that all reasonable men and women—reasonable, that is, by any other standard—will find the constraints of Rawlsian public reason equally confining. Rawlsian liberalism imposes on religious people, but not on their unbelieving fellow citizens, a painful and debilitating form of internal division. An unwillingness to pay for liberal social programs is the predictable result of the taxation without moral representation that Rawls imposes on many of his fellow citizens.

On Rawls's own showing, the requirements of public reason are a matter of social and historical contingency. What the public reason of a given society ends up allowing depends on the world-views its various members hold, how persuasive the advocates of these world-views are, and how they are applied in practice. Sometimes accepting the arguments of dissident citizens means accepting their world-view as a whole, although we may expect such conversions to be rare. Sometimes it may be possible to see the point of their arguments, or their emotional and imaginative appeals, and incorporate their conclusions within the corpus of our own beliefs, without becoming full converts. To dismiss such possibilities in advance of argument is cultural arrogance disguised as philosophy.

In fact, some of those who reject Rawlsian public reason—such as Mother Theresa and Alexander Solzshenitsyn—get an audience for their views despite the best efforts of the liberal censors. Rawls, though without fully noticing what he is doing, concedes the central point: he acknowledges that citizens may appeal to their comprehensive views, as long as the end result is to strengthen public reason (Lect. VI, sec. 8). He is even prepared to say that Lincoln's

Second Inaugural with its prophetic (Old Testament) interpretation of the Civil War as God's punishment for the sin [of] slavery, falling equally on North and South . . . does not violate public reason as . . . it applied in his day, . . . since what he says has no implications bearing on constitutional essentials or matters of basic justice. [!] (p. 254)

But that Lincoln's rhetoric strengthened public reason reflected the fact that many Americans found his "nonpublic" reasons compelling.

Michel Foucault writes:

A certain fragility has been discovered in the very bedrock of existence—even, and perhaps above all, in those aspects of it that are most familiar, most solid, and most intimately related to our bodies and to our everyday behaviour.[36]

In this context of newly discovered fragility, he supports what he calls "an *insurrection of subjugated knowledges.*"[37] But this consciousness of the fragility of the experienced order, combined with the resurgence of "knowledges" suppressed by establishment intelligentsia, precisely characterizes the Religious Right and other movements challenging liberal humanist orthodoxy.

Rawls, in reply, could abandon his proceduralist presuppositions and affirm the inherent dignity of human beings as well as the limits our inherent dignity places on the legitimate forms of social policy, on substantive Kantian grounds. But such an approach would require him to defend a general Kantian approach to normative questions, in a way that the whole thrust of his argument is designed to avoid.

Greenawalt

Kent Greenawalt is a secularist in the sense that he treats the common sense of contemporary liberal democratic societies as the criterion of public justification. But, unlike Rawls, he sees that contemporary common sense is frequently ambiguous in a way that leaves openings for religious (and other) people to bring their distinctive visions to bear. Thus, or so Greenawalt reasons, "citizens . . . have to reach beyond shared premises and publicly accessible reasons to determine their positions," and these may include religious reasons (p. 47).[38] (This position is elaborated and applied throughout the book, especially in chapters 6–10.) But in his version of liberal democracy the fact that an act is, from a religious point of view, wrong, is not an acceptable reason for making that act a crime (ch. 5).

Greenawalt announces positions that are not supported by his argument, and actually are in some tension with it. He favors "a rule of nondiscrimination [against practicing homosexuals] in public employment, including school teaching" (p. 94), even though such a rule may conflict with the, in his view, legitimate conscientious objections of parents to entrusting their children to the care of such persons. And, although he believes that *Roe v. Wade* was wrongly decided, he opposes its reversal (p. 120)—though a "states rights" resolution of the constitutional issue would better reflect the varying religious climates of different parts of the country than does the pro-choice orthodoxy imposed by the Court.

Furthermore, Greenawalt's notion of "publicly accessible reasons" (cf. ch. 4) is dependent on the strength or weakness of religious influences within a given liberal democracy. One's reading of his criteria of acceptable public reasons will be affected by one's outlook (and if one is religious, one's religious outlook) in much more profound ways than he realizes.

For example, Lord Devlin's suggestion that deviant sexual acts might be legally restricted for the sake of social solidarity (discussed by Greenawalt at pp. 90, 93) is consistent with a form of atheism, suggested by Durkheim, that holds that society must replace God and provide its members with a meaningful structure wherewith to conduct their lives. Persons whose religious beliefs emphasize the interconnectedness of all human beings will find a religious analogue of Durkheim's social philosophy more plausible than will persons, believers or not, of a more individualistic outlook. It is easier to propose a moral belief as a basis for social solidarity if one believes it to be true, even if its truth does not enter directly into one's political argument for its enforcement.

Whether so strong an emphasis on social solidarity is consistent with liberal democracy is a matter of definition. The question of definition cannot be settled, certainly not in an individualist direction, on historical grounds.[39] A philosophy that heavily emphasizes social solidarity poses no problem for majority rule, and even allows some scope for minority rights, to religious conscience, for example. If, as Greenawalt argues, we are entitled to draw on religious premises to resolve questions of fetal rights, animal rights, and the claims of the environment, we are also entitled to draw on them to resolve ambiguities in liberal democratic theory on the basis of membership in American society.

Besides these ambiguities, Greenawalt's argument is subject to one important limitation. There are reasons, and indeed religious reasons, for acting so far as possible "as good liberal citizens" (p. 209). But these reasons cannot in the nature of the case be absolute. To believe in God is to believe in an authority that can, and sometimes does, trump earthly authority of every sort, even that established in liberal democracies. Prophecy in the radical sense is a rare and dangerous exercise, but cannot be excluded by any political or constitutional theory.

Carter

Stephen L. Carter has summed up the objection to liberal "gag rules" with admirable bluntness.

The truth—an awkward one for guardians of the public square—is that tens of millions of Americans rely on their religious traditions for the moral knowledge that tells them how to conduct their lives, including their political lives. They do not like being told to shut up. (p. 67)[40]

Yet by Carter's own admission, certain issues cannot be satisfactorily resolved if one takes seriously both the autonomy of religious groups and secular conceptions of equality (at least in the version he prefers) (p. 155). One example is the refusal of religiously affiliated institutions to hire avowed, practicing homosexuals.

Carter's proposal for affirmative action for minority religions (p. 126) threatens him with both theoretical and practical disaster. For it is neither unjust, nor evidence of injustice, that "fringe" religious groups gain fewer adherents than do major churches, unless of course the doctrines of the fringe groups happen to be true (and even here *injustice* is not perhaps the most appropriate word). The root of the difficulty is Carter's relativism: his argument that religious groups have an "epistemology" different from that of the secular state (p. 284 n.33). This kind of relativism turns all issues into power politics, even against Carter's own inclination. Thus his last word to parents who want their children taught creation science is that might makes right. "We win because you lose. We have the power and you don't" (p. 182). Relativism of this sort erodes the possibility of finding common ground when religious and secular imperatives conflict, and entails that such conflicts must be decided on grounds of power politics or of sentiment (or of some combination of the two).

"SECULAR HUMANISM" AND EDUCATION

I now examine the claim of many religious conservatives that American public education, contrary to its professions of religious neutrality, indoctrinates students in a religion called "secular humanism."[41] One difficulty with this thesis consists in identifying the "secular humanist" world-view, which is somewhat elusive both in the writings of its advocates and in those of its critics.

At least two different outlooks go under the name "secular humanism." One—"scientific humanism"—derives from the Enlightenment (though without the deism of the leading Enlightenment figures); it teaches that reality is entirely comprehensible by science and entirely open to manipulation by technology. There is no reason, on such premises, why enlightened scientists should respect the liberty of their benighted subjects: even moral objections to nontherapeutic experimentation on human subjects are at best questionable on such premises. The other—"Romantic humanism"—affirms human dignity but places that dignity in our ability to reshape ourselves however we please; it favors maximum personal liberty even at some social cost. One source of difficulty is that groups as well as individuals wish to reshape themselves (more exactly: individuals may wish to reshape the groups to which they belong), and there is no preestablished harmony between these two kinds of reshaping.

These outlooks are in a quite reasonable sense "religious" although they do not involve belief in a deity, they do involve an implicit world-picture, accepted on faith, and conveyed in irreducible part through imaginative representations. In the case of the scientific humanist outlook, this feature is paradoxical, for scientific humanism proposes to do entirely without myth. Yet when Copernicus, Galileo, and Newton are portrayed as prophets of atheism, despite the fact that all three of them held relatively traditional forms of religious belief, there can be no doubt that the myth-making imagination has been at work.

Whether public school students are indoctrinated in either or both of these outlooks is a complex question. But textbooks are written from one of these perspectives, or from some (muddled) attempt to combine them, and few public school teachers attempt to inform students of the existence of alternatives (let alone require them to attempt to understand them). The implicit message is that scientific and Romantic humanism are the only ideas worthy of examination, and the only conflict worthy of discussion is the conflict between the two "humanist" outlooks. In the absence of explicit intent, the word *indoctrination* is a bit strong. Nonetheless, for believers in traditional religion (as well as for believers in liberal education), the situation is little different than one of explicit indoctrination. For militant secularists business as usual may be better than explicit antireligious propaganda, which is likely to generate resentments and an interest in the forbidden.

(Discussions of "secular humanism" also point to the New Age movement. This movement is almost infinitely distant from scientific humanism, although it has important affinities with the Romantic variety. Though very amorphous, and for that reason hard to discuss, it is clearly a religion and should be treated as such for all intellectual and social purposes.)

The danger of secularist education is not so much that it will make religion somehow go away: even without relying on theological guarantees of the survival of the Church, this seems unlikely. It is more that banishing religion from the mind entails banishing mind from religion, with a range of results from the cult of Elvis to dangerous sects like the Branch Davidians. Even within established religions, strange results follow if people are not encouraged to think consequently about religion (something even professional philosophers have a hard time doing these days). Even from the point of view of secular society, the proliferation of cranky and fanatical forms of religion is hardly to be welcomed; if one believes that an acceptable religion must somehow bring together faith and reason, the results are disastrous.

Even when overtly irrational religion does not result, secularist pressures distort religion in one of two ways. (These ways are inconsistent, but some people are irrational enough to attempt to combine them.) One is to treat religion as a private fantasy or hobby, as a "lifestyle choice" rather like a taste for chocolate or bird watching, not to be taken seriously when engaging in politics, business, or other "real-world" activities. (Rawls's "public reason" encourages this sort of religion.) Or religion is treated as an adjunct to politics—a way of maintaining morale within a group struggling against opposition for some program—whether "liberal" or "conservative" does not matter.

Warren A. Nord (especially chs. 6–7) presents, as an alternative to secularist public education, a form of education that takes religion and its truth-claims seriously. But Nord's educational program is designed with some care to favor liberal Protestantism, against both its conservative and its "secular humanist" adversaries (see especially pp. 220–225). There is no doubt about his willingness to contest doctrinaire scientism: he proposes, for example, that students "be taught 'about' science just as they are taught 'about' religion" (p. 253). Nonetheless, he is far more concerned about fairness to non-Christian religions than about fairness to conservative forms of Christianity or Judaism (p. 233). Conservatism in religion, let us recall, is not a doctrine but a way of holding doctrines alien to the liberal mind, whose demands are not met by treating conservative ideas fairly within a liberal framework as Nord proposes (cf. pp. 257–258). At the deepest level, he assumes that it is possible to step outside of our cultural heritage to understand and evaluate radically alien positions, however difficult it may be to make truth-claims when one has done so (pp. 237–238).

Once we see that ignoring religion is in no sense neutral, it follows that religiously neutral education is impossible. Even a system of vouchers would require the state either to set limits on what forms of religion are publicly acceptable or to endorse a form of relativistic tribalism (cf. ch. 12). (This is not to say that vouchers may not be preferable to a public school system hostile to religion.) And what constitutes fairness—what points of view are reputable enough to deserve a hearing—will vary according to one's outlook. When we venture outside the range of positions familiar in the contemporary West, and confront popular Hinduism or Russian Old Belief, it becomes clear that there are many world-views most of us cannot take seriously enough even to refute them. And to make influence the decisive criterion is to endorse a version of the view that might makes right.

PROSPECTS FOR DIALOGUE

Secularism cannot be imposed on a diverse society without thereby destroying the very liberty it attempts to protect. Similarly, the effects of attempts to impose, say, Evangelical Christianity on such a society are also unattractive. Instead, adherents of every faith—whether or not conventionally regarded as religions—need to express their creeds openly and charitably, and to enter into practical and theoretical dialogue with one another.[42]

When called upon to spell out their presuppositions, liberals show themselves to be of divided mind.[43] Sometimes they are toned-down Nietzscheans who assume, on grounds not clear to me, that the demands of social peace override private visions. At other times they take disagreement about ultimates as a fact, without necessarily regarding it as permanent or desirable, and they look for those forms of proximate agreement necessary to maintain peace and mutual cooperation within pluralistic societies.[44] Only the second form of liberalism is tenable, since the first generates wider and wider disagreements, that will strain past the breaking point, whatever institutions we may devise to preserve social peace.

Serious questions remain about our ability to find a stable mean between the extremes of secularism and theocracy. For religious tolerance is from one perspective a strange, almost unnatural, phenomenon. Suppose some group appeals to revelation to establish a proposition to which other vocal groups strenuously object. If God has indeed spoken, then how dare we put the rules of civil society above His manifest will? If He has not, the claim to speak for Him is blasphemy, to which no tolerance is due. At least this is the case if appeals to God's will produce violations of the rules of civil society, or create an outlook for which issues like the size of the federal budget are an occasion for nonnegotiable demands.

When some political actors take unreasonable positions, the others have every incentive to refuse to compromise as well. This refusal may be expressed in entirely secular terms, but if political actors can make it more creditable by using religious language, some of them are sure to do so. What Laurence Tribe has called the "clash of absolutes" is therefore endemic to any form of politics that forsakes the path of pragmatic compromise. But if pragmatic compromise is given unlimited scope, there are no limits to the proposals—say, mass euthanasia for the homeless—that may be put forward. (In fact, limitless willingness to compromise favors the extremist.)

Even so, the prospects for dialogue are not hopeless. An important part of the good life is the search for the good life, in dialogue with like-minded others as well as those whose outlooks challenge our own. Our common humanity provides a basis for dialogue among diverse men and women—however unclear the character of that humanity might be, and however difficult such dialogue might appear in practice. From this common dialogue, no one is excluded except those who exclude themselves. To be sure, initially it rests, on a moral and political postulate rather than a theoretical insight.[45] But we have every reason to make this postulate, and we can find subsequent practical confirmation of its truth.

Believers in revelation must defend a conception of God which (unlike Aristotle's, for example) makes revelation possible. They must also show, not that any reasonable person would accept the Bible (say) as a vehicle of divine revelation, but that some reasonable people might. They must defend the inferences they draw from the vehicle of revelation they accept by principles of interpretation that are at least somewhat intelligible to outsiders. They must take part in dialogue on the question, On what terms can believers and disbelievers in biblical revelation live together in peace and mutual respect? The same issue arises concerning those whose "Bible" is a different set of documents and those who understand the same Bible in seriously different ways.

Other elements in our society must engage in parallel inquiries depending on the exact nature of their commitments. In the end, each party must decide for itself, in the light of its own commitments, which issues require martyrdom and which admit of compromise.

Yet the political problem remains. Religion is fragmented in American society, and there does not seem to be any way of changing that fact by morally acceptable means (and even nasty methods would probably not succeed). While those whose religious outlooks are importantly different— for example, Catholics and Evangelicals[46]—can work together for shared political purposes, in order to do so they will have to forget about theological issues that they may regard as extremely important in other contexts. Yet persons of a wide variety of religious outlooks can unite in repudiating strategies that would give one of the outlooks competing for our allegiance—that of atheistical or agnostic Northeastern liberals—the right unilaterally to define the ground rules for public discussion.

NOTES

1. I defend my own views in my book *Relativism, Nihilism, and God* (Notre Dame, Ind.: University of Notre Dame Press, 1989).

2. For an account of this phase of the history of our cultural conflicts, see Philip Gleason, *Speaking of Diversity* (Baltimore, Md.: Johns Hopkins University Press, 1992), ch. 8.

3. Harold Bloom, *The Western Canon* (New York: Harcourt Brace, 1994) defends a "canon" both too large and too eccentric for curricular purposes, perhaps because he is looking for a new Scripture.

4. Among "baby boomers," 42 percent of whom are "dropouts" from organized religion, 96 percent believe in God and 70 percent desire a return to stricter moral standards. (Statistics from W. Clark Roof, *A Generation of Seekers* [San Francisco: Harper, 1994], pp. 73, 96, 155.) As Stephen L. Carter has pointed out, black Americans are significantly more devout than white Americans and are thus unlikely knowingly to support a program that implies consigning traditional religious outlooks to the closet. See *The Culture of Disbelief* (New York: Basic Books, 1993), p. 69.

5. For a useful compendium of data on American religion, see Richard John Neuhaus, ed., *Unsecular America* (Grand Rapids, Mich.: Eerdmans, 1986), Appendix; on the Bible, see Table 12. For discussion of the significance of the data, see "The Story of an Enounter," ibid., pp. 67–114.

6. See R. Laurence Moore, *Selling God* (New York: Oxford University Press, 1994), especially ch. 3. Barry Alan Shain, *The Myth of American Individualism* (Princeton, N.J.: Princeton University Press, 1994), argues that religious (and specifically Protestant) conceptions have had a central influence on the formation of American conceptions of liberty and the public good.

7. Shain's anti-individualist reading of the Declaration of Independence (pp. 246ff.) seems to me strained.

8. See Orlando Patterson, "Ethnicity and the Pluralist Fallacy," *Change* 7 (March 1975): 15–16.

9. Moore puts it well. "Thumbing through J. Gordon Melton's *Encyclopedia of American Religions* is a humbling exercise. In addition to the more or less standard families, we find thick chapters labeled, 'Christian Science and Metaphysical Family,' 'Spiritual, Psychic, and New Age Families,' 'Ancient Wisdom Families,' and 'Magick Families.' Melton's book is not a historical catalogue. It is a guide to the present" (p. 256).

10. See ibid., *passim*.

11. Roof, *A Generation of Seekers*, p. 214.

12. See Thomas Day, *Why Catholics Can't Sing* (New York: Crossroad, 1992).

13. On how this happened, see George M. Marsden, *The Soul of the American University* (New York: Oxford University Press, 1994).

14. Moore, *Selling God*, p. 10.

15. See Kent Greenawalt, *Religious Convictions and Political Choice* (New York: Oxford University Press, 1988), ch. 3.

16. The defeated "Moderates" are represented by Walter Shurden, ed., *The Struggle for the Soul of the SBC* (Macon, Ga.: Mercer University Press, 1993).

17. A good short account of this development, which proposes nothing useful by way of a remedy, is Benton Johnson, "Winning Lost Sheep," in Robert S. Michaelsen and Wade Clark Roof, eds., *Liberal Protestantism* (New York: Pilgrim, 1986), ch. 13.

18. A good history of the Cold War, attending to its psychodynamics on the American side is H. W. Brands, *The Devil We Knew* (New York: Oxford University Press, 1993). On the role of the theologian Reinhold Niebuhr in constructing the Cold War ideology, see pp. 34–35.

19. Mary Daly, *Outercourse* (San Francisco: HarperSanFrancisco, 1992), p. 1n.

20. Ibid., p. 1.

21. Ibid. pp. 19, 20.

22. Ibid., p. 144.

23. See Mark Juergensmeyer, *The New Cold War?* (Berkeley: University of California Press, 1994).

24. Celia Wolf-Devine called my attention to this issue.

25. *Ecology* appears in the index neither of Robert Wuthnow's *Restructuring of American Religion* (Princeton, N.J.: Princeton University Press, 1988) nor of George Marsden's *Religion and American Culture* (San Diego: Harcourt Brace, 1990). It is also lacking in Roof's account of the elective spirituality of the "baby boom" generation, and in Moore's account of the marketing of American religion, despite the fact that Moore himself is a worshipper at the ecological shrine (pp. 273–274; note his use of words such as *stewardship* and *apocalyptic*).

26. This is Greenawalt's inquiry.

27. See my article, "On the Definition of 'Religion,' " *Faith and Philosophy* (July 1986). See further the Appendix.

28. Marsden, *Religion and American Culture*, p. 6.

29. Pierre Manent confuses theocracy with Christianity in his generally perceptive book *An Intellectual History of Liberalism*, Rebecca Balinski, trans. (Princeton, N.J.: Princeton University Press, 1994).

30. See, for example, Laurence Tribe, "Toward a Model of Roles in the Due Process of Life and Law," *Harvard Law Review* 87 (1973): 1–55.

31. On American secularism and its hopes for cultural dominance, see George M. Marsden, "Are Secularists the Threat?" in Neuhaus, ed., *Unsecular American*, pp. 31–51.

32. Moore, *Selling God*, p. 253.

33. Isaiah Berlin, *The Magus of the North*, Henry Hardy, ed. (London: John Murray, 1993); quotation, p. xv.

34. John Rawls, *A Theory of Justice* (Cambridge, Mass.: Harvard University Press), pp. 3, 4.

35. John Rawls, "Kantian Constructivism in Ethics," *Journal of Philosophy* 77 (1980): 515–572; "Justice as Fairness: Political not Metaphysical," *Philosophy & Public Affairs* 14 (1985): 223–251; and "The Idea of Overlapping Consensus," *Oxford Journal of Legal Studies* 7 (1987): 1–25. Rawls's later work is brought together in his *Political Liberalism* (New York: Columbia University Press, 1993), to which I make parenthetical reference in this subsection.

36. Michel Foucault, *Power/Knowledge*, Colin Gordon, ed., Colin Gordon et al. trans. (New York: Pantheon, 1980), p. 80.

37. Ibid., p. 36.

38. Parenthetical references in this subsection are to Greenawalt's *Religious Convictions and Political Choice*.

39. See Shain, *The Myth of American Individualism*.

40. Parenthetical references in this subsection are to *The Culture of Disbelief*.

41. I have benefited from the balanced discussion in Warren A. Nord, *Religion and American Education* (Chapel Hill: University of North Carolina Press, 1995), ch. 5. Parenthetical references in the remainder of this section are to this book.

42. I thus welcome the dialogical liberalism suggested by James S. Fishkin, *The Dialogue of Justice* (New Haven, Conn.: Yale University Press, 1992).

43. Rawls has repudiated the metaphysics attributed to him by Michael Sandel, *Liberalism and the Limits of Justice* (Cambridge: Cambridge University Press, 1982). What metaphysics he would accept remains uncertain; for another liberal writer, see the pair of quotations from Bruce Ackerman, *Social Justice and the Liberal State* (New Haven, Conn.: Yale University Press, 1980), cited in Sandel, p. 176 n.2.

44. This formulation derives ultimately from John Courtney Murray, *We Hold These Truths* (New York: Sheed and Ward, 1966); its immediate source is a lecture by Father J. Bryan Hehir at Providence College in the fall of 1994.

45. See chapter 6 under "The Humanist Program."

46. Odd things are happening in American religion these days. In 1995 I received a notice for a Tent Revival at the La Sallette Shrine (in Attleboro, Massachusetts).

Conclusion

I have been contending that dealing with human diversity requires a shared conception of our common humanity and that the more aware we are of the pervasiveness of diversity, the more important such a conception of human nature will be. At least for most people, this will mean a conception of human nature that is understood in traditional religious (and in America, in Christian) terms. These conclusions are of special importance in a society in which, as Gary Wills puts it, "the authority of government can no longer be assumed"[1]—in part because it has come to be seen as waging war against the moral and religious beliefs of the majority. It remains to develop this line of thought in detail and to examine the "Christian America" thesis—a view that many of my readers will find offensive or even threatening.

THE RELEVANCE OF GOD

Traditional arguments for and against the existence of God, or the rationality of belief in Him, are systematically unconvincing. The issue of the rationality of belief in God quickly resolves itself into that of canons of rational belief and meaningful discourse. Whether *God* is even a meaningful word, whether it makes sense to suppose that physical and moral evil are somehow remedied by other goods, and whether the sense of *cause* used in the Five Ways is a coherent one, are contested among philosophers, as are the various theories invoked to resolve them. Some of these theories have been designed with the explicit intention of excluding religious discourse from the sphere of rationality or even of meaningfulness. The concept of *meaning* is contested, too: what Jones finds profoundly meaningful, Smith finds cognitively meaningless, and often for roughly the same reasons.

This chapter argues, in the light of the discussion so far, that belief in God speaks significantly to cultural and political questions, and that we can dismiss it as meaningless or inherently irrational only at our peril. My apologetic aims are very modest: to persuade the reader that the question of the existence and nature of God is worth asking, and that outlooks that exclude it *a priori* are for that very reason questionable.

All discussion proceeds within a set of background assumptions concerning the kind of world we live in and the way we are well advised to conduct ourselves within it. A man or woman's view of the world affects, among other things, his or her conception of what data have evidentiary force (and how much). Where background pictures differ, therefore, disputes will be particularly intractable. It is thus easy to argue that claims about Ultimate Reality are implicated in disputes of every variety,[2] and to view those whose picture of the world is different from our own as irrational or mad. In fact, however, Christians and atheists share some assumptions and thus can see one another as, in a minimum sense, rational. Virtually no one accepted Sir Isaac Newton's personal theology; yet his physics was accepted by naturalists, Christians, and deists.

On the other hand, many contemporary philosophers begin with a policy of dogmatic closedness to the transcendent. If such people are right, *God* is not even a word, and any kind of causation that implies the existence of a Transcendent Cause is ruled out of court for that reason alone. Positivistic and semi-positivistic criteria of meaningfulness and rationality express and enforce such a policy, but the policy is antecedent to and independent of the particular criteria some philosopher or group of philosophers may advocate.

My argument begins with observations about human beings and their cultural traditions. The emergence of culture, including our own, is something of a mystery. We can explain how improved hunting techniques enable a tribe to survive periods when game is scarce, or how a shared religion may favor group survival by enhancing solidarity in times of distress. But evolution can explain neither the distinctive human capacities involved in cultural creation nor the particular creations that make up a cultural mix. Hence if a poet tells us that his work comes from the Muse, or a tribe tells us that its institutions were supplied by the gods, we cannot regard such explanations as unacceptable in principle.

What is true of culture in general is true of the cultures of contemporary liberal democracies. Liberalism and democracy invoke principles that are, at least in their origin, Jewish and Christian. That each of us is capable of judging what is good for ourselves and our society, and that each of us has a dignity and inviolability that even society as a whole is not entitled to override, are propositions that are most naturally supported by the belief that each of us was created in the image of God. We can, of course, affirm human dignity as an unreasoned axiom, or as part of our cultural heritage, or as part of some "secular" philosophy such as that of Kant, without accepting the religion within which this belief arose. But we cannot dismiss the claim that men and women were created in the image of God as inherently absurd. It is in the highest degree imprudent for those who believe in human dignity to adopt theoretical perspectives that exclude from public dialogue important sources of support for their central moral axiom. This is so even if they regret some of the implications drawn from a religious understanding of human dignity.

Let us suppose for the sake of argument that some philosopher could articulate, in terms of clear concepts and self-evident axioms, a comprehensive view of human existence, and that this philosophy supported some form of (perhaps expanded) democracy capable of being embodied in contemporary America. Let us even suppose that this philosophy fails to support those moral requirements of which many contemporary educated people are most eager to rid themselves. The adherents of such a philosophy would still be very few. although philosophers may hope to say everything clearly, most people use myths (in a nonderogatory sense) to express what they take to be the most important truths.

Nor is supporting democracy with a religion of democracy a likely prospect: the very majority to which democrats appeal will reject it as, to put it at the lowest, boring. As Talleyrand advised those of his day who proposed to found a new religion for political purposes, "Die and rise from the dead, and then we can talk about it."

The worship of democracy means the worship of ourselves (collectively), and nothing good has ever come of self-worship. What democracy needs, in any case, is not the self-celebration implied in turning it into a religion, but to overcome the many obstacles to its functioning that pervade the contemporary social world. Of the many such obstacles, I here limit myself to two that bear directly on cultural conflicts.

First, many members of the elite have isolated themselves, morally as well as materially, from the common herd. As Christopher Lasch puts it,

The culture wars that have convulsed America since the sixties are best understood as a form of class warfare, in which an enlightened elite (as it thinks of itself) seeks not so much to impose its values on the majority (a majority perceived as incorrigibly racist, sexist, provincial, and xenophobic), much less to persuade the majority, as to create parallel or "alternative" institutions in which it will be no longer necessary to confront the unenlightened at all.[3]

Second, the majority has more and more withdrawn from a political process it perceives to be an (often sordid) spectacle created for their entertainment. Hence they have not taken the trouble to acquire the information necessary for informed political choice, especially about painful and complex issues. To quote Lasch again, "In the absence of democratic exchange, most people have no incentive to master the knowledge that would make them capable citizens."[4]

To restore communication across social boundaries, we need a common frame of reference, which philosophy alone cannot provide. For one thing, philosophy, despite its aspiration toward clarity and rigor, always ends up acknowledging places where clarity is impossible. In contemporary secular philosophy,[5] these dark spots are at least four.

First, secular philosophers cannot explain how one can reasonably take some normative principles as overriding other legitimate concerns, and in particular how the demands of human dignity can require displacement of entrenched social customs. It took a bloody civil war to end slavery in America.

Second, liberals assume that we each have a fairly well-defined plan of life, with an equally well defined hierarchy of ends, and that our only problem is gaining or preserving our freedom to pursue them. Many men and women live their lives in happy indifference to ultimate questions, until some identity-threatening crisis arises, and many drift from choice to choice, without any sense of direction whatever. But identity-threatening crises, the most important of which is the approach of death, cannot be wholly avoided.

Third, communities need to define their identities, and the source of their claims on their members, while giving these members reasons to believe that their individual good is in harmony with the good of society. These problems become particularly intense in times of war and economic stringency, but they are also acute when a society has been deprived of a familiar enemy.

Liberals have characteristic problems explaining why it is that the present generation is obliged to continue the institutions and practices that their moral and physical ancestors created. They also have difficulty with parent-child relationships: small children are unable to make decisions for themselves in the way liberals want us to do, and in particular to measure the obedience due their parents by some philosophically defensible standard. Liberals also have difficulty explaining the larger claims of society on its members. John Rawls, for example, takes for granted "society [as] a more or less self-sufficient association of persons," in such a way that when he argues that "the difference principle represents . . . an agreement to regard the distribution of talents as a common asset,"[6] he does not see the need to ask "common among whom?" But when we ask this question, his theory falls apart.

Fourth, human beings are endlessly, and sometimes perversely, creative. Good students will not let a professor get away with saying, *Nobody thinks that . . .* , and thereby escape the need to reflect on his reasons for rejecting the proposition in question. The maxim *If you can think of it, someone will have done it* (with the corollary that *someone will have defended it*) implies a need to establish limitations on the possibilities for legitimate thought and action.[7] We need to show how reality checks can be established on the epistemological-metaphysical-linguistic fantasies of men and women, and in particular how these checks can be rich enough to enable people from diverse starting points to converge on the same (or at least compatible) results.

Religious traditions provide answers to the questions left unanswered by philosophy, though not in the lucid terms philosophers desire. I make this case for Christianity here but do not suppose that only Christianity is able to make it.

First, Christians hold that we are created in the image of God and therefore may not be treated in certain ways. Murder is prohibited, and the casuistry that distinguishes murder from justifiable homicide is governed by a strong presumption against easy exceptions. Slavery is wrong, as are all forms of social relationship akin to it.

Second, it is God Who establishes and maintains unity among the various elements of the self, even when circumstances threaten that unity. Each of us stands in a unique relationship to God, which defines our task here on earth, and may override communal attachments. Like Abraham, we may be required to depart from our father's house to find a new home.

Third, Christians do not face the problems secular liberals do in defining communal identity and asserting communal ties. We are created as social beings and commanded, though not unconditionally, to obey the authorities set over us. Many problems remain, but the fact of moral bonds among human beings is not among them.

The family, for example, makes better sense in Locke's (at least semi-Christian) view than on contemporary liberal premises. What most people want to say about parent-child relations makes best sense on the assumption that children are entrusted to their parents by God, but that He has also authorized others to intervene when parents abuse or neglect their children beyond tolerable limits.[8] The same is true of questions of justice outside the family: Locke starts from the assumption that "God . . . hath given the world to men in common,"[9] though he would never extend this argument to our talents and labors as Rawls does (nor would he accept Rawls's practical limitation of common ownership to the citizens of some nation-state). It is their shared divine origin that makes it possible to hope that the needs of the individual and the society will be, in the end, compatible, although their full reconciliation may have to take place outside the confines of the present world.

Fourth, God created us as part of a world independent of ourselves, which we can know and control only in part. Human beings take part in, and are able to create, a variety of institutions and cultural forms, but these forms are nonetheless subject to the strictures of the created order. Those who neglect the limits imposed by the created order will, sooner or later, be made to feel their power. The way the world constrains our inquiries and endeavors varies from science to politics to ethics to religion, and from time to time and from place to place. Exactly how these limits are established requires a great deal more discussion, and a final resolution of all questions concerning them is possible only at the Eschaton.

I have attempted to show that there is a God-shaped gap in our world and thus that religious questions (and hence also religious answers) are meaningful. I have not attempted, however, to supply a coercive argument against those for whom *God* is incapable of designating anything. Dogmatic closedness to the transcendent can, like any other viewpoint, be held against all objections, although its adherents must be prepared to pay the theoretical and practical costs.

To argue for the relevance of God as I have is not to imply that God exists, so to speak, in order to be relevant to us. Modernist critics of religion like Freud[10] interpret it as assuring us that we are the favored creatures of Omnipotence. Sometimes they call upon us to reject this belief in the name of maturity; sometimes they acknowledge that illusions are necessary for at least some people. In its most radical forms, however, religion challenges such complacency and calls upon us to love a world we did not create and which we only in part understand.

Much of what I have said on behalf of Christians might also be said on behalf of other religions. Both Christians and adherents of other religions will also want to defend the relevance of their special doctrines—in the Christian case, the doctrines of the Trinity[11] and the Incarnation. All I can do as a philosopher is to urge the widest possible dialogue, and as much mutual tolerance as our situation and convictions permit. The rest must be left, as the theists among us would put it, to God.

CHRISTIAN AMERICA?

Politics has two aspects, which cannot be disentangled in practice. One is the struggle for material advantage, and the other a struggle among various ways of understanding and evaluating the world—including the importance of material advantage. Without denying the importance of "who gets what?" questions, I have attempted here to say something useful about cultural politics.

Standard liberal answers to questions of cultural politics are inadequate. Rawls's attempt to wall off such larger questions, and in so doing silence expressions of what may be true and rationally held beliefs, is unacceptable.[12] Simply accepting the incoherence of our institutions, as liberals of a postmodern stripe would do, leaves us paralyzed in the fact of internal and external challenge. Unless somehow rooted in a larger scheme, liberty means the freedom to exploit others and to disregard the requirements of the common good, without constraint. The fear of a slippery slope toward social Darwinism motivates many welfare liberals to support programs about which they entertain considerable doubts, especially in the absence of any coherent philosophy in terms of which they might generate and justify alternatives. Deifying change has dismal results: it is hardly prudent to take radical positions on questions of political economy without a coherent moral framework in terms of which we can assess both economic institutions and programs for changing them. Otherwise there is no end to the dreary process by which oppressed become oppressors.

Appeals to collective memory[13] are important in all societies, and the declining fortunes of political correctness have made them possible once again, even in elite academic circles.[14] But these appeals will inevitably require us to consider the religion of our (literal or metaphorical) ancestors.[15] External enemies are always a fruitful source of solidarity, but I at least find seeking them out both dangerous and morally questionable. And vague appeals to the Judeo-Christian tradition offend both serious Jews and serious Christians.

For these reasons, we must look again at the "Christian America" thesis. This thesis (which would not hold for Japan, for example) is that our institutions, on those occasions when they are more than a set of ad hoc compromises among competing contenders for power, make sense only in a context of Christian belief.[16] To have any plausibility, it must refer to a generic Christianity—neither Protestant nor Catholic—and it requires, not an established church, but a coalition of religious communities concurring on issues of political importance. This thesis is logically independent of the truth of Christianity itself, although when held by an atheist it produces the disturbing problems summed up in Dostoevsky's Grand Inquisitor and the Platonic doctrine of the noble lie. From a Christian point of view, it raises the possibility that Christianity itself will be distorted by its political uses.

The Christian America thesis faces powerful historical and political objections. Many of the Founding Fathers were deists, and pantheism subsequently became important in the formation of the American mind. Jewish and agnostic Kantian (and now Buddhist, Hindu, and Islamic) citizens should not be excluded from public discourse. The popularity of New Age religious doctrines also creates a political problem. Among these groups, Jews have an importance disproportionate to their numbers: for one thing, many people alienated from their Christian origins have felt drawn to the Jewish tradition.[17]

But deism has more or less died out, and is thus unavailable for political purposes, so that the philosophy of the Declaration of Independence requires another kind of support. Competent and well-informed philosophers describe the Enlightenment as atheistic, showing how much the deism of most Enlightenment figures has been effaced.[18] It is hard to see how one can distinguish, on pantheist principles, between moral or political good and moral or political evil. Judaism and so forth are destined to be the views of minorities (except in Hawaii, where Buddhism appears to have become the majority religion).[19] The possibly corrupting influence of "Christian America" on Christianity itself is a matter for intra-Christian dialogue.

Elite nihilism undermines concern for the poor and the afflicted, our capacity to work together for common ends, and in the end even social tolerance. One of democracy's strengths is that it enables diverse people to work out common problems, while respecting one another's right to differ, and in that way discovering one another's humanity. Even Rawls found it necessary, in his early work at least, to conclude with a muted appeal to Christian concepts: "Purity of heart, if one could attain it, would be to see clearly and act with grace and self-command from this point of view."[20] A Christian approach to politics need not mean unwillingness to look at the dark side of a market economy, including a tendency to legitimate selfish hedonism, to break up communities, and to sanction indifference by the fortunate to the well-being of the poor.[21] (This is not to say that there is a case for getting rid of markets altogether.)

In short, democracy is now in alliance with a nuanced appeal to our Christian heritage.[22] Perhaps the most judicious formula is that we are a predominantly Christian society, except on the many occasions when we are devoted to the selfish pursuit of pleasure, power, and prestige, and that our political and legal institutions, even when in the formal sense religiously neutral, rest and are intended to rest on a believing society. My conclusion concerns society, not the state; hence it need not mean that we should dismantle what is (not very aptly) called the "wall of separation" between church and state.[23] Accepting the Christian America thesis, however, will have an impact on the way this idea is applied; one must take care to prevent a large and invasive secular government from undermining the legitimate religious beliefs of the people. Forms of public education which silently—and for that reason all the more effectively—convey the message that religion is irrelevant to thought (and hence that thought is irrelevant to religion) are open to severe objections on this ground.

Even the most judicious appeal to the concept of Christian America must, however, face the charge of implicit anti-Semitism (not surprisingly, since many arguments like mine have lapsed into it). Protestations of goodwill toward Jewish friends and colleagues will not refute this charge, since arguments have a logic independent of the intentions of their authors. A more adequate approach begins with a distinction between the modern, racial variety of anti-Semitism, which does not care whether the object of its hatred is Jewish or Christian (or, for that matter, Buddhist) in its religious beliefs; and traditional religious anti-Semitism (more accurately, anti-Judaism). The first and more virulent sort of anti-Semitism is, from a Christian point of view, absurd (though many Christians have fallen into it). As St.

Ignatius Loyola put it, I would be proud to be related to the Virgin Mary. Intolerance is a constant temptation to anyone who takes his beliefs seriously, and is by no means limited to Christians. Outside a dogmatic theological context, I can only cite the consensus of contemporary reflective Christians, both Protestant and Catholic, that religious freedom deserves protection on Christian as much as on worldly grounds.

Any structure (even a chaotic one) will marginalize some people and thus threaten to oppress them. It is possible to steer a middle course between oppression of minorities and allowing aggressive secularizers to exploit feelings of collective guilt to destroy the framework that, in the end, is the source of the principles that protect minorities. The problem of respecting minority rights without hamstringing the majority is a perpetual problem of democratic politics, and it cannot be evaded by denying the majority the right to vote their convictions.

NOTES

1. Gary Wills, "The New Revolutionaries," *New York Review of Books* 42, 13 (August 18, 1995): 54.

2. See Roy A. Clouser, *The Myth of Religious Neutrality* (Notre Dame, Ind.: University of Notre Dame, 1990).

3. Christopher Lasch, *The Revolt of the Elites* (New York: Norton, 1995), pp. 20–21.

4. Ibid., p. 12.

5. I regard Hilary Putnam as one of the best among the secular philosophers, despite his avowal of Judaism in *Renewing Philosophy* (Cambridge, Mass.: Harvard University Press, 1992). He has done next to nothing toward applying a Jewish perspective to normative, let alone metaphysical and epistemological, issues.

6. John Rawls, *A Theory of Justice* (Cambridge, Mass.: Harvard University Press, 1971), pp. 4, 101. Allen Buchanan cites an unpublished manuscript in which Rawls speaks of his contractors as joined in "one co-operative scheme in perpetuity" in *Secession* (Boulder, Colo.: Westview, 1991), p. 5. My critique of Rawls at this point derives from Sandel.

7. See my forthcoming book, *The Search for Moral Absolutes*.

8. See the contrast between Locke and Rawls's follower Jeffrey Blustein, drawn by Joshua Jacob Ross in *The Virtues of the Family* (New York: Free Press, 1994), pp. 139–140.

9. John Locke, *Of Civil Government*, sec. 26. Found in John Somerville and Ronald E. Santoni, *Social and Political Philosophy* (Garden City, N.Y.: Doubleday Anchor, 1963), p. 175.

10. As opposed to Enlightenment critics, who are content to argue that core religious claims are false; and postmodern critics, who oppose to Christianity and Judaism a mythology of their own.

11. John Milbank's difficult book, *Theology and Social Theory* (Oxford: Basil Blackwell, 1990), suggests the crucial social relevance of the doctrine of the Trinity.

12. See chapter 11 of this volume under "Theoretical Perspectives," paragraph 1.

13. For a study of this phenomenon, see Michael Kammen, *Mystic Chords of Memory* (New York: Knopf, 1992).

14. David Hackett Fischer, Warren Professor of History at Brandeis, makes repeated reference to Paul Revere's "message for our time" in his *Paul Revere's Ride* (New York: Oxford University Press, 1995); for example, see p. 344.

15. See Kammen, *Mystic Chords of Memory*, ch. 7, on the replacement of traditional religion by filiopietism.

16. Eugene Genovese appears to endorse this thesis in his review of Barry Allan Shain, *The Myth of American Individualism*, in *First Things* 55 (August-September 1995): 45–47.

17. For example, Edmund Wilson; Jeffrey Meyers, *Edmund Wilson* (Boston: Houghton Mifflin, 1995), pp. 355–363.

18. See Peter Van Inwagen, "Quam Dilecta," in Thomas V. Morris ed., *God and the Philosophers* (New York: Oxford University Press, 1994), pp. 49ff. There is, however, a World Deist Society (P.O. Box 178, Webster, Wisconsin 54893–0178 USA), which advocates, among other things, vegetarianism and nudism. (I am indebted to Stanley Azaro, O.P., for this information.)

19. Warren A. Nord, *Religion and American Education* (Chapel Hill: University of North Carolina Press, 1995), p. 206.

20. Rawls, *A Theory of Justice*, p. 587.

21. A leading American conservative observes that "the three pillars of modern conservativism are religion, nationalism, and [capitalist] economic growth," blandly ignoring the conflicts among these "pillars." Irving Kristol, "Foreword," in Michael Cromartie, ed., *Disciples and Democracy* (Washington, D.C.: Ethics and Public Policy Center, 1994), p. viii.

22. Nominal Christians make up 85 percent of the American population: the closest thing to a consensus that one can expect in the present world. (Jews make up 2 percent of the population, and Muslims 0.5 to 2 percent, making a majority of 87.5 to 89 percent for some form of theism. Hindus and Buddhists make up another 1 percent, and 11 percent claim no religion.) Figures from Nord, *Religion and American Education*, p. 286.

23. No one, to my knowledge, has formulated American church-state doctrine adequately. Nord does as good a job as anyone when he defends "substantive neutrality," which requires government to act affirmatively to minimize the negative impact of its secular programs on religious belief. This means, for example, that fair-minded examination of religious ideas should be mandatory in the public schools (ibid., p 247), whereas school "vouchers" are constitutionally permissible (though they may not be a good idea) (p. 373). But, as he acknowledges, "judgments about what is substantively neutral may require a measure of subtlety" (p. 131).

Appendix: Four Problem Concepts

This appendix is analytic in character and includes material that would otherwise break the flow of the main argument. It seeks to clarify four difficult concepts that have an important role in any discussion of the culture wars—setting aside normative questions so far as possible. (They cannot be avoided entirely.) The concepts considered here are *conservatism*, *culture*, *modern*, and *secular*.

CONSERVATISM

Sometimes *conservative* means "pro-capitalist," a formulation that limits conservatism to one family of issues, marginal to the concerns of this book. The sense of conservatism favored by many Americans, advocacy of small government, in fact designates a species of liberalism. Some policies now thought of as conservative—such as free speech and academic freedom, and race-blind educational policies—were once thought liberal or even radical. Sometimes a "conservative" is anyone who invokes the reality principle to control the epistime-metaphysico-linguistic fantasies of intellectuals. In this sense, Karl Marx and V. I. Lenin were conservatives. Many other "conservatives" are severe critics of existing institutions who fail to fit the standard left-liberal paradigm.

In the simplest sense, a conservative resists innovation, whether out of interest, inertia, love of the status quo, identification with the powerful, or fear of the alternatives. Up to a point, conservatives will try to reverse changes of recent vintage—although there is no clear way of answering the question "how recent?" Beyond that point, however, they are prepared to tolerate those aspects of the status quo they dislike for the sake of those they treasure. If they attempt to reverse changes that occurred before a certain undefined point, they are called *reactionary* or, more politely, *restorationist*. The recognition of the irreversibility of historical change is a characteristic feature of reflective conservative thought.[1] But the point at which a conservative is obliged to accept change as irreversible is ambiguous, especially in the present climate.

Conservatives define justice, as far as possible, as conformity to the laws and customs of one's society, and they resist claims that these laws and customs are themselves unjust. A radical, by way of contrast, presses just this sort of claim, though of late Nietzsche's invasion of the Left has eroded radical claims of justice in favor of demands for power. In any event, radicals need be in little agreement with one another, since there is not one but many ways in which we might depart from the status quo. Some of those called "conservative" are in fact radicals, the adoption of whose ideas would mean massive and quite possibly destabilizing changes in the structure of our society.

But the status quo is in constant flux. Hence conservatives are concerned primarily with stability and will propose changes of a moderately large sort for its sake.[2] But when they advocate change, including reversal of changes of recent vintage, they do so in part at least to stabilize existing laws and customs. These changes may turn out to be far larger in their implications than conservatives realize. Moreover, real-life conservatives are prepared under some circumstances to go into radical opposition, although conservatism as such cannot define what the limits of their acquiescence in innovation might be.

The maxim, *When it is necessary to change, it is necessary not to change*, has distinct limitations in a world in which our institutions, like it or not, are constantly bringing about changes. For example, conservatives are always shutting their eyes, and that of their readers, to the massive social changes a market economy generates. Reversing such changes, or stopping them at their source, will require political and economic, and perhaps even cultural, change of an unsettling nature. When the status quo becomes confusing beyond a certain point, the word *conservative* loses its utility, whether as a term of censure or as a term of blame. For the issue is frequently not *whether* to change, but *in what way* to do so. At this point, the instinctual conservatism of the human species does not provide an adequate response.

One sort of conservative endeavors to maintain and repair a community's moral, religious, and cultural traditions. Cultural and political-economic conservatism are potentially in great conflict with one another. For those in power can use it to exempt themselves from shared moral traditions and in that and other ways weaken the force of those traditions throughout the community. The pursuit of wealth and power within the existing framework frequently disrupts those communities that sustain such traditions. Nonetheless, effective cultural conservatism may require cultural as well as political and economic change. The Hebrew prophets are equally concerned with the oppression of the rich and powerful, and with transgressions of religious law, but they were not interested in preserving the cultural status quo as such.

CULTURE

Definitions of *culture* need to steer a middle course between two extremes. The anthropological sense includes all features of the life of a society, however trivial. On the other hand, "high culture" is too narrow: on any reasonable understanding, baseball is as much a part of American culture as Dante or even Whitman. I thus define the culture of a society as the conglomerate of norms and standards, epistemic as well as moral, which its members (often incoherently and half-consciously) share. I assume the existence of discrete and even somewhat independent cultures only for the sake of simplicity: in fact, each individual has a unique implicit world-view, derived from a number of sources. But even the most reflective individual makes only a small contribution to the formation of such a view.

A culture is thus an implicit world-picture, which tells its adherents how things are and must be and ought to be, and how these three aspects of their world are related. It provides a picture of the natural world and of the social world (what Charles Taylor calls "the social imaginary"),[3] and sometimes of the supernatural world as well. It includes religion, language, etiquette and sports as well as art and literature; but it does not include rules of technique assessed in strictly pragmatic terms.

A rough synonym for *culture* is *background*, which Taylor explains as follows:

Our explicit beliefs about our world and ourselves are held against a background of unformulated (and perhaps in part unformulable) understandings, in relation to which these beliefs make the sense they do. In one dimension, the background incorporates matters that *could* be formulated as beliefs, but aren't functioning as such in our world (and couldn't *all* function as such because of their unlimited extent). . . . In other dimensions, I have this kind of understanding of myself as an agent with certain powers, of myself as an agent among other agents. And I want to add: an agent moving in certain kinds of social spaces, with a sense of how both I and these spaces inhabit time, a sense of how both I and they relate to the cosmos and to God or whatever I recognize as the source(s) of good.[4]

MODERNITY

In the strict chronological sense, the modern world is the world now in place, and the referent of this description is constantly changing. There seems to be no reason why we must embrace or reject modernity as such, but people frequently do. As Clifford Geertz puts it, "modern is what some of us think we are, others of us wish desperately to be, yet others despair of being, or regret, or oppose or fear, or, now, desire somehow to transcend."[5]

I thus consider the use of the word *modern* in an evaluatively charged context. The most important feature of the modern world, for evaluative purposes, is rapid change; and what is not the same thing, intense awareness of change, especially in the implicit norms governing belief and conduct. Ideas and attitudes that are avant garde at one time are conventional at another and old-fashioned at yet another. Even more confusingly, ideas that are old-fashioned at one time are avant garde at another.

One can imagine, following Bernard Williams, a *hypertraditional* society in which reasoning is merely the application of inherited standards. One can also imagine a *hypermodern* society in which change occurs so quickly and decisively as to free the members of society from troubling memories. To imagine such societies is to imagine what we are not. One important consequence of rapid change in law and custom is the loss of an unquestionable background against which discussion can proceed. "Old-fashioned" ideas persist, but even their adherents come to view them as such rather than as self-evident truths.

Taylor has distinguished two different understandings of modernity.[6] The *acultural* understanding regards modernity as the result of human capacities for good or evil, independent of the particular history and cultural configurations of our civilization, which all societies are destined to realize in fundamentally the same way. It is thus easy to applaud or condemn modernity as such, depending on whether one believes the human capacities realized in it are virtuous, sinful, or mixed. (An example of a mixed view is the position of some writers—Leo Strauss and his followers perhaps—that modernity consists in the acquisition of forms of knowledge which, though compelling for the elite, cannot be safely shared with the mass.)

According to the *cultural* understanding, modernity involves a distinct culture, as different in its own way from medieval Europe as each of them is from traditional Japan. As such, it contains a distinctive vision of the social, physical, and spiritual universe, which makes room for distinctively modern virtues such as responsible autonomy understood in broadly Kantian terms. On such a view of modernity, the task of evaluation is much more difficult (which is not to say impossible).

One thing that makes it even more difficult is that modernity has no clear meaning, even when understood as a distinctive culture rather than as a universal human capacity for enlightenment or sin. Thus Geertz sums up the experience of "emergent" nations very well when he writes:

What was surprising, and disorganizing as well, was that modernity turned out to be less a fixed destination than a vast and inconstant field of warring possibilities, possibilities neither simultaneously reachable nor systematically connected, neither well defined nor unequivocally attractive.[7]

Nonetheless, modernity does involve a world of rapid change and enormous possibilities, good, bad, and equivocal. Such a world provides the occasion for the exercise of important virtues, but *even when the change in question is altogether welcome*, it also provides the occasion for lives of the shallowest and most selfish sort.

Four different attitudes toward modernity are possible. *Modernism* affirms the authority of the modern world: it proposes to drag others, not always kindly, "kicking and screaming into the twentieth century." Paradoxically, poets who are modernist in their style are frequently disgusted with the modern world and in search of new values in old places. In this respect, they might be compared with those contemporary Southern Baptists who exploit contemporary communications technology to maximum advantage. Modernism undergoes crisis when a new generation arises, which rejects the work of the previous generation as old hat: other schools of thought can dismiss such charges, but not modernism. Moreover, the war on "old-fashioned" ideas sooner or later undermines every criterion by which some changes as opposed to others can be regarded as progressive and others reactionary. *Antimodernism*, in contrast, rejects the modern world, while accepting the modernists' terms of reference.

Postmodernism—to use the paradoxical expression now customary—is despairing modernism. The postmodernist despairs of getting the chaos of the modern world to produce a new order, of stopping the process of change that creates the problem, or even of ending the disturbing persistence of premodern attitudes and practices within the modern world. He therefore is content to play idly with a decaying tradition.

A fourth attitude could also be called postmodern, but to avoid confusion I prefer the equally paradoxical expression *neotraditionalist*. Like the other people I have considered, the neotraditionalist confronts the confusion created by a rapidly changing world, and the threat of nihilism implicit in attacks on inherited standards. But he uses them as an occasion to apply half-forgotten ideas in an innovative way. In fact, the most important "conservative" thinkers have always been innovators of this sort. Such thinkers include Pascal, Berkeley, Burke, Leo XIII, and in our own age Alasdair MacIntyre. A complementary class of neotraditionalists are thinkers who apply thoroughly traditional ideas in support of political or economic innovation. They include the American Founding Fathers, Frederick Douglass, Gandhi, Abraham Lincoln, and Martin Luther King, Jr.

THE SECULAR

In its origins, *secular* is a term in Christian tradition. It refers to the affairs of the society controlled by the human desire for pleasure, power, and prestige as opposed to the community created by the love of God and neighbor. St. Augustine took the Roman Empire as his prime example of the city of man and the Christian Church as his prime example of the city of God, though in neither case can one assert a strict identity.

In the crudest understanding of the spiritual-secular distinction, therefore, secularization means nothing less than the triumph of evil, and secularists are for that reason the minions of Satan. As used by a student of comparative religions, however, the word cannot have quite that meaning. For even if Christianity (or "orthodox" Christianity) were to die out utterly, this would not necessarily produce a secular society, since other religions could—and very likely would—fill the resulting gap.

A definitional strategy at the other end of the spectrum marks out certain experiences, problems, and needs as spiritual in character, and distinguish, as secular, those institutions and ideas that do not attempt to address them. The spiritual in this sense can be evil: after all, not all spirits are of God. And the secular may be entirely good (though no doubt incomplete). Yet this definition questionably requires us to distinguish religious from worldly aspects of our lives, independent of any particular religious framework.

Let us therefore begin afresh. We know that Christianity is a religion. If we ask whether Scientology, for example, is a religion as well, we are asking whether it resembles Christianity sufficiently to be treated in the same way for (say) legal purposes. And if we do conclude that Scientology is a religion, we can expect to distinguish those matters that are "sacred" for its adherents, from those matters that they regard as secular. A sacred matter will be one to which the teachings of Scientology are directly relevant, whereas their relevance to a profane issue, while not for that reason nonexistent, will be at least oblique.

But the Christian tradition has many features, the presence or absence of which may lead us to call a tradition religious, or refuse it that designation. There is no reason, at least so far, to suppose that the distinction between secular and sacred enjoys a privileged place among these features. We do not yet have a way of understanding the claim that a society, such as Japan, in which Christianity has never played much of a role, is highly secular. Nor can we expect Muslims to accept arguments for tolerance, if these include a distinction between sacred and secular alien to Islamic thought.

Escape from this impasse requires a rudimentary philosophical anthropology. Human beings, we may say, are among other things animals. We are conceived and born, we eat and excrete; we mate, care for our young, and die, in ways that at least resemble the patterns to be found in the lives of birds and mammals. We are also social beings—in many obvious and subtle ways dependent on one another for our survival and flourishing.

Hence we govern our lives, in the first instance, by inherited norms taught, upheld, and enforced by the other members of our society. We make up for the relative weakness and indeterminacy of instinct through individual and collective habits, which can have almost the force of instinct. Yet our lives contain features and episodes that require us to step outside inherited patterns of life, and ask ourselves questions concerning their meaning and validity. There is no way of formulating these questions that is entirely neutral across cultural and religious traditions; nonetheless "What's it all about?" approximates neutrality more closely than "What must I do to be saved?"

Among the events that put our lives in question, the chief is death, or rather its prospect. The same is true of the breakups and re-formation of societies—indeed, of all historical change, whether welcome or unwelcome, that redefines our world. It is not surprising that some of our most important religious texts come from a small nation, caught between larger powers, that was first destroyed by external invasion, and then managed to reestablish itself (and has in fact done so twice).

Religious expressions are distinguished from those of art and literature by their claim to convey a truth that belongs to a larger community rather than an individual's private vision. (This line is often unclear, especially with the Romantic poets.) Religious expressions are distinguished from those of philosophy by their use of imaginative representations (in a non-derogatory sense, "myth") to establish their coherence; and by their invocation of suprahuman powers, on whose favor the welfare of the believer and his community is thought to depend. (Some religions contain only one of these features.)[8]

We may thus distinguish religion from that of the routine pursuit of ends, such as the making of a living, whose value and significance are taken as indisputable. Religion has to do, first, with the coherence of a life taken as a whole; and, second, with a Good that cannot be adequately expressed in the language of ordinary life.

We may thus define the *secular* as the sphere of life in which ultimate questions are kept at bay. *Secularization* is a process of banishing ultimate questions from daily discourse, and a *secular society* is one in which this repression has been carried out. (The advantages and disadvantages of repressing ultimate concerns are similar to those of repressing sexuality.) More and more of life comes to be carried on according to routines, and in accordance with technical principles, to which ultimate concerns are irrelevant, and which are in turn irrelevant to questions of ultimate concern.

A consequence of these definitions is that secularism and atheism are not the same. Some believers ignore their beliefs with remarkable efficiency, and some atheists believe that Christianity (or whatever religion is widely believed in their society), though false, nonetheless plays an indispensable social role. Moreover, there are forms of religion characteristic of secular society—as a fantasy disconnected with "real-world" activities such as politics and business, and as a morale-building adjunct to those activities. One can, for example, conclude, on entirely secular grounds, that we must retard or reverse the fragmentation characteristic of modern societies, and invoke religion instrumentally for this end (for example, as a way of dealing with tensions within a family, or as a ground for denouncing the "secular humanists" who oppose this program).

CONCLUDING NOTE

A culture begins with a powerfully held and socially cohesive set of beliefs—a religion in the broad sense. Secularization means that more and more of the life of society gets done without explicit reference to these beliefs, so that it becomes easier to disbelieve or violate them while remaining a member in good standing of society. Some individuals continue to accept the governing beliefs of their tradition, even fervently. But as the lessening of its social supports changes, the quality of their belief changes, sometimes in an admirable way, sometimes in the direction of laxity or fanaticism. Sometimes the shared beliefs around which people organize their lives become less fervently held, where they are not denied outright; at other times, they lose definition even as they gain energy.

Up to a point, this fading of shared belief is consistent with social health, and even with great creative activity (and even with personal sanctity), as men and women struggle with its implications. But at some point the danger of disintegration becomes acute. Then either the governing beliefs of society need to be revived, perhaps in a modified form, or else some new tradition moves into the resulting vacuum. Under such circumstances, the threat of anarchy is acute—or more likely, the threat of a pitiless regime put into power with the promise of maintaining order.

Perhaps the succession of cultures represents the progress of a master tradition from strength to strength, even if through periods of decline. Perhaps it represents a decline, even if punctuated by brief rallies, from some past epoch of cultural purity (though it has always been difficult for traditionalists to specify persuasively when this epoch was). It may also represent an endless cycle of rise and decline, without there being any larger story. We may have hopes and fears about such things but hardly knowledge.

There was a time when many scholars held that the decline of religion, or at least of public religion, was irreversible. But a one-time prophet of the "secular city" now writes: "Today it is secularity, not spirituality, which may be headed for extinction."[9] As for what journalists will be saying three decades from now, I prefer not to speculate, though without doubt they will tell a story in which our present situation is a waystation to theirs.

NOTES

1. For example, T. S. Eliot: "We cannot revive old factions, we cannot restore old policies/ Or follow an antique drum./ These men, and those who opposed them/ and those whom they opposed/ Accept the constitution of silence/ and are folded in a single party" ("Little Gidding," Pt. III).

2. The contrast between stability and justice derives from Peter Steinfels, *The Neoconservatives* (New York: Simon and Schuster, 1979), especially pp. 53–55.

3. Charles Taylor, "Two Theories of Modernity," *Hastings Center Report* 23, 2 (March-April 1995): 29.

4. Ibid., p. 28. Taylor (p. 33 n.4) cites the following philosophers as sources for this concept: Martin Heidegger, Maurice Merleau-Ponty, Ludwig Wittgenstein, Michael Polyani, John Searle, and Hubert Dreyfus.

5. Clifford Geertz, *After the Fact* (Cambridge, Mass.: Harvard University Press, 1995), p. 136.

6. Taylor, "Two Theories of Modernity," especially pp. 24–27. See also his book, *The Ethics of Authenticity* (Cambridge, Mass.: Harvard University Press, 1992).

7. Geertz, *After the Fact*, p. 138.

8. See my article, "On the Definition of 'Religion,' " *Faith and Philosophy*, July 1986.

9. Harvey Cox, *Fire from Heaven* (Reading, Mass.: Addison-Wesley, 1995), p. xv. He quotes (p. xvii) Gilles Kepel on "the revenge of God."

Selected Bibliography

PERSPECTIVES

The classification is rough. I apologize to those who dislike the company in which I have placed them.

The Cultural Right

Arkes, Hadley. "Strauss and the Religion of Reason." *National Review* 47, 12 (June 26, 1995): 60ff. This essay by a disciple confirms that Leo Strauss was an atheist.

Cromartie, Michael, ed. No Longer Exiles. Washington, D.C.: Ethics and Public Policy Center, 1993.

Fleming, Thomas. *The Politics of Human Nature*. New Brunswick: Transaction, 1988.

John Paul II. "Verititatis Splendor." *Origins* 23 (1993): 297–336.

Johnson, Phillip E. "Do You Sincerely Want to Be Radical?" *Stanford Law Review* 36 (1984): 247–291. A probing critique of the Critical Legal Studies Movement (see Unger, below), which does not endorse the "liberal rationalist" alternative, either.

———. *Reason in the Balance: The Case against Naturalism in Science, Law, and Education*. Downers Grove, Ill.: InterVarsity Press, 1995.

Lasch, Christopher. *The True and Only Heaven*. New York: W. W. Norton, 1991.

Limbaugh, Rush. *See, I Told You So*. New York: Pocket Books, 1993.

MacIntyre, Alasdair. *After Virtue*. Rev. ed. Notre Dame, Ind.: University of Notre Dame Press, 1984.

———. *Three Rival Versions of Moral Enquiry*. Notre Dame, Ind.: University of Notre Dame Press, 1990.

Neuhaus, Richard John. *America Against Itself.* Notre Dame, Ind.: Notre Dame University Press, 1992.

Robertson, Pat. *The Turning of the Tide.* Dallas, Tex.: Word Publishing, 1994. Shows the addiction of even the most conservative Americans to historical optimism.

Scruton, Roger. *The Meaning of Conservatism.* Totowa, N.J.: Barnes and Noble, 1980.

———. *The Philosopher at Dover Beach.* New York: St. Martin's, 1990.

Shils, Edward. *Tradition.* Chicago: University of Chicago Press, 1981.

Strauss, Leo. *Persecution and the Art of Writing.* Glencoe, Ill.: Free Press, 1952. A poorly understood and often unacknowledged presence in cultural debates, Strauss is the Machiavelli of the intellectual life.

The Cultural Center

Dewey, John, and James H. Tufts. *Ethics.* Rev. ed. New York: Henry Holt, 1932.

Fishkin, James S. *The Dialogue of Justice.* New Haven, Conn.: Yale University Press, 1992.

Frank, Manfred. *What Is Neostructuralism?* Sabine Wilke and Richard Gray, trans. Minneapolis, Minn.: University of Minnesota Press, 1989.

Gates, Henry Louis, Jr. "Beyond the Culture Wars." *Profession* 93 (1993): 6–11.

Hackney, Sheldon. "Toward a National Conversation." *The Responsive Community* 4, 3 (summer 1994): 16–20.

Hunter, James Davison. *Culture Wars.* New York: Basic, 1991.

Kekes, John. *The Morality of Pluralism.* Princeton, N.J.: Princeton University Press, 1993.

Kennan, George. *Around the Cragged Hill: A Personal and Political Philosophy.* New York: Norton, 1993.

Lasch, Christopher. *The Revolt of the Elites and the Betrayal of Democracy.* New York: Norton, 1995.

Putnam, Hilary. *Realism with a Human Face.* James Conant, ed. Cambridge, Mass.: Harvard University Press, 1990.

———. *Words and Life.* James Conant, ed. Cambridge, Mass.: Harvard University Press, 1994.

Rawls, John. *Political Liberalism.* New York: Columbia University Press, 1993.

———. *A Theory of Justice.* Cambridge, Mass.: Harvard University Press, 1971.

Sandel, Michael. *Liberalism and the Limits of Justice.* Cambridge, Mass.: Cambridge University Press, 1982.

Steiner, George. *Real Presences.* Chicago: University of Chicago Press, 1989.

Steinfels, Peter. *The Neoconservatives.* New York: Simon and Schuster, 1979.

Taylor, Charles. *The Ethics of Authenticity.* Cambridge, Mass.: Harvard University Press, 1992.

Trilling, Lionel. *The Liberal Imagination: Essays in Literature and Society.* Garden City, N. Y.: Doubleday Anchor, 1953.

The Cultural Left

Daly, Mary. *Outercourse.* San Francisco: HarperSanFrancisco, 1992.

Derrida, Jacques. *The Gift of Death*. David Wills, trans. Religion and Postmodernism, Mark C. Taylor, ed. Chicago: University of Chicago Press, 1995. This book appeared too late for me to take into account here.

———. *Of Grammatology*. Baltimore: Johns Hopkins University Press, 1976.

Fish, Stanley. *Doing What Comes Naturally*. Durham, N.C.: Duke University Press, 1988.

Foucault, Michel. *The Order of Things: An Archaeology of the Human Sciences: A Translation of Les Mots et les Choses*. R. D. Laing. ed., *World of Man: A Library of Theory and Research in the Human Sciences*. New York: Pantheon Books, 1970.

———. *Power/Knowledge: Selected Interviews and Other Writings, 1972–1977*. Colin Gordon ed., Leo Marshall et al., trans. New York: Pantheon Books, 1980.

Gless, Darryl J., and Barbara Herrnstein Smith, eds. *The Politics of Liberal Education*. Durham, N.C.: Duke University Press, 1992.

Greenblatt, Stephen, and Giles Gunn, eds. *Redrawing the Boundaries: The Transformation of English and American Literary Studies*. New York: Modern Language Association, 1992.

List, Peter, ed. *Radical Environmentalism*. Belmont, Calif.: Wadsworth, 1993.

Murphy, John W. *Postmodern Social Analysis and Criticism*. Westport, Conn.: Greenwood, 1988.

Nietzsche, Friedrich. *Twilight of the Idols*. R. J. Hollingdale, trans. Harmondworth: Penguin, 1988.

Norris, Christopher. *Derrida*. Cambridge, Mass.: Harvard University Press, 1987.

Rainbow, Paul, ed. *The Foucault Reader*. New York: Pantheon, 1984.

Rorty, Richard. *Consequences of Pragmatism*. Minneapolis: University of Minnesota, 1982.

———. *Contingency, Irony, Solidarity*. Cambridge: Cambridge University Press, 1989.

Sontag, Susan. "What's Happening to America?" *Partisan Review* 34 (winter 1967).

Unger, Roberto Magnabeira. *The Critical Legal Studies Movement*. Cambridge, Mass.: Harvard University Press, 1986.

West, Cornel. *The Ethical Dimension of Marxist Thought*. New York: Monthly Review Press, 1991.

ISSUES

Education

Bloom, Allan. *The Closing of the American Mind*. New York: Simon and Schuster, 1987.

Bromwitch, David. *Politics by Other Means: Higher Education and Group Thinking*. New Haven, Conn.: Yale University Press, 1992.

Devine, Philip E. "Allan Bloom: Nihilistic Conservative." *New Oxford Review* (October 1988).

Friedman, Marilyn, and Jan Narveson. *Political Correctness: For and Against*. James P. Sterba and Rosmarie Tong, eds., Point/Counterpoint. Lanham, Md.: Rowman and Littlefield, 1995.

Gates, Henry Louis, Jr. "Beyond the Culture Wars." *Profession* 93 (1993): 6–11.

Graff, Gerald. *Beyond the Culture Wars*. New York: Norton, 1992.

Kimball, Roger. *Tenured Radicals*. New York: Harper and Row, 1990.

Marsden, George M. *The Soul of the American University: From Protestant Establishment to Established Nonbelief*. New York: Oxford University Press, 1994.

Nord, Warren A. *Religion and American Education: Rethinking an American Dilemma*. Chapel Hill: University of North Carolina Press, 1995.

Oakeshott, Michael. *The Voice of Liberal Learning: Michael Oakeshott on Education*. Timothy Fuller, ed. New Haven, Conn.: Yale University Press, 1989.

Shaw, Peter. *The War Against the Intellect*. Iowa City: University of Iowa Press, 1989.

Creation and Evolution

Buell, Jon, and Virginia Hearn, eds. *Darwinism: Science or Philosophy?* Richardson, Tex.: Foundation for Thought and Ethics, 1994.

Dawkins, Richard. *The Blind Watchmaker*. New York: Norton, 1986.

Dennett, Daniel C. *Darwin's Dangerous Idea*. New York: Simon and Schuster, 1995.

Denton, Michael. *Evolution: A Theory in Crisis*. Bethesda, Md.: Adler and Adler, 1986.

Gould, Stephen. *The Panda's Thumb*. New York: W. W. Norton Co., 1989.

———. *Wonderful Life*. New York: W. W. Norton 1989.

Grizzle, Raymond E., and Phillip E. Johnson. "Two Views: Science and the Christian Faith." *Touchstone* 8, 1 (winter 1995): 5–7.

Horgan, J. "In the Beginning . . ." *Scientific American* (February 1991).

Kitcher, Philip. *Abusing Science: The Case against Creationists*. Cambridge, Mass.: MIT Press, 1982.

Johnson, Phillip E. *Darwin on Trial*. Washington, D.C.: Regnery Gateway, 1991.

———, et al. *Evolution as Dogma*. Dallas, Tex.: Haughton Publishing, 1990. This pamphlet was originally published in *First Things*, October and November 1990.

Monod, Jacques. *Chance and Necessity*. Austryn Wainhouse, trans. New York: Knopf, 1991.

Moreland, J. P., ed. *The Creation Hypothesis*. Downers Grove, Ill.: InterVarsity, 1994.

Noll, Mark A. *The Scandal of the Evangelical Mind*. Grand Rapids, Mich.: Eerdmans, 1994. Chs. 7 and 8.

Numbers, Ronald L. *The Creationists*. Berkeley: University of California Press, 1992.

Putnam, Hilary. *Renewing Philosophy*. Cambridge, Mass.: Harvard University Press, 1992.

Ruse, Michael. *Darwinism Defended*. London: Addison-Wesley,1982.

———, ed. *But Is It Science?: The Philosophical Question in the Creation/Evolution Controversy*. Buffalo, N.Y.: Prometheus, 1988.

St. Augustine. *On Genesis*. Roland J. Teske, S. J., trans. The Fathers of the Church, Thomas J. Halton et al., eds. Vol. 84. Washington, D.C.: Catholic University of America Press, 1991.

Free Speech and Political Correctness

Beckwith, Francis J., and Michael E. Bauman, eds. *Are You Politically Correct?* Buffalo, N.Y.: Prometheus, 1993.

Berman, Paul, ed. *Debating P.C.* New York: Laurel, 1992.

Bernstein, Richard. *Dictatorship of Virtue.* New York: Knopf, 1994.

Choi, Jung Min, and John W. Murphy. *The Philosophy and Politics of Political Correctness.* Westport, Conn.: Praeger, 1993.

Fish, Stanley. *There's No Such Thing as Free Speech and It's a Good Thing, Too.* Oxford: Oxford University Press, 1994.

Leo, John. *Two Steps Ahead of the Thought Police.* New York: Simon and Schuster, 1994.

"The Politics of Political Correctness." Special Issue. *Partisan Review* 60 (4) (1993).

Relativism and Neo-Tribalism

Buchanan, Allen. *Secession: The Morality of Political Divorce from Fort Sumter to Lithuania and Quebec.* Boulder, Colo.: Westview, 1991.

Crnobrnja, Mihailo. *The Yugoslav Drama.* Montreal: McGill-Queens, 1994.

Devine, Philip E. "Relativism, Abortion, and Tolerance." *Philosophy and Phenomenological Research* 48 (1987): 131–38.

_____. *Relativism, Nihilism, and God.* Notre Dame, Ind.: University of Notre Dame Press, 1989.

Fussell, Paul. *Class.* New York: Dorset, 1983.

Geertz, Clifford. *After the Fact.* Cambridge, Mass.: Harvard University Press, 1995.

Kotkin, Joel. *Tribes.* New York: Random House, 1993.

Lakatos, Imre. "Falsification and the Methodology of Research Programmes." In Imre Lakatos and Alan Musgrave, eds., *Criticism and the Growth of Knowledge*, pp. 90–196. Cambridge: Cambridge University Press, 1972.

Margolis, Joseph. *The Truth About Relativism.* Oxford: B. Blackwell, 1991.

Moynihan, Daniel Patrick. *Pandaemonium.* Oxford: Oxford University Press, 1993.

Novick, Peter. *That Noble Dream: Objectivity and the American Historical Profession.* Ideas in Context, Richard Rorty et. al. eds. Cambridge: Cambridge University Press, 1988. Especially Pt. IV.

O'Brien, Conor Cruise. "Ireland's Fissures, and My Family's." *The Atlantic Monthly* (January 1994): 50–72.

Patterson, Orlando. "Ethnicity and the Pluralist Fallacy." *Change* 7 (March 1975): 15–16.

Rodriguez, Richard (interviewed by Virginia Postrel and Nick Gillespie). "On Borders and Belonging." *Utne Reader* (March-April 1995): 75–79.

Schmooker, Andrew Bard. *The Parable of the Tribes.* Berkeley: University of California Press, 1984.

Schwartz, Benjamin. "The Diversity Myth." *The Atlantic Monthly* May 1995: 57–67.

Taylor, Charles, et al. *Multiculturalism and the "Politics of Recognition."* Amy Guttman, ed. Princeton, N.J.: Princeton University Press, 1992.

Wong, David. *Moral Relativity.* Berkeley: University of California Press, 1984.

Yates, Steven. "Multiculturalism and Epistemology." *Public Affairs Quarterly* (October 1992): 435–56.

Religion

Barr, James. *Fundamentalism.* London: SCM, 1977.

Beale, David O. *In Pursuit of Purity: American Fundamentalism Since 1850.* Foreword by Bob Jones. Greenville, S.C.: Unusual Publications, 1986.

Boone, Kathleen C. *The Bible Tells Them So.* Albany, N.Y.: SUNY Press, 1989.

Carter, Stephen L. *The Culture of Disbelief.* New York: Basic Books, 1993.

Clouser, Roy A. *The Myth of Religious Neutrality.* Notre Dame, Ind.: University of Notre Dame Press, 1990.

Cohen, Norman J., ed. *The Fundamentalist Phenomenon.* Grand Rapids, Mich.: Eerdmans, 1990.

Colson, Charles, and Richard John Neuhaus, eds. *Evangelicals and Catholics Together: Toward a Common Mission.* Dallas, Tex.: Word Publishing, 1995. A manifesto of "co-belligerency" in the culture wars.

Cromartie, Michael, ed. *Disciples & Democracy.* Washington, D.C.: Ethics and Public Policy Center, 1994.

Cuddihy, John Murray. *No Offense: Civil Religion and Protestant Taste.* New York: Seabury, 1978.

Danzger, M. Herbert. *Returning to Tradition: The Contemporary Revival of Orthodox Judaism.* New Haven, Conn.: Yale University Press, 1989.

Douglass, R. Bruce, and David Hollenbach, eds. *Catholicism and Liberalism: Contributions to American Public Philosophy.* Robin W. Lovin, general ed. Cambridge Studies in Religion and American Public Life. Cambridge: Cambridge University Press, 1994.

Greenawalt, Kent. *Religious Convictions and Political Choice.* New York: Oxford University Press, 1988.

John Paul II. *Crossing the Threshold of Hope.* Jenny McPhee and Martha McPhee, eds. Vittorio Messori, trans. New York: Knopf, 1994.

Jurgensmeyer, Mark. *The New Cold War? Religious Nationalism Confronts the Secular State.* Paperback ed. Berkeley, Calif.: University of California Press, 1994.

Marsden, George M. *Fundamentalism and American Culture.* New York: Oxford University Press, 1980.

———. *Religion and American Culture.* San Diego, Calif.: Harcourt Brace, 1990.

Marty, Martin, and R. Scott Appleby, eds. *Fundamentalisms Observed.* Chicago, Ill.: University of Chicago Press, 1991.

Milbank, John. *Theology and Social Theory.* Oxford: Basil Blackwell, 1990.

Moore, R. Laurence. *Selling God: American Religion in the Marketplace of Culture.* New York: Oxford University Press, 1994.

Neuhaus, Richard John, ed. *Unsecular America.* Encounter Series, no. 2. Richard John Neuhaus, general ed. Grand Rapids, Mich.: Eerdmans, 1986.

Quinn, Philip L. "Political Liberalisms and their Exclusions of the Religious." *Proceedings and Addresses of the American Philosophical Association* 69, 2 (November 1995): 35–56.

Sandeen, Ernest R. *The Roots of Fundamentalism.* Chicago, Ill.: University of Chicago Press, 1977.

Scruton, Roger, "Godless Conservatism." *The Wall Street Journal,* April 5, 1996.

Shurden, Walter, ed. *The Struggle for the Soul of the SBC.* Macon, Ga.: Mercer University Press, 1993.

Strozier, Charles B. *Apocalypse.* Boston: Beacon Press, 1994.

Tipton, Steven M. *Getting Saved from the Sixties: Moral Meaning in Conversion and Cultural Change.* Berkeley: University of California Press, 1982.

Wertheimer, Jack. *A People Divided.* New York: Basic Books, 1993.

Wright, Stuart A., ed. *Armageddon in Waco: Critical Perspectives on the Branch Davidian Conflict.* Chicago, Ill.: University of Chicago Press, 1995. How much tolerance for deviant religions is possible?

Sex and Gender Issues (Including Abortion)

Daly, Mary. *Gyn/Ecology.* Boston: Beacon Press, 1990.

Devine, Philip E., and Celia Wolf-Devine, eds. *Sex and Gender: A Spectrum of Views.* Jones and Bartlett Series in Philosophy. Robert Ginsberg, general ed. Boston: Jones and Bartlett, forthcoming.

Duden, Barbara. *Disembodying Women: Perspectives on Pregnancy and the Unborn.* Lee Homacki, trans. Cambridge, Mass.: Harvard University Press, 1993.

Ford, Norman, S.D.B. *When Did I Begin?* Cambridge: Cambridge University Press, 1988.

Gilmore, David D. *Manhood in the Making: Cultural Concepts of Masculinity.* New Haven, Conn.: Yale University Press, 1990.

Green, Ronald. "Conferred Rights and the Fetus." *Journal of Religious Ethics* (spring 1974).

Grisez, Germain. "When Do People Begin?" In Stephen J. Heaney ed. *Abortion: A New Generation of Catholic Responses,* ch. 1. Braintree, Mass.: Pope John Center, 1993.

Haack, Susan, advisory ed. "Feminist Epistemology: For and Against." *Monist* 77, 4 (October 1994).

Hunter, James Davison. *Before the Shooting Begins: Searching for Democracy in America's Culture War.* New York: Free Press, 1994. Mainly on abortion.

McAlister, Pam, ed. *Reweaving the Web of Life.* Philadelphia, Penn.: New Society Publishers, 1982.

Okin, Susan Moller. *Justice, Gender, and the Family.* New York: Basic Books, 1989.

Patai, Daphne, and Norette Koertege. *Professing Feminism.* New York: Basic Books, 1994.

Pluhar, Werner. "Abortion and Simple Consciousness." *Journal of Philosophy* 24 (1977): 159–72.

Poijman, Louis P., and Francis J. Beckwith, eds. *The Abortion Controversy.* The Jones and Bartlett Series in Philosophy. Robert Ginsberg, general ed. Boston: Jones and Bartlett, 1994.

Ross, Jacob Joshua. *The Virtues of the Family.* New York: Free Press, 1994.

Schechter, Susan. *Women and Male Violence: The Visions and Struggles of the Battered Women's Movement.* Boston: South End Press, 1982.

Scruton, Roger. *Sexual Desire.* New York: Free Press, 1986.

Thomson, Judith Jarvis. "A Defense of Abortion." *Philosophy and Public Affairs* 1 (1971).

Tribe, Laurence. "Toward a Model of Roles in the Due Process of Life and Law." *Harvard Law Review* 87 (1973): 1–53.

Wilcox, John T. "Nature as Demonic in Thomson's Defense of Abortion." *New Scholasticism* 79 (autumn 1989): 463–84.

Wolf-Devine, Celia. "Abortion and the Feminine Voice." *Public Affairs Quarterly* 3 (July 1984): 81–97.

Wreen, Michael. "The Power of Potentiality." *Theoria* 5 (1986): 16–40.

OF GENERAL INTEREST

Berry, Wendell. *Sex, Economy, Freedom, and Community*. New York: Pantheon, 1993.

Curti, Merle. *Human Nature in American Thought: A History*. Madison, Wisc.: University of Wisconsin Press, 1980.

Elshtain, Jean Bethke. *Democracy on Trial*. New York: Basic Books, 1995.

Genovese, Eugene. "Class Power, Again." *Crisis* (September 1994).

_____. "The Question." *Dissent* (summer, 1994).

_____. "The Riposte." *Dissent* (summer, 1994).

Gleason, Philip. *Speaking of Diversity: Language and Ethnicity in Twentieth Century America*. Baltimore, Md.: Johns Hopkins University Press, 1992.

Harvey, David. *The Condition of Postmodernity: An Inquiry into the Origin of Cultural Change*. Cambridge, Mass. and Oxford: Blackwell, 1990.

Kammen, Michael. *Mystic Chords of Memory: The Transformation of Tradition in American Culture*. New York: Knopf, 1992.

Lifton, Robert Jay. *The Protean Self: Human Resilience in an Age of Fragmentation*. New York: Basic Books, 1993.

Manent, Pierre. *An Intellectual History of Liberalism*. Rebecca Bulinksi, trans. Thomas Pavel and Mark Lilla, eds. New French Thought. Princeton, N.J.: Princeton University Press, 1994.

May, Henry F. *The End of American Innocence*. Oxford: Oxford University Press, 1979.

Rosen, Stanley. *Hermeneutics as Politics*. Josué Odéon, V. Harari, and Vincent Descombes, general eds. New York: Oxford University Press, 1987.

Seligman, Adam B. *The Idea of Civil Society*. New York: Free Press, 1992.

Shain, Barry Alan. *The Myth of American Individualism*. Princeton, N.J.: Princeton University Press, 1994.

Index

About the Author

PHILIP E. DEVINE is Professor of Philosophy at Providence College in Rhode Island. He is the author of *The Ethics of Homicide* (1978) and *Relativism, Nihilism, and God* (1989).

ISBN 0-275-95205-3

90000>

EAN

9 780275 952051

HARDCOVER BAR CODE